essentials
of
Symbolic
Logic

essentials
of
Symbolic
Logic

R. L. Simpson

broadview press

Canadian Cataloguing in Publication Data

Simpson, R.L.
  Essentials of symbolic logic

revised edition

Includes index.

ISBN 1-55111-250-7

1. Logic, symbolic and mathematical. I Title.
BC135.S556 1999   160   C98-932753-1

> N.B. This title was originally published by Routledge in 1989 (ISBNs 0-415-01870-6 hc, 0-415-01871-4 pb); *Essentials of Symbolic Logic* is now available worldwide exclusively in this new Broadview Press edition, which incorporates substantial revisions.

Broadview Press Ltd. is an independent, international publishing house, incorporated in 1985.

North America:

PO Box 1243, Peterborough, Ontario, Canada K9J 7H5

3576 California Road, Orchard Park, NY, USA 14127

phone, fax and e-mail addresses for North America: (705) 743-8990 (phone); (705) 743-8353 (fax); 75322.44@COMPUSERVE.COM

UK and Europe:

Turpin Distribution Services Ltd., Blackhorse Rd., Letchworth, Hertfordshire, SG6 1HN United Kingdom (01462) 672555 (phone); (01462) 480947 (fax)

Australia:

St. Clair Press, PO Box 287, Rozelle NSW 2039 (02)818 1942

elsewhere:

Please order through local wholesalers or direct from North America.

www.broadviewpress.com

Broadview Press Ltd. gratefully acknowledges the financial support of the Government of Canada through the Book Publishing Industry Development Program for our publishing activities.

PRINTED IN CANADA

ACKNOWLEDGEMENTS

This book owes much to more people than can be listed here. Over the years, many of my students have pointed out errors and omissions in various versions of the text. Among the former students who have been particularly helpful are Sandy Bannikoff, John Davison and Dan Rubin.

Various teachers of logic have given advice and encouragement. Norman Swartz in particular spent an extraordinary amount of time and effort when the enterprise of writing a new text seemed overwhelming. I have also received help and encouragement from Skip Bassford, Bob Goldman, Michael Picard and James Young.

I am indebted to the readers at Broadview Press. They caught many minor errors and more than one major one. The readers made suggestions and criticisms, some accepted and some rejected. Many suggestions were ignored on the grounds that a short book could not deal with the suggested changes or additions. A number of readers had serious criticisms of a few claims made in the text. In several cases I rejected them on the basis that I did not agree. All the criticisms, rejected or not, were helpful. Where I disagreed, I tried to reword the text so that contentious issues are not presented in a way that suggests that opposing views are not worth considering.

My family, of course, has had to put up with my preoccupation with the book. In the future, I hope it will be possible to eat a meal in a restaurant without asking someone for a slip of paper to write down a new idea.

CONTENTS

CHAPTER ONE

CHAPTER TWO

CHAPTER THREE

CHAPTER FOUR

CHAPTER FIVE

CHAPTER SIX

INDEX

SYMBOLS

The symbols used in the text are introduced at the indicated pages. Various symbols mentioned only in Chapter 6 are not included.

~	10
∧	10
∨	10
⊃	10
≡	10
(	10
)	10
†††	12
∃	140
∀	142
{	156
}	156
X|X	156
∅	166
{ }	166
⟨	167
⟩	167

GREEK LETTERS

Several Greek letters are used in the text. They are listed below with their names and a rough guide to pronunciation.

Upper-Case Letters:

Φ	phi	rhymes with 'pie' – 'ph' as in 'PHone'
Ψ	psi	rhymes with 'pie' – 'ps' as in 'tiPSy'
Ω	omega	oh ME ga or oh MAY ga

Lower-Case Letters:

χ	chi	rhymes with 'pie' – 'ch' as in 'loCH'
τ	tau	rhymes with 'cow'

CHAPTER ONE

INTRODUCTION

§1.1: THE AIMS OF THIS BOOK

... God has not been so sparing to men to make them barely two-legged creatures, and left it to Aristotle to make them rational... God has been more bountiful to mankind than so. He has given them a mind that can reason, without being instructed...

John Locke, *An Essay Concerning Human Understanding,*
Bk. IV, Ch. XVII.

This quotation reflects Locke's belief that one can reason logically without having studied the subject called 'logic'. I share Locke's view. The study of logic, of course, is far different now from what it was in Locke's time; the student of today is likely to spend much more time on symbolic logic than on the logic of Aristotle. Notwithstanding the great differences between Aristotelian logic and contemporary symbolic logic, the view that one should learn logic in order to reason properly is still prevalent. I do not deny that the study of logic can – and often does – sharpen one's ability to reason; what I deny is that this is the only, or even the primary, reason for studying the subject.

A common approach to the teaching of logic begins with the claim or at least the strong suggestion that the student can neither evaluate arguments nor construct decent arguments without some formal training in logic. Coupled with the equally dubious claim or suggestion that knowledge of logically respectable argumentation is useful in producing persuasive arguments, this approach to logic leads – by a decidedly shaky inference – to the claim that every student should study logic, preferably symbolic logic with a battery of esoteric symbols to impress the uninitiated. There are at least three reasons why it is wrong to promote the study of logic in this way.

First, people of any intelligence, from the time of Sextus Empiricus to the present, have realized that logicians do not have a monopoly on rationality. The suggestion that one needs to study logic in order to deal with everyday arguments is manifestly false. The very enterprise of studying logic requires the ability to reason, and students recognize this. To begin the study of logic with an attempt to establish a conclusion by means of an obviously unsound argument is hardly a way to encourage people to assess their beliefs on some rational basis.

Second, the claim that logic should be studied only because it is 'useful' belittles the subject. Proving the obvious is a sophisticated activity; pretending that the obvious is not obvious until it is demonstrated is both dishonest and pedagogically unhelpful. The study of symbolic logic is a worthwhile activity in itself; there is no need to invent spurious justifications for learning something about an intellectually exciting activity.

Third, the all too common practice of attempting to express every philosophical claim and argument in symbolic terms frequently ignores subtleties which are comparatively clear in English and completely lost in the symbolic language. Although the use of symbols may not, as some claim, be the last resort of the philosophical scoundrel, students who complain about 'philosophical squid' hiding in an inky cloud of symbols often have a legitimate complaint.

The study of symbolic logic has, of course, practical benefits, but these benefits are not primarily skills in applying a testing procedure to arguments. Over the years I have dealt with hundreds of logic students. My experience has been that most students gain two things from an introductory course in symbolic logic. First, translating statements and arguments from English into a symbolic language makes the student read and write carefully. For the most part, post-secondary students do not need to *learn* how to read and write carefully; they already know how. Nevertheless, translating from English into a symbolic language forces students to use the knowledge they have, and in many cases habits of close reading and disciplined writing which are helpful to the students in all their studies are developed. Second, producing derivations in a natural deduction system is an exercise in problem-solving. The problem of getting a formula in the right place using only a particular set of rules is challenging. The similarities between problems of this sort and problems facing students in computer science will be obvious to anyone with any experience in programming computers. Many students have told me that their work with derivations has helped them in their computer science courses. Whatever the student goes on to study, the habit of taking a systematic approach to problems is worth developing. The study of logic, like the study of any intellectually respectable subject, tends to inculcate this.

Given this perception of what in fact is learnt by most students in an introductory course, the choice of a text is not easy. There are many excellent texts available. My primary objection to most of them is that they cover much more than would be taught in an introductory course, with the result that the students have to pay for material which they do not use and are intimidated by a text of forbidding length and complexity. After teaching several courses using notes prepared by myself and others, I decided to write the material in just the way I want to present it in class. The result is *Essentials of Symbolic Logic.*

In producing this book, my concern is to produce a text which is short and affordable. Many topics are simply ignored, but the experience of teaching over the years has convinced me that there is enough material here for a respectable course.

§ 1.2: PRIMARILY FOR THE STUDENT

Many students take a course in symbolic logic only because it is a required course for a degree or diploma. Others take such a course because they have come across various strange symbols and want to know what people are doing with them. Whatever one's reasons for studying symbolic logic, the study can be interesting and fruitful.

Essentials of Symbolic Logic was written for neither fools nor illiterates. It was not written to teach anyone 'how to think properly' – whatever that may mean. It was written to supply a short text which would make the student familiar with a standard set of logical symbols and reasonably adept at using those symbols. The major part of the book is concerned with solving derivation problems, the problems discussed in Chapter 3 and Chapter 5. These problems can often be baffling, but considerable care has been taken to provide the student with a way of approaching problems that minimizes frustration.

Chapter 2 and Chapter 3 deal with sentence logic, the relationship between sentences and clauses that can stand alone as meaningful sentences. Chapter 4 and Chapter 5 deal with predicate logic, which is concerned with the internal structure of sentences. An understanding of Chapter 2 is necessary to understand anything that follows. However, if one wants to skip the material on derivations in Chapter 3, one can go straight from Chapter 2 to Chapter 4. Chapter 5, the discussion of derivations in predicate logic, relies heavily on the previous treatment of derivations, and should not be approached until one has mastered the material in all of the earlier chapters.

Logic is a serious discipline and cannot be learnt without serious intellectual effort. However, learning some elementary symbolic logic is far easier than it might appear at first glance; the symbols which initially seem so confusing were developed to make matters simpler, not more difficult. In working through the text, students should become clearer in their understanding of the logical structure underlying English sentences and develop problem-solving skills as they work at producing derivations. In the process, many students actually enjoy themselves.

§1.3: PRIMARILY FOR THE INSTRUCTOR

Various versions of *Essentials of Symbolic Logic* have been used for some dozen years with students of varying abilities and interests. While no text can anticipate all the problems which students might have, care has been taken to address recurrent difficulties.

Metatheory is not considered for three reasons. First, it would add to the length and cost of the book. Second, many students are not concerned with metatheoretical questions; their interests and career plans lead them in quite different directions. Third, most students need to be very familiar with some system of logic before they can address the problems of metatheory seriously.

There is not *very* much time spent on instructions for translating English sentences and arguments, although these are important skills. Most students already have an understanding of English which is sufficient to cope with quite complicated sentences and arguments; they do not read and write with care because they have not been forced to do so. Average students are quite capable of distinguishing between 'if' and 'only if' without being instructed. Similarly, any student who can read this text can identify the premises and conclusions of quite complex arguments. It is not necessary to spend much time on *teaching* such things; simply demanding careful work (and grading exercises accordingly) forces students to use the knowledge and skills they already have.

This text has been written with the recognition that many students will go on to study more logic from other texts. Since there are different conventions current, it is impossible to avoid some inconsistencies. There are also a couple of eccentricities which require explanation. First, the way in which the columns of truth tables are numbered may strike some instructors as being potentially confusing to the students. I have marked thousands of truth tables, and getting the students to number the columns in the way I suggest is the only way I have found which forces them to complete every column on the truth table and to indicate clearly what they take to be the main operator in each formula. Second, I have deliberately avoided the common practice of writing variables in italics. As far as possible, I have tried to set up formulas, tables, arguments and derivations in a way that any student can duplicate with no great calligraphic skills. Neither of these departures from the more usual conventions should cause any difficulty for the student who moves on to another text.

I use the caret symbol, '∧', rather than the more common ampersand or dot. Dots produced by students are often shapeless blobs or virtually invisible, and many students have great difficulty in writing a legible ampersand. Students have better things to do with their time than to struggle with such difficulties. In accordance with almost universal usage in logic, I refer to the '~' as a 'tilde' although strictly speaking it is called a 'swing dash'. (Typographers will insist that the tilde is a diacritical mark which appears over a character, as in 'cañon'.) I refer to parentheses as 'brackets'. This usage is formally correct in some countries and colloquially common wherever English is spoken. Students will not be confused by the use of either word.

The material can, of course, be supplemented by whatever other material the instructor sees fit. In the past, I have adjusted the course to the interests and capabilities of the students by introducing a discussion of set theory and Venn diagrams in one case, and some work on electrical analogues of the truth-functional operators in another. The common procedure of using incomplete truth tables is not discussed. Capable students can see when a truth table need not be completed, and incomplete truth tables can be discussed in class. My own practice in teaching has been to be sure above all else that the basics are thoroughly understood. Additions, such as those above or a bit of metatheory, can be added as time permits.

As far as possible, I have kept the technical vocabulary to an absolute minimum. Students already have to learn several unfamiliar terms, and learning unnecessary vocabulary distracts students from understanding logical concepts and dealing with logical problems.

To keep the book short and inexpensive, there are not many exercises. The exercises cover all the major topics, and it will not be onerous for instructors to create their own exercises. Solutions to exercises in texts tend to be circulated after a text has been used for a while, and there is no substitute for producing fresh exercises for each new class.

Students are not given solutions for any of the exercises in the book. The problem with providing solutions to exercises is that students almost invariably look at the solution when they run into any difficulty, realize that there is no insurmountable problem, and think they have learnt something when in fact they have not.

A brief discussion of several topics not discussed in the main text is included as Chapter 6. A very short discussion of truth trees is included in that chapter. Additional rules such as *modus tollens* and various replacement rules are also mentioned in this chapter. Understanding the basic set of rules is essential to understanding symbolic logic. While the additional rules make shorter derivations possible, they add little of theoretical interest.

Some instructors have suggested that the insistence on reiteration makes derivations unnecessarily long. In Chapter 6, I mention the possibility of avoiding reiterations, but this is not a practice I would recommend to students. It is easy to see how the reiteration steps could have been skipped in a completed derivation. However, in the process of constructing derivations, particularly in predicate logic, reiterating formulas onto the scope line on which one is working makes the problems more manageable and helps to avoid serious errors.

CHAPTER TWO

SENTENCE LOGIC

§2.1: THE FUNDAMENTALS

The first part of this chapter will deal with a simple artificial language and the relationship between English and that language. The second part of the chapter will use the artificial language to deal with some matters which are most easily dealt with by using a non-natural language. It is not claimed that the artificial language which will be developed is better than a natural language such as English; the claim is merely that for some purposes the artificial language is more convenient than a natural language.

The basic unit to be considered is a declarative sentence, the sort of thing which can be true or false. For example, 'Rome is an ancient city' is a sentence having a **truth value,** which is just another way of saying that it can be true or false. By contrast, 'Is Rome an ancient city?' is neither true nor false; it does not have a truth value. Similarly, a request like 'Please shut the door' cannot be said to be either true or false. The only sentences which will be considered in this book are sentences having truth values.

The sentence 'The equator is to the south' is true when uttered in England and false when uttered in Australia. Similarly, the sentence 'My name is Bill' is true when uttered by Bill and false when uttered by John. The fact that the truth value of a sentence can depend on the occasion of its utterance has led some logicians to make a distinction between a *statement* or *proposition* which strictly speaking has a truth value and a *sentence* which is a meaningful sequence of words. This distinction is not without its difficulties, but there is no need to consider them here. For present purposes, the distinction can simply be ignored. In this book the word 'sentence' is to be understood as referring to the sort of thing that can be true or false, and will be used accordingly.

Two points about truth and falsity should be noted here. First, determining the truth or falsity of a sentence such as 'The Chinese invented gunpowder' is not necessary for present purposes; one can simply assume that it is true or assume that it is false. In the terminology of logic, to make an assumption about the truth or falsity of a sentence is to **assign a truth value** to the sentence. Second, there is no need to complicate matters by considering the possibility of differing degrees of truth or falsity. Various logicians have attempted to develop logics in which one can deal with this sort of thing, but this book will deal with only two truth values. Thus, the sentence 'Wine helps the digestion' will have to be regarded simply as true or false, and not partly true or true for some people. It should be noted that this places no restriction on what one can say. If one wants to say that wine drunk in moderation helps the digestion of some people, one can say just that by using the sentence 'Wine drunk in moderation helps the digestion of some people.'

§2.2: TRUTH FUNCTIONS

A sentence such as 'Jack is a lawyer and John is an accountant' is usually called a compound sentence. It is formed by combining the two simple sentences, 'Jack is a lawyer' and 'John is an accountant.' In order to tell whether or not the compound sentence is true, one need only know whether or not 'Jack is a lawyer' is true and whether or not 'John is an accountant' is true. The truth value of 'Jack is a lawyer and John is an accountant' is a function of the truth value of 'Jack is a lawyer' and the truth value of 'John is an accountant.' Such functions are **truth functions**. The word 'and' in the compound sentence serves as a **truth-functional operator** between the two simple sentences.

It is easy to find other examples of truth-functional operators in everyday English. The word 'or' in the sentence 'Either Bill will go to the wedding or John will go to the wedding' serves as a truth-functional operator. The truth value of the compound sentence can be determined from the truth values of the simple sentences. For example, if one knows that Bill will go to the wedding, one knows that the compound sentence is true. Similarly, if one knows that Bill will not go to the wedding and one knows that John will not go to the wedding, then one knows that the compound sentence is false.

Although the phrase 'It is false that ...' does not connect two simple sentences, if one knows the truth value of 'Mary is married to Brian', one knows the truth value of 'It is false that Mary is married to Brian.' The truth value of 'It is false that Mary is married to Brian' is a function of the truth value of 'Mary is married to Brian.' Accordingly, the phrase 'It is false that ...' serves a role which is analogous to the role served by 'and' and 'or' in the sentences just discussed, and it is a truth-functional operator. Truth-functional operators are often called 'truth-functional connectives', and in much writing in logic the word 'connective' is frequently used when 'operator' is used in this book. It is because 'connectives' often do not in any straightforward sense do any connecting that 'operator' is the preferred vocabulary in this book.

Many sentences are formed by words or phrases which plainly do not serve as truth-functional operators. For example, the truth value of 'He is irritable because he lost the game' cannot be determined from the truth value of 'He is irritable' and the truth value of 'He lost the game'; one can know that he is irritable and know that he lost the game without knowing that his irritation is the result of his losing the game. Similarly, the truth value of 'I went home before I went to the play' cannot be determined from the truth values of 'I went home' and 'I went to the play.' Phrases such as 'It is obvious that ...' and 'It is necessarily the case that ...' are logically different from phrases such as 'It is false that ...' This is shown by the fact that one cannot determine the truth value of 'It is obvious that Smith is guilty of the crime' from the truth value of 'Smith is guilty of the crime.' These examples of words and phrases which do not serve as truth-functional operators are mentioned in order to help clarify the limits of sentence logic. Sentence logic is concerned with truth-functional operators. In the next few sections, five different truth-functional operators will be discussed.

§2.3: SENTENCE LETTERS AND SYMBOLS

When the notion of a truth function was introduced in §2.2, simple sentences such as 'Mary is married to Brian' were picked arbitrarily. It should be clear that the particular sentences involved did not matter. For purposes of doing logic, rather than writing out arbitrarily picked sentences, one can use letters to stand for sentences. The symbolic language to be developed in this chapter will use any upper-case Roman letter to represent a sentence, so such expressions as 'It is false that G' and 'R or S' can be used to discuss truth functions. Although one is restricted to twenty-six letters, there is no theoretical limit to the number of distinct sentences which can be represented by sentence letters. The need will never arise, but it is possible to extend the stock of sentence letters by using subscripts. Thus, one can write 'A_5 and B_8' or 'It is false that G_{32}.' Use of subscripts for this purpose should be avoided because it is unnecessary. The possibility of using more than twenty-six sentence letters is mentioned only to make the theoretical point that the symbolic language does not restrict one to a limited number of sentences.

There are advantages in using sentence letters rather than sentences. As a matter of simple convenience, it is just quicker to write a letter than to write a sentence. More important, in considering the way logical operators work, one should be careful not to let the content of the sentences confuse the issue. Using sentence letters allows one to see clearly the logical connections between various simple and compound sentences without judging issues of truth and falsity on the basis of the content of particular sentences.

Similar considerations make it desirable to use symbols instead of English words or phrases for the various truth-functional operators. This will become increasingly apparent as the symbols and their approximate English equivalents are discussed. Five symbols will be defined and the relationship between those symbols and various English words and phrases will be considered. A very crude account of the way these symbols are used follows:

1 '~ A' is the rough equivalent of 'It is false that A.'
   The '~' is the **tilde**.

2 '(A ∧ B)' is the rough equivalent of 'A and B.'
   The '∧' is the **caret**.

3 '(A ∨ B)' is the rough equivalent of 'A or B.'
   The '∨' is the **vel** sometimes called the 'wedge'.

4 '(A ⊃ B)' is the rough equivalent of 'If A, then B.'
   The '⊃' is the **horseshoe** sometimes called the 'hook'.

5 '(A ≡ B)' is the rough equivalent of 'A, if and only if B.'
   The '≡' is the **triplebar** sometimes called 'tribar'.

All the elements of the symbolic language which will be developed for sentence logic have now been exhibited. They are very simple, and consist of three kinds of items:

1 A stock of twenty-six sentence letters, in principle supplemented by subscripted letters.

2 Five symbols for creating new sentences from existing sentences.

3 A left bracket '(' and a right bracket ')' which serve as the only punctuation marks.

§2.4: METALANGUAGE

Now that a very sketchy outline of an artificial language has been given, it is time to consider a reasonable approach to discussing this language. Most speakers of English who learn French are taught about the foreign language in their native language. Thus, a beginning student of French may learn some French by hearing or reading the English sentence, 'The French word "et" has the same meaning as the English word "and".' The language being discussed, French in this case, is the **object language**. The language used to discuss the object language, English in this case, is the **metalanguage**. The symbolic language of logic which is discussed in this book is the object language. It will be talked about in a metalanguage, which is English supplemented by a few symbols borrowed from the object language and by a handful of Greek letters.

English speakers, of course, do not study only foreign languages; they also study their own language. When they do, the object language and the metalanguage are one and the same. In practice, this works quite well. Given some grasp of basic English, one can understand a grammar text written in English. There are, however, theoretical problems about using a single language as both object language and metalanguage, and the symbolic language in this text will never be used to talk about itself.

The difficulty in using the same language as both the object language and the metalanguage can easily be seen by considering the problems one would have in trying to show in written English the use of quotation marks in English. It would be hard to avoid writing something which does not presuppose an understanding of how English quotation marks are used. The following sentence, for example, looks decidedly strange and it is hard to see how anyone could learn anything by reading it:

> In English, the convention is to begin quotations with " " " and end quotations with " " ".

By contrast, the following sentence does not look so strange and it is easy to see how someone could learn something by reading it:

> In French, the convention is to begin quotations with " « " and end quotations with " » ".

For purposes of illustration, double quotation marks are used in both examples. The same problems would arise if single quotation marks were used or a combination of single and double quotation marks.

Akin to the distinction between an object language and a metalanguage is the distinction between what can be shown *within* a logical system and what can be shown *about* that logical system. Within the logical system to be developed in this book, several rules will be given for doing such things as deriving one sentence in the symbolic language from another sentence.

These rules will simply be presented with the implied claim that they are logically respectable, but no attempt will be made to give a clear account of what that involves. Such an account is a question in **metatheory**; it is a matter of discussing the logic of the system rather than using it. Metatheory embraces this and many other topics, but none of them will be considered in this book.

Unlike the rules of English spelling and grammar, the rules of the symbolic language are extremely simple and completely consistent. Questions of spelling do not arise, and the only punctuation marks are the left and right brackets. In this book, the rules of the object language will be followed scrupulously – with one exception. The one permissible departure from the rules is discussed in §2.5. Many of the quirks of everyday English, however, will remain in the metalanguage.

§2.5: WELL-FORMED FORMULAS

Just as English has rules of grammar, so the symbolic language has rules. Some combinations of symbols conform to the rules. These are **well-formed formulas**. A well-formed formula is a **WFF**. The usual pronunciation of 'WFF' is 'whiff' or 'woof'. The terms 'well-formed formula' and 'WFF' will be used interchangeably in this book. The rules for creating well-formed formulas will be explained as the language is developed. Other combinations do not conform to the rules. When these are shown for purposes of illustration, they will be flagged with three daggers ('†††') to emphasize that what has just been written is mistaken in some way. (Throughout this book, the three daggers will be used to mark errors.)

A sentence letter standing alone is an **atomic formula**. Thus, 'A' is an atomic formula, and '~ A' is not. Any atomic formula is a WFF. Thus, 'A' is a well-formed formula, as are 'B', 'C' and 'Y'. Putting a tilde in front of any WFF results in another WFF, the **negation** of the original WFF. Thus, '~ A', '~ G' and '~ M' are all WFFs. Since '~ A' is a WFF, '~ ~ A' is a WFF, as are '~ ~ ~ A', '~ ~ ~ ~ A' and '~ ~ ~ ~ ~ A'. Using the Greek letter 'Φ' to stand for any well-formed formula whatever, '~ Φ' is a well-formed formula. (It should be noted that 'Φ' is not a WFF in the symbolic language. It is part of the metalanguage used to discuss the symbolic language.)

Using the 'Φ' and 'Ψ' to stand for any well-formed formulas, '(Φ ∧ Ψ)' is a WFF, '(Φ ∨ Ψ)' is a WFF, '(Φ ⊃ Ψ)' is a WFF and '(Φ ≡ Ψ)' is a WFF. Strictly speaking, the brackets are essential; 'Φ ∧ Ψ', 'Φ ∨ Ψ', 'Φ ⊃ Ψ' and 'Φ ≡ Ψ' are not WFFs, although the lack of brackets causes no confusion. Throughout the rest of this book, when dropping brackets causes no ambiguity, they will usually be dropped.

For various purposes, different conventions have been established to disambiguate arithmetical expressions. However, for a normal reader, an expression such as '6 + 4 ÷ 2' is ambiguous. Is one to add 6 and 4 and then divide the result by 2, or is one to divide 4 by 2 and then add 6 to the result? Adding brackets in the appropriate places make it clear whether it is the first or second which is intended: plainly, '(6 + 4) ÷ 2' means something different from '6 + (4 ÷ 2)'. In just the same way, 'A ∨ B ⊃ C' ††† is not a WFF because it is ambiguous between 'A ∨ (B ⊃ C)' and '(A ∨ B) ⊃ C'. The former should be read as 'Either A, or if B then C', while the latter should be read as 'If either A or B, then C'. Strictly speaking, neither 'A ∨ (B ⊃ C)' nor '(A ∨ B) ⊃ C' is a WFF, but the absence of the outer brackets does not create any ambiguity.

In fact, the absence of the outer brackets makes formulas easier to read, and there is no reason to add them every time one uses '∧', '∨', '⊃' or '≡'. However, it is important to add brackets as more complex formulas are created. For example, the two formulas 'S' and 'P ≡ Q' can be used in various more complex formulas such as 'S ∨ (P ≡ Q)', '(P ≡ Q) ∧ S' and 'S ⊃ (P ≡ Q)'. In each case, brackets must be added to 'P ≡ Q' in order to avoid such ambiguous expressions as 'S ∨ P ≡ Q' †††, 'P ≡ Q ∧ S' ††† and 'S ⊃ P ≡ Q' †††.

Every formula which is not an atomic formula has a **main operator**. In the formula 'S ∨ (P ≡ Q)', '∨' is the main operator; in the formula '(P ≡ Q) ∧ S', '∧' is the main operator; and in the formula 'S ⊃ (P ≡ Q)', '⊃' is the main operator. The main operator of any formula in sentence logic can be determined by considering the way in which the WFF is built up either from another formula in the case of the tilde or from other formulas in the case of the other operators. The last operator which is added is the main operator. If there is no way of determining which operator is the main operator of a formula, then that formula is not a WFF.

§2.6: EXERCISES

Which of the following are *strictly speaking* well-formed formulas?

1 ~ ~ ~ B

2 ((A) ⊃ B)

3 (F ∧ (G ∨ H))

4 ((F ∧ G) ∨ H)

5 ((F ∧ G ∨ H))

6 ~ (~ M ⊃ ((R ∨ G) ≡ S))

7 ~ (~ M ⊃ (((R ∨ G) ≡ S))

8 ((F ∨ G) ∧ (F ∨ G))

9 R ∨ S

10 (f ⊃ (g ∨ s))

§2.7: SIMPLE TRANSLATION: NEGATION

It is now possible to do a little translation from English into the symbolic language. For example, one can translate 'Jack is greedy' as 'G'. Then, if one wants to assert that Jack is not greedy, that it is false that Jack is greedy, one can write '~ G'. Similarly, if the sentence letter 'R' is used to represent the English sentence 'Robert is my brother', the denial of the statement that Robert is my brother is represented by '~ R'.

As a general rule, in translating English sentences into the symbolic language, one should try to use atomic formulas and operators to reflect the logical structure of the English sentence. Using 'M' for 'Martin went to the party' and translating 'It is false that Martin went to the party' as '~ M' is an example of a good translation. Using 'M' for 'It is false that Martin went to the party' is an example of a poor translation.

'It is false that Martin went to the party' is not, of course, the most colloquial way of saying that he did not go. The 'It is false that ...' locution has been used until now because the English negation is before the sentence it negates, just as the tilde is before the formula it negates. In ordinary English, however, there are very many ways of expressing negation, few of them involving a negating clause at the beginning of a sentence. A knowledge of basic English is all that is required to recognize them, but a few are listed here:

It is not true that Sam is old.

O: Sam is old.

~ O

John is not coming.

C: John is coming.

~ C

It is false that she is abnormal.

N: She is normal.

~ ~ N

This is illegal.

L: This is legal.

~ L

It is not true that this is not illegal.

L: This is legal.

~ ~ ~ L

They are dissatisfied.
S: They are satisfied.
~ S

He is incompetent.
C: He is competent.
~ C

It is irregular.
R: It is regular.
~ R

One must always use care in translation and pay serious attention to the meaning of the English sentence. For example, to translate 'He is infamous' as 'It is false that he is famous' is plainly wrong; to say that someone is infamous is not to deny that the person in question is famous. Similarly, to translate 'Everyone is dissatisfied' as 'It is false that everyone is satisfied' is to change the meaning of the original sentence.

§2.8: SIMPLE TRANSLATION: CONJUNCTION

A formula such as 'A ∧ B' is a **conjunction**, and the two formulas flanking the caret are **conjuncts**.

Using 'M' to represent 'Mary studies biology' and 'K' to represent 'Kate studies philosophy', one can translate 'Mary studies biology and Kate studies philosophy' as 'M ∧ K'. Adding the sentence letter 'J' to represent 'Jane studies history', one can translate 'Mary studies biology, Kate studies philosophy and Jane studies history' as '(M ∧ K) ∧ J'. 'M ∧ (K ∧ J)' would also be a correct translation, but 'M ∧ K ∧ J' ††† would not. This is because the formula is not well formed; it could not be produced by placing '∧' between two WFFs. Even with the inclusion of outer brackets, '(M ∧ K ∧ J)' ††† is ambiguous between '(M ∧ K) ∧ J' and 'M ∧ (K ∧ J)' and therefore not a WFF. The fact that in this case the ambiguity is of no consequence does not make the formula well formed.

There are many ways in which conjunctive sentences are written in English. As with negation, recognizing these involves no more than a little care and knowledge of English. Some of the more common locutions are given below:

Bill is a dentist and John is a lawyer.
B: Bill is a dentist.
J: John is a lawyer.
B ∧ J

Bill and John are dentists.

B: Bill is a dentist.

J: John is a dentist.

B ∧ J

She was poor but she was honest.

P: She was poor.

H: She was honest.

P ∧ H

Although cigarette smoking is a common habit, it is dangerous.

C: Cigarette smoking is a common habit.

D: Cigarette smoking is dangerous.

C ∧ D

Carl plays tennis and jogs.

T: Carl plays tennis.

J: Carl jogs.

T ∧ J

Paul is successful; his brother, however, is not.

P: Paul is successful.

B: Paul's brother is successful.

P ∧ ~ B

In translating English into symbols, pronouns should be replaced whenever possible by the nouns or noun phrases to which they refer. Someone reading the translation of one sentence should be able to understand it without having to refer to another sentence. In translating conjunctive sentences, one needs to pay careful attention to the sense of the English. It would be ludicrous to translate 'No one is a Protestant and a Muslim' as the conjunction of 'No one is a Protestant' and 'No one is a Muslim', for example.

One reason for care in translating the word 'and' is that it is often used in English as something other than a simple conjunction. When 'and' is used in such a way, it cannot be treated as a conjunction without some loss of meaning. For example, 'We had dinner and went to the theatre' is naturally taken to mean that we had dinner before we went to the theatre. 'He caught pneumonia and died' is usually taken to mean that he died as a result of the pneumonia. In most contexts, 'Sam and Janet are married' should be understood as meaning that they are married to each other. Where something of consequence other than simple conjunction is expressed, an English sentence cannot be translated into two formulas flanking a caret.

§2.9: SIMPLE TRANSLATION: DISJUNCTION

A formula such as 'M ∨ P' is a **disjunction**, and the two formulas flanking the vel are **disjuncts**. 'F ∨ G', 'F ∨ ~ G' and 'F ∨ (G ∧ H)' are all disjunctive formulas. Using 'P' to represent 'Lana is in Paris', 'R' to represent 'Lana is in Rome' and 'B' to represent 'Lana is in Brussels', one can translate 'Lana is in Paris, Rome or Brussels' in several ways. 'P ∨ (R ∨ B)' and '(P ∨ R) ∨ B' are both correct translations. Although there is nothing to choose between these two translations, '(P ∨ R ∨ B)' ††† is not a good translation because it is not a WFF.

In English, the word 'or' is sometimes taken to mean 'either but not both' and sometimes taken to mean 'either and perhaps both'. The former is the **exclusive** sense of 'or' and the latter is the **inclusive** sense of 'or'. In most cases, the context makes it perfectly clear which sense is intended, but one often sees expressions such as 'and/or' and 'one or the other but not both' when these are needed to make the meaning perfectly clear. The symbol '∨' expresses the inclusive sense of 'or'. (In Latin, the exclusive sense of 'or' is 'aut' while the inclusive sense of 'or' is 'vel'. This explains the symbol and its name.)

There are not so many ways of expressing disjunction in English as there are ways of expressing conjunction. A few typical examples follow:

Bob or Charlie will win a scholarship.
B: Bob will win a scholarship.
C: Charlie will win a scholarship.
B ∨ C

Bob or Charlie, but not both, will win a scholarship.
B: Bob will win a scholarship.
C: Charlie will win a scholarship.
(B ∨ C) ∧ ~ (B ∧ C)

Either Jane or Mary will come to the party.
J: Jane will come to the party.
M: Mary will come to the party.
J ∨ M

Either Jack will come to the picnic or Sam won't.
J: Jack will come to the picnic.
S: Sam will come to the picnic.
J ∨ ~ S

Mary will go, or Jill and Sally will go.
M: Mary will go.
J: Jill will go.
S: Sally will go.
M ∨ (J ∧ S)

Mary or Jill will go, and Sally will go.

M: Mary will go.

J: Jill will go.

S: Sally will go.

$(M \lor J) \land S$

Either Peter's mother will be upset or he is doing his homework.

M: Peter's mother will be upset.

H: Peter is doing his homework.

$M \lor H$

Peter's mother will be upset unless he is doing his homework.

M: Peter's mother will be upset.

H: Peter is doing his homework.

$M \lor H$

Translating both 'Either Peter's mother will be upset or he is doing his homework' and 'Peter's mother will be upset unless he is doing his homework' as disjunctions may strike some readers as odd. Treating 'unless' as a disjunction produces the most economical translation, but the word can be translated in other ways. The claim that Peter's mother will be upset unless he is doing his homework can be thought of as claiming that Peter's mother will be upset if he is not doing his homework, and translating the sentence in this way is perfectly correct. This will be made clearer in §2.10 and in §2.18 where truth-functional equivalences are discussed.

Translating disjunctive sentences is straightforward if one is careful not to distort the meaning of the English sentences. It requires no logical sophistication to recognize that 'Every number is odd or even', for example, cannot be translated as the disjunction of 'Every number is odd' and 'Every number is even.'

§2.10: SIMPLE TRANSLATION: THE HORSESHOE

Using 'P' to represent 'Peter will go to France' and 'J' to represent 'Jim will go to France', the sentence 'If Jim goes to France, Peter will go' can be translated as 'J ⊃ P'.

The formula to the left of the horseshoe, the 'if' part, is the **antecedent**. The formula to the right of the horseshoe, the 'then' part, is the **consequent**. Both antecedents and consequents can be atomic formulas or complex formulas. 'If ... then' sentences are often called 'conditional' sentences.

There are many ways of expressing conditional sentences in English. Some of the more common ones follow:

If it is sunny, I will go.
S: It is sunny.
G: I will go.
S ⊃ G

I will go if it is sunny.
S: It is sunny.
G: I will go.
S ⊃ G

If Peter is not doing his homework, his mother will be upset.
M: Peter's mother will be upset.
H: Peter is doing his homework.
~ H ⊃ M

Peter's mother will be upset unless he is doing his homework.
M: Peter's mother will be upset.
H: Peter is doing his homework.
~ H ⊃ M

Assuming that I don't lose my job, I'll buy a new car this year.
L: I will lose my job.
B: I will buy a new car this year.
~ L ⊃ B

If you are an American citizen by birth, you can be President, provided that you are at least thirty-five years old.
C: You are an American citizen by birth.
P: You can be President.
O: You are at least thirty-five years old.
C ⊃ (O ⊃ P)

You cannot castle when you have moved your king.
C: You can castle.
K: You have moved your king.
K ⊃ ~ C

James will get the scholarship only if he learns a little German.
J: James will get the scholarship.
L: James learns a little German.
J ⊃ L

There is fire only if there is oxygen.
F: There is fire.
O: There is oxygen.
F ⊃ O

The everyday expression 'only if' confuses many people when they are translating. 'There is fire only if there is oxygen' means that oxygen is necessary for fire – if one sees fire, one knows that oxygen is present. It does *not* mean that if oxygen is present then fire is present. The distinction between 'if' and 'only if' is clearly shown in the expression 'if and only if' which is discussed in §2.11.

In most cases, translating English 'if ... then' sentences into symbols is not difficult. As always, one needs to be sure that the meaning of the English sentence is not changed. For example, 'If something is a cow, then it is a mammal' certainly cannot be translated as 'If something is a cow, then something is a mammal.' The former sentence asserts that all cows are mammals, while the latter is far less informative. There are some special complexities concerning the horseshoe which will become apparent when this symbol is formally defined. These complexities will be discussed later in this chapter.

§2.11: SIMPLE TRANSLATION: THE TRIPLEBAR

Some examples of formulas which contain a triplebar are 'K ≡ L', '~ J ≡ ~ M' and 'S ≡ (V ⊃ H)'. Translating 'I will apply for the job' as 'A' and translating 'Peter resigns' as 'P', one can translate the sentence 'I will apply for the job if and only if Peter resigns' as 'A ≡ P'. A sentence using 'if and only if' is often called a 'biconditional' sentence.

Expressions such as 'if and only if' are relatively rare in colloquial English. When people use such expressions they are usually speaking carefully, which tends to make the task of translation straightforward. Some of the more common ways of expressing 'if and only if' follow:

You are eligible if and only if you are a student.
E: You are eligible.
S: You are a student.
E ≡ S

You can go when and only when the light is green.
G: You can go.
L: The light is green.
G ≡ L

Saying that it is an acid is equivalent to saying that it is a proton donor.
A: It is an acid.
P: It is a proton donor.
A ≡ P

Provided, but only provided, that there are no objections from the major shareholder, the merger will take place.

S: There are objections from the major shareholder.

M: The merger will take place.

$\sim S \equiv M$

The equipment will be used just in case there is a fire.

E: The equipment will be used.

F: There is a fire.

$E \equiv F$

John will take the course iff Kate takes it.

J: John will take the course.

K: Kate will take the course.

$J \equiv K$

'Iff' in the final example is not a misspelling; it is logicians' shorthand for 'if and only if'. It is pronounced 'if-if' and the triplebar can always be used in translating it.

Translating English sentences into formulas which contain a triplebar is usually quite straightforward, but of course one must not translate blindly with no attention to the meaning of the sentence under consideration. For example, 'I am taking my umbrella just in case it rains' is not to be understood as 'I am taking my umbrella if and only if it rains.' Similarly, 'Every animal has a heart if and only if it has a kidney' must not be read as 'Every animal has a heart if and only if every animal has a kidney.'

§2.12: TRANSLATING COMPLICATED SENTENCES

A knowledge of how the truth-functional operators work in simple cases, together with an ordinary grasp of the English language, is all that is required to deal with very complicated sentences. One need only pay careful attention to the meaning of the sentence being translated. A few examples should show this.

The sentence 'If Sam goes to the chess club or visits his sister, he will be late for the play' can be broken up into three simple sentences which are joined by truth-functional operators. One should begin the translation by assigning sentence letters to the three simple sentences. The choice of sentence letters is arbitrary, but one might as well use letters which help one to remember which letter represents which sentence. 'C' can represent 'Sam goes to the chess club', 'S' can represent 'Sam visits his sister' and 'P' can represent 'Sam will be late for the play.' The sentence asserts that if Sam does either of two things he will be late for the play; if he either goes to the chess club or visits his sister, then he will be late for the play. Thus, a correct translation of the original sentence is '$(C \vee S) \supset P$'. (There are other correct translations of this sentence. The various possibilities will be discussed later in this chapter.) One can now write the original and the translation in a clear way:

> If Sam goes to the chess club or visits his sister, he will be late for the play.
> C: Sam goes to the chess club.
> S: Sam visits his sister.
> P: Sam will be late for the play.
> $(C \lor S) \supset P$

Four points about this translation should be noted.

First, the reader is given a clear indication of what is being translated, which sentence letter represents which simple sentence, and what the translation of the original sentence is.

Second, each sentence letter is assigned to a complete English sentence – something which has a truth value. 'If Sam goes to the chess club' and 'or visits his sister' are not, of course, grammatical sentences. It is often necessary to do a little rewording in order to have a grammatical simple sentence to which one can assign a sentence letter.

Third, wherever possible, pronouns are replaced. As far as possible, each sentence letter should be assigned to a sentence which does not require reference to some other sentence for an understanding of its meaning.

Fourth, the position of the brackets is extremely important. Unlike '$(C \lor S) \supset P$', '$C \lor (S \supset P)$' says that either Sam goes to the chess club or he will be late for the play if he visits his sister. Plainly, this is not the meaning of the original sentence. 'If Sam goes to the chess club or visits his sister, he will be late for the play' is a conditional sentence, while 'Either Sam goes to the chess club or he will be late for the play if he visits his sister' is a disjunctive sentence. The two sentences have different main operators.

In translating a sentence from English into the symbolic language, the brackets should reflect the structure of the English sentence. It would be hard to misread the sentence about Sam which was just discussed. The presence of a comma in 'If Sam goes to the chess club or visits his sister, he will be late for the play' makes it completely clear that this is a conditional sentence. However, one cannot rely on the presence of punctuation marks. One must often determine the intended meaning of a sentence by keeping in mind what someone might be expected to mean by that sentence. This means that one frequently has to depend on the context to determine how a sentence is to be understood.

The position of the brackets does not always affect the meaning of the sentence. It does not matter, for example, in translating 'Jones, Smith or the butler did it.' '$(J \lor S) \lor B$' and '$J \lor (S \lor B)$' are both perfectly good translations. '(J ∨ S ∨ B)' †††, however, is not a good translation because there is no way of telling which vel is the main operator.

In everyday English, most sentences are quite short. Occasionally, however, one comes across a long sentence which can cause some confusion. In such cases one should break up the sentence in stages. The following sentence is grammatically correct, although far too lengthy from a stylistic point of view:

> If Jack is neither on the track nor in the pits, then his car has broken down or he has crashed and a caution flag is out; but if a caution flag is out, all the cars will slow down and everyone will know it.

This is a conjunctive sentence, with 'but' serving as the main operator. The first part of the sentence is a complex 'if … then' clause and the second part of the sentence is a less complex 'if … then' clause. The first thing to do is to identify the simple sentences. There are seven.

> If Jack is neither on the track nor in the pits, then his car has broken down or he has crashed and a caution flag is out; but if a caution flag is out, all the cars will slow down and everyone will know it.
> T: Jack is on the track.
> P: Jack is in the pits.
> B: Jack's car has broken down.
> C: Jack has crashed.
> F: A caution flag is out.
> S: All the cars will slow down.
> K: Everyone will know that a caution flag is out.

Since it is the simplest, one can tackle the second 'if … then' clause first. This is easily translated as 'F ⊃ (S ∧ K)'. The first 'if … then' clause is not much more difficult. The antecedent of the clause, 'Jack is neither on the track nor in the pits', can be translated either as '~ (T ∨ P)' or as '~ T ∧ ~ P'. Since the former is slightly shorter, it will be used. The consequent of the clause, '… his car has broken down or he has crashed and a caution flag is out', is easily translated as 'B ∨ (C ∧ F)'. Accordingly, the whole clause can be translated as '~ (T ∨ P) ⊃ (B ∨ (C ∧ F))'. The entire sentence is simply the conjunction of the two clauses:

$$(\sim (T \lor P) \supset (B \lor (C \land F))) \land (F \supset (S \land K))$$

There are, of course, other correct translations.

The procedure for translating an English sentence into the symbolic language consists of five steps. One should:

1 Read the complete sentence carefully to grasp its meaning.

2 Determine how many simple sentences there are. Every English sentence should be broken up into as many simple sentences as possible in order to let the operators show the logical structure. One should replace pronouns where possible.

3 Assign letters to each simple sentence, providing the reader with a clear indication of which letter represents which simple sentence.

4 Check to be sure that insignificant differences in wording have not resulted in any redundant sentence letters.

5 Write the sentence in the symbolic language, being sure that this translation is a WFF and that it captures the meaning of the original sentence.

One can then remove any unnecessary brackets.

Translating English sentences into symbols is usually not very difficult if one takes things a step at a time. On occasion, a piece of English is so unclear that one does not know which of several different translations is an expression of the intended meaning. If the context does not make the sentence clear, the best one can do is to produce as many translations as there are reasonable interpretations of the sentence.

§2.13: EXERCISES

§2.13 Part 1

Using the given sentence letters, translate each of the following sentences.

     B: Brian drives a BMW.
     M: Michael drives a Mercedes Benz.
     P: Paul drives a Porsche.

1 Paul does not drive a Porsche.

2 Brian drives a BMW only if Michael drives a Mercedes Benz.

3 If Michael doesn't drive a Mercedes Benz or Paul doesn't drive a Porsche, then Michael doesn't drive a Mercedes Benz and Paul doesn't drive a Porsche.

4 Unless Paul drives a Porsche, either Michael drives a Mercedes Benz or Brian drives a BMW.

5 Brian drives a BMW if and only if either Paul doesn't drive a Porsche or Michael drives a Mercedes Benz.

6 Paul drives a Porsche; Brian, however, drives a BMW.

7 Michael drives a Mercedes Benz or Brian drives a BMW, but it is not true that Michael drives a Mercedes Benz and Brian drives a BMW.

8 If Paul drives a Porsche, Michael drives a Mercedes Benz if Brian drives a BMW.

9 Provided that Michael drives a Mercedes Benz, Paul drives a Porsche only if Brian drives a BMW.

10 If it is false that Paul drives a Porsche and Michael drives a Mercedes Benz, then either Paul drives a Porsche and Brian does not drive a BMW or Michael drives a Mercedes Benz and Brian does not drive a BMW.

§2.13 Part 2

Translate each of the following sentences into symbols, being sure to specify clearly the meanings of the sentence letters.

1 I am not guilty.

2 My grandfather is old, but he is very active.

3 My grandfather is not old, but he is not very active.

4 She doesn't own her car; she leases it.

5 That exercise is neither enjoyable nor useful.

6 The old are wise and cautious; the young are foolish and brave.

7 Neither of my parents has blue eyes.

8 He was an officer but no gentleman.

9 There is no heavy industry in the eastern or northern regions.

10 They do not ask politely; they either snarl or grovel.

11 When you're hot, you're hot; when you're not, you're not.

12 Copper can be soldered but stainless steel must be welded.

13 If the rates on our loans remain the same and the rise in the market does not slow down, we are bound to become millionaires.

14 John will buy a new car only if he can sell his old one.

15 I've not only made a fortune in the market; I've made some money as a financial journalist.

16 The star doesn't sing, dance or do any comic routines.

17 If mortgage rates go down, I will buy a house if my wife still wants me to do so.

18 You will be caught unless you slow down and/or buy a radar detector.

19 Either the theory of the supply-siders is right and that of the traditional economists is wrong, or the theory of the traditional economists is right and that of the supply-siders is wrong.

20 Provided, but only provided, that two members make an objection in
    writing, the chairman is obliged to reopen the question of Smith's
    membership if Smith still wants to join the club.

§2.14: DEFINING THE OPERATORS

The five truth-functional operators have been introduced as being roughly
equivalent to certain English words or phrases. There are serious problems
connected with defining some of the terms of a natural language such as
English. For example, most English speakers would be hard pressed to
provide a strict definition of 'or', and reference to a dictionary in such a case
is of little help. However, these problems do not arise in connection with the
symbolic operators. Since these operators are truth-functional, it is possible
to provide formal definitions of them in terms of truth values. This can most
easily be done by considering all of the different possibilities on a **truth table**.

The simplest case is the tilde. If the sentence 'Zinc is an element' is true,
the sentence 'It is false that zinc is an element' is false. Similarly, if the
sentence 'Zinc is an element' is false, the sentence 'It is false that zinc is an
element' is true. The negation of any sentence 'Φ' is false if 'Φ' is true and is
true if 'Φ' is false. There are only two possibilities: either 'Φ' is true or 'Φ' is
false. The truth table for the tilde follows:

Φ	$\sim \Phi$
T	F
F	T

The formulas to be considered, 'Φ' and '$\sim \Phi$', are placed above the line in
the table. There are two rows beneath the line, since there only two
possibilities. The first row shows the truth value of '$\sim \Phi$' if 'Φ' is true, while
the second row shows the truth value of '$\sim \Phi$' if 'Φ' is false. The meaning of
the tilde is determined by this truth table. Although '$\sim$' is defined truth-
functionally, it corresponds roughly to phrases like 'It is false that ...' in
English.

The truth table for conjunction is a little more complicated, since the
truth values of two formulas joined by '$\wedge$' must be considered. For any two
formulas 'Φ' and 'Ψ', there are exactly four possibilities:

1 'Φ' and 'Ψ' are both true.

2 'Φ' is true while 'Ψ' is false.

3 'Φ' is false while 'Ψ' is true.

4 'Φ' and 'Ψ' are both false.

The following truth table covers all these possibilities:

Φ	Ψ	Φ ∧ Ψ
T	T	T
T	F	F
F	T	F
F	F	F

As would be expected, 'Φ ∧ Ψ' is true only if 'Φ' is true and 'Ψ' is true; in all other cases it is false. Although the caret suffices to express some uses of 'and', 'but' and other English expressions, it is defined by the truth table.

The truth table for disjunction reflects the same four possibilities:

Φ	Ψ	Φ ∨ Ψ
T	T	T
T	F	T
F	T	T
F	F	F

Bearing in mind that '∨' is the rough equivalent of the inclusive sense of 'or', there is nothing surprising in this truth table. 'Φ ∨ Ψ' is true if either 'Φ' is true or 'Ψ' is true; it is false only if both 'Φ' and 'Ψ' are false. '∨' is defined by the truth table, and this definition does in fact capture the sense of many uses of 'or' in English.

So far, the truth tables for the operators have been just as one would expect them to be from an understanding of English. The truth table for the horseshoe does not follow this pattern. As before, there are four possibilities, but the final two rows of the truth table are not what one might expect:

Φ	Ψ	Φ ⊃ Ψ
T	T	T
T	F	F
F	T	T
F	F	T

The important point to remember is that the horseshoe is defined by this truth table. The easiest way to remember the truth table for the horseshoe is to think about how an English conditional sentence could be shown to be false. The sure way to show that a conditional sentence in English is false is to provide an example in which the antecedent is true and the consequent is false. If a man claims that he will eat his hat if Brown wins the election and Brown does not win, it is hard to establish whether his claim is true. If, on the other hand, Brown does win the election and the man does not eat his hat, the falsity of his claim is clearly established.

The horseshoe is a truth-functional operator, and the truth values of many conditional sentences in English are not functions of the truth values of their antecedents and consequents. For example, the sentence 'If Mexico had a king, peaches would grow well in Iceland' is most naturally taken as making a causal claim which is manifestly false; whether or not there is a king of Mexico has nothing whatever to do with the climate of Iceland. However, letting 'M' represent 'Mexico has a king' and 'P' represent 'Peaches grow well in Iceland', the sentence is symbolized as 'M ⊃ P'. When this formula is put on the following truth table, row 4 of the truth table indicates that the formula is true, since as a matter of fact both the antecedent and consequent are false.

M P	M ⊃ P
T T	T
T F	F
F T	T
F F	T

It is clear that there are many conditional sentences in English which can be judged to be true or false on some basis other than the truth values of their antecedents and consequents. What this means is that there are many sentences in English in which 'if ... then' does not function as a truth-functional operator, and this fact has raised serious problems in some areas of logic. However, for purposes of dealing with all the logic covered in this book, these problems can simply be ignored; the horseshoe can always be used to translate English 'if ... then' sentences.

The last operator to be considered is the triplebar. The truth table for the triplebar follows:

Φ ψ	Φ ≡ ψ
T T	T
T F	F
F T	F
F F	T

The resemblance between the triplebar and the '=' sign is not entirely coincidental; 'Φ ≡ ψ' is true when 'Φ' and 'ψ' have the same truth values and false when 'Φ' and 'ψ' have different truth values. This is just what one would expect from an understanding of English phrases such as '... if and only if ...' However, it should be kept in mind that the symbol is defined by the truth table.

Truth tables have been introduced to define the five sentence operators. In each case, all the possibilities of truth and falsity have been considered.

Since every complete truth table covers all possibilities, there is a row on every complete truth table which corresponds to the actual world. For purposes of doing logic, however, there is no need to determine which row that is.

All the truth tables discussed so far have dealt with formulas having a single operator. The next topic to be considered is the development of truth tables for more complex formulas.

§2.15: TRUTH TABLES

One can use the simple truth tables for the five sentence operators to calculate the truth values of complicated formulas such as '~ (R ∧ G)'. If both 'R' and 'G' are true, then 'R ∧ G' is true. If 'R ∧ G' is true, then '~ (R ∧ G)' must be false. Similarly, if 'R ∧ G' is false, then '~ (R ∧ G)' must be true. In developing the truth table for '~ (R ∧ G)', one has to determine the truth value of 'R ∧ G' before one can determine the truth value of '~ (R ∧ G)', because the '~' is the main operator of the formula. Truth tables should be developed on a column-by-column basis, with the column under the main operator being done last. An example follows:

G	R	~	(R ∧ G)
T	T	F	T
T	F	T	F
F	T	T	F
F	F	T	F
		1	2

Three conventions are observed in this truth table.

1 In assigning the different truth values for 'R' and 'G' in the first two columns, the sentence letters are arranged in alphabetical sequence. In principle, this sequence does not matter, but in practice the initial columns for the sentence letters should always be arranged alphabetically. This convention is almost universally observed, and setting out one's sentence letters in any other way creates unnecessary work for anyone checking the truth table.

2 Still concerning the initial columns for the sentence letters, the right column (under 'R') has alternate 'T's and 'F's, while the column immediately to the left of that one (under 'G') has two 'T's followed by two 'F's. If there were three columns, the column on the extreme left would have four 'T's followed by four 'F's. This pattern of arranging the initial columns for the sentence letters when there are three or more sentence letters is exemplified later in this section. There are other

arrangements of 'T's and 'F's which would ensure that all the possible combinations are included, but this is the most common way of setting out a truth table, and it should always be used.

3 The number '1' is put under the column for the main operator of the formula. Different conventions are used to indicate which operator is the main operator, but in this book the columns will be numbered in the reverse order to that in which they are completed.

'~ R ∧ G' is a completely different formula from '~ (R ∧ G)', and this difference is shown in the difference between the truth table for '~ (R ∧ G)' which has just been given and the truth table for '~ R ∧ G' which follows:

G	R		~	R	∧	G
T	T		F		F	
T	F		T		T	
F	T		F		F	
F	F		T		F	
			2		1	

The truth table for a more complicated formula follows:

C	D	E		~	(C	∨	D)	⊃	(D	≡	~	E)
T	T	T		F		T		T		F	F	
T	T	F		F		T		T		T	T	
T	F	T		F		T		T		T	F	
T	F	F		F		T		T		F	T	
F	T	T		F		T		T		F	F	
F	T	F		F		T		T		T	T	
F	F	T		T		F		T		T	F	
F	F	F		T		F		F		F	T	
				4		5		1		2	3	

The truth table was begun by setting up the initial columns in alphabetical order for each of the distinct sentence letters which occur in the formula. In this case there were three letters, so eight rows were required on the truth table. In all cases, the number of rows on a truth table is a function of the number of distinct sentence letters. If there is one sentence letter, two rows are required; if there are two sentence letters, four rows are required; if there are three sentence letters, eight rows are required; if there are four sentence letters, sixteen rows are required, and so on. As the number of rows increases geometrically, truth tables rapidly become so complex that they are unmanageable. In principle, however, there is no limit to the number of rows on a truth table.

The next step was to fill in the columns under the sentence operators. The horseshoe is the main operator, so the column under it had to be completed last. The last column to be completed is always column 1. The first column to be completed was the column under the vel. The truth values for this column were determined from the truth values of 'C' and 'D' which appear at the left side of the truth table, and the truth-table definition of '∨'. There are five columns to be completed, so this column was labelled '5'. One could have begun by completing the column under the second '~' and determining the truth values for this column by reference to the truth values of 'E' and the truth-table definition of '~'. There is nothing to choose between these different ways of beginning the truth table. However, one could not have begun with the column under the '≡', since the truth values for this column are determined by reference to the truth values of 'D' and the truth values of '~ E'. Plainly, one must have completed the column for '~ E' before one could complete the column for 'D ≡ ~ E'. Similarly, one could not have completed the column for '~ (C ∨ D)' before one had completed the column for 'C ∨ D'. The final column, of course, could not have been completed before the column for '~ (C ∨ D)' and the column for 'D ≡ ~ E' were completed.

One more example should suffice to make these points clear. Since '(L ⊃ ~ ~ N) ∧ (M ∨ (O ⊃ L))' has four distinct sentence letters, the truth table for this formula has sixteen rows:

L	M	N	O	(L ⊃ ~ ~ N)	∧	(M ∨	(O ⊃ L))
T	T	T	T	T T F	T	T	T
T	T	T	F	T T F	T	T	T
T	T	F	T	F F T	F	T	T
T	T	F	F	F F T	F	T	T
T	F	T	T	T T F	T	T	T
T	F	T	F	T T F	T	T	T
T	F	F	T	F F T	F	T	T
T	F	F	F	F F T	F	T	T
F	T	T	T	T T F	T	T	F
F	T	T	F	T T F	T	T	T
F	T	F	T	T F T	T	T	F
F	T	F	F	T F T	T	T	T
F	F	T	T	T T F	F	F	F
F	F	T	F	T T F	T	T	T
F	F	F	T	T F T	F	F	F
F	F	F	F	T F T	T	T	T
				4 5 6	1	2	3

As in the previous example, there is some choice in the order in which the columns are completed. One could have begun with the column for 'O ⊃ L', for example. Since the truth value of '∼ ∼ N' is always the same as the truth value of 'N', one might be tempted to skip column 6. However, a complete truth table requires that there be a complete column for every occurrence of an operator. Accordingly, the column for '∼ N' should be included; the truth table would be incomplete if column 6 were missing. Producing truth tables is a completely mechanical procedure. Once one has learned the truth tables for the sentence operators and understands the way in which the position of the brackets determines what the operators do, the whole business tends to become boring. However, some interesting things can be shown with truth tables, and it is worth taking the time to complete them carefully.

§2.16: EXERCISES

Produce a complete truth table for each of the following formulas, numbering each column as was done in §2.15.

1 ∼ (M ∨ N)

2 ∼ ∼ ∼ (F ≡ G)

3 S ⊃ (V ∨ K)

4 (S ⊃ V) ∨ K

5 ∼ (P ⊃ ∼ ∼ P)

6 (S ∧ R) ∧ ∼ Q

7 S ∧ (R ∧ ∼ Q)

8 ∼ ((F ≡ G) ∧ (G ⊃ H))

9 (R ⊃ G) ⊃ S

10 (M ∧ N) ∧ ∼ (O ∨ K)

§2.17: TYPES OF FORMULAS

When one produces a truth table for certain formulas, the final column consists of nothing but 'T's. Such formulas are **truth-functionally true**. 'M ∨ ∼ M' is an example of a truth-functionally true formula:

M	M ∨ ∼ M
T	T F
F	T T
	1 2

Another example of a truth-functionally true formula is '~ (K ∧ ~ K)':

K	~ (K ∧ ~ K)
T	T F F
F	T F T
	1 2 3

The mark of a truth-functionally true formula is that it is true no matter what truth values are assigned to the atomic formulas of which it is made up. No matter what sentence is represented by 'K', one can be certain of the truth of '~ (K ∧ ~ K)'. Whenever the final column of a truth table for a given formula consists of nothing but 'T's, that formula is truth-functionally true.

The final columns of the truth tables for some formulas consist of nothing but 'F's. Such formulas are **truth-functionally false**. 'R ∧ ~ R' is an example of a truth-functionally false formula:

R	R ∧ ~ R
T	F F
F	F T
	1 2

'~ (S ∨ ~ S)' is another example of a formula which is truth-functionally false:

S	~ (S ∨ ~ S)
T	F T F
F	F T T
	1 2 3

A truth-functionally false formula is always false regardless of what truth values are assigned to the atomic formulas of which it is made up. No matter what sentence is represented by 'S', one can be certain that '~ (S ∨ ~ S)' is false. Whenever the final column of a truth table for a given formula consists of nothing but 'F's, that formula is truth-functionally false.

The second example of a truth-functionally true formula, '~ (K ∧ ~ K)', is the negation of a truth-functionally false formula, 'K ∧ ~ K'. Similarly, the second example of a truth-functionally false formula, '~ (S ∨ ~ S)', is the negation of a truth-functionally true formula, 'S ∨ ~ S'. In all cases, the negation of a truth-functional truth is truth-functionally false and the negation of a truth-functional falsehood is truth-functionally true.

Between the two extremes of truth-functional truth and truth-functional falsehood are formulas whose truth values are dependent upon the truth values of the atomic formulas of which they are made up. Such formulas are

truth-functionally indeterminate. They can be recognized by the appearance of at least one 'T' and at least one 'F' in the final columns of their truth tables.

The mark of a truth-functionally indeterminate formula is that its final column includes at least one 'T' and at least one 'F'. The final column of the following truth table has this feature. Accordingly, '(P ⊃ Q) ∨ ~ P' is truth-functionally indeterminate.

P Q	(P ⊃ Q) ∨ ~ P
T T	T T F
T F	F F F
F T	T T T
F F	T T T
	3 1 2

The final column of the next truth table also includes at least one 'T' and at least one 'F'. Thus, '(K ∧ L) ⊃ (~ L ∨ R)', too, is truth-functionally indeterminate:

K L R	(K ∧ L) ⊃ (~ L ∨ R)
T T T	T T F T
T T F	T F F F
T F T	F T T T
T F F	F T T T
F T T	F T F T
F T F	F T F F
F F T	F T T T
F F F	F T T T
	4 1 3 2

§2.18: TRUTH-FUNCTIONAL EQUIVALENCES

Any two formulas of sentence logic, 'Φ' and 'Ψ', are **truth-functionally equivalent** if and only if '$\Phi \equiv \Psi$' can be shown to be truth-functionally true on a truth table. As an example, the truth-functional equivalence of '$A \wedge B$' and '$B \wedge A$' is shown on the truth table for '$(A \wedge B) \equiv (B \wedge A)$':

A	B		$(A \wedge B)$	$\equiv$	$(B \wedge A)$	
T	T		T	T	T	
T	F		F	T	F	
F	T		F	T	F	
F	F		F	T	F	
			3	1	2	

Joining two formulas with a triplebar and seeing whether the resulting formula is truth-functionally true is not necessary for purposes of checking the truth-functional equivalence of two formulas. Simply putting both formulas on a single truth table will serve as well. Then, if the columns under their main operators are identical, those two formulas are truth-functionally equivalent. Doing this is not only simpler; it allows one to check the truth-functional equivalence of three or more formulas. As an example, the intuitively clear truth-functional equivalence of '$(A \vee B) \vee C$', '$A \vee (B \vee C)$' and '$(B \vee A) \vee C$' is shown on the following truth table:

A	B	C	$(A \vee B)$	$\vee C$	$A \vee$	$(B \vee C)$	$(B \vee A)$	$\vee C$
T	T	T	T	T	T	T	T	T
T	T	F	T	T	T	T	T	T
T	F	T	T	T	T	T	T	T
T	F	F	T	T	T	F	T	T
F	T	T	T	T	T	T	T	T
F	T	F	T	T	T	T	T	T
F	F	T	F	T	T	T	F	T
F	F	F	F	F	F	F	F	F
			2	1	1	2	2	1

Although there is some variation in the different number 2 columns, all number 1 columns are identical. This shows that the three formulas are truth-functionally equivalent.

Since the final column of the truth table for a truth-functionally true formula consists of nothing but 'T's, it follows that all truth-functionally true formulas are truth-functionally equivalent. The following truth table for two arbitrarily picked truth-functionally true formulas shows this to be so:

M R	M ∨ ~ M	R ⊃ R
T T	T F	T
T F	T F	T
F T	T T	T
F F	T T	T
	1 2	

Similarly, since the final column of the truth table for a truth-functionally false formula consists of nothing but 'F's, it follows that all truth-functionally false formulas are truth-functionally equivalent. The following truth table for two arbitrarily picked truth-functionally false formulas demonstrates this:

P Q	P ∧ ~ P	~ (Q ∨ ~ Q)
T T	F F	F T F
T F	F F	F T T
F T	F T	F T F
F F	F T	F T T
	1 2	1 2 3

The statement 'John studies chemistry or John studies physics' can be represented as 'C ∨ P'. Saying that John studies chemistry or John studies physics amounts to saying that the conjunction 'John does not study chemistry and John does not study physics' is false, which one can represent as '~ (~ C ∧ ~ P)'. The truth-functional equivalence of these two statements is shown on the following truth table:

C P	C ∨ P	~ (~ C ∧ ~ P)
T T	T	T F F F
T F	T	T F F T
F T	T	T T F F
F F	F	F T T T
	1 4	2 3

It should be clear from this example that whenever one has a disjunctive formula one can produce a truth-functionally equivalent formula using the caret and the tilde. This means that '∨' is not strictly necessary in the symbolic language; everything done with it can be done with '∧' and '~'.

There is another way in which one can dispense with '∨'. The statement 'John studies chemistry or John studies physics' tells one two things: if John does not study chemistry, then he studies physics; and, if John does not study physics, then he studies chemistry. This suggests a truth-functional equivalence between 'C ∨ P', '∼ C ⊃ P' and '∼ P ⊃ C' which is confirmed by a truth table:

C	P	C ∨ P	∼ C ⊃ P		∼ P ⊃ C	
T	T	T	F	T	F	T
T	F	T	F	T	T	T
F	T	T	T	T	F	T
F	F	F	T	F	T	F
		2	1	2	1	

Just as one can do without '∨', one can also dispense with '∧'. 'John studies chemistry and John studies physics' can be represented as 'C ∧ P'. To say that John studies both chemistry and physics is to say that it is false that John does not study chemistry or does not study physics, which one can represent as '∼ (∼ C ∨ ∼ P)'. Again, the truth table shows the truth-functional equivalence:

C	P	C ∧ P	∼	(∼ C	∨	∼ P)
T	T	T	T	F	F	F
T	F	F	F	F	T	T
F	T	F	F	T	T	F
F	F	F	F	T	T	T
		1	4	2	3	

Since one can use '∼' and '∨' instead of '∧', and '∼' and '⊃' instead of '∨', it follows that one can express 'C ∧ P' using only '∼' and '⊃'. The following truth table shows this to be correct:

C	P	C ∧ P	∼	(C ⊃	∼ P)	∼	(P ⊃	∼ C)
T	T	T	T	F	F	T	F	F
T	F	F	F	T	T	F	T	F
F	T	F	F	T	F	F	T	T
F	F	F	F	T	T	F	T	T
		1	2	3		1	2	3

'John studies both chemistry and physics' is an example of plain English, whereas what has just been shown to be its truth-functional equivalent, 'It is false that, if John studies physics, then he does not study chemistry', is such a strange example of English that it might seem unintelligible. The study of an artificial language of the sort developed in this book helps one to avoid the trap of supposing that something is unintelligible simply because it is unusual.

It is easy to eliminate the triplebar. 'John studies chemistry if and only if John studies physics' means just what it says: 'John studies chemistry if John studies physics, and John studies chemistry only if John studies physics.' The following truth table shows that 'C ≡ P' is truth-functionally equivalent to '(P ⊃ C) ∧ (C ⊃ P)':

C	P	C ≡ P	(P ⊃ C)	∧	(C ⊃ P)
T	T	T	T	T	T
T	F	F	T	F	F
F	T	F	F	F	T
F	F	T	T	T	T
			3	1	2

Since one knows how to dispense with '∧' by using '~' and '⊃', one can express 'C ≡ P' as '~ ((C ⊃ P) ⊃ ~ (P ⊃ C))', as is shown by the truth table:

C	P	C ≡ P	~	((C ⊃ P)	⊃	~	(P ⊃ C))
T	T	T	T	T	F	F	T
T	F	F	F	F	T	F	T
F	T	F	F	T	T	T	F
F	F	T	T	T	F	F	T
			1	5	2	3	4

Using the arbitrarily chosen sentences, 'John studies chemistry' and 'John studies physics', and the arbitrarily chosen sentence letters, 'C' and 'P', it has been shown how it is possible to do everything done with the five operators, '∨', '∧', '⊃', '~' and '≡', using only '~' and '⊃'. The same possibilities obtain if one uses other formulas, which need not be atomic formulas, instead of 'C' and 'P'. It can also be shown that all the work done by '~' together with '⊃' can be done by either '~' together with '∨' or '~' together with '∧'. The additional operators are not essential, but they are helpful in two ways. First, they allow one to represent certain statements more concisely than would otherwise be possible. Second, the extra operators are close approximations to many English words which serve as operators, making translation relatively simple.

Understanding some of the different ways in which certain operators can be eliminated is useful in that it leads to an understanding of various truth-functional equivalences. Moreover, the possibility of reducing the number of operators is of theoretical interest in logic, since one of the recurring interests of logicians is accomplishing more with less.

§2.19: EXERCISES

§2.19 Part 1

Produce a complete truth table for each of the following formulas. Use the truth table to determine whether the formula is truth-functionally true, truth-functionally false or truth-functionally indeterminate.

1 ~ (F ⊃ G) ∧ ~ (G ⊃ H)

2 ~ (R ∧ ~ ~ R) ∧ (~ R ⊃ R)

3 (L ⊃ M) ∧ (~ L ⊃ M)

4 (L ⊃ M) ∧ ~ (L ⊃ M)

5 (C ⊃ (~ K ∧ ~ B)) ∧ (~ K ⊃ S)

6 ((F ⊃ ~ G) ∧ (F ⊃ H)) ∧ (G ∨ ~ S)

§2.19 Part 2

Produce a single complete truth table for each of the following pairs of formulas. Use the truth table to determine whether or not the formulas in each pair are truth-functionally equivalent.

1 (F ⊃ G) ∧ (F ⊃ H)
   F ⊃ (G ∧ H)

2 (F ∧ G) ⊃ H
   (F ⊃ H) ∧ (G ⊃ H)

3 K ∨ L
   K ∨ (~ K ∧ L)

4 R ⊃ (S ⊃ R)
   S ⊃ (R ⊃ S)

5 M ⊃ N
   ~ N ⊃ (M ⊃ N)

6 R ⊃ (S ∨ L)
   (R ⊃ S) ∨ (R ⊃ L)

§2.20: ARGUMENTS

The term 'argument', as used in logic, does not refer to disputes, fights or anything of that sort. An **argument** is simply a collection of statements. The only arguments to be considered in this book are **deductive** – arguments in which the truth of some statements of the collection, the **premisses**, is supposed to guarantee the truth of another statement of the collection, the **conclusion**. If the truth of the premisses does guarantee the truth of the conclusion, the argument is **valid**. If the truth of the premisses fails to guarantee the truth of the conclusion, the argument is **invalid**. There are no degrees of validity; any deductive argument which is not valid is invalid and worthless.

In writing arguments, the universal practice is to list the premisses, draw a line under them and write the conclusion, much in the way that sums in arithmetic are written. Two examples follow:

$$\frac{A}{A \lor B}$$

$$\frac{S}{S \supset R}$$
$$R$$

Valid arguments are **truth-preserving**. That is to say, if all the premisses are true, the conclusion must be true. To say that an argument is valid is not to say that the premisses are in fact true or that the conclusion is in fact true; it is only to say that there cannot be a situation in which the conclusion is false while all the premisses are true.

To determine the **truth-functional validity** of an argument, one should put all the premisses and the conclusion on a single truth table. If there is a row on which all the premisses are true and the conclusion is false, the argument is **truth-functionally invalid**. If there is no such row, the argument is truth-functionally valid. It should be clear that the truth-functional invalidity of an argument can be shown by reference to a single row on a truth table, while the truth-functional validity of an argument can be shown only by checking every row.

The second example of an argument given in this section was:

$$\frac{S}{S \supset R}$$
$$R$$

The four rows of the truth table for this argument cover all possibilities.

R	S	S	S ⊃ R	R
T	T	T	T	T
T	F	F	T	T
F	T	T	F	F
F	F	F	T	F

The only row on which both premisses are true is row 1. On this row, the conclusion is true. Thus, the argument is truth-functionally valid.

Another example of an argument follows:

~ K

K ⊃ L
_____

~ L

The truth table gives the truth values for both premisses and the conclusion:

K	L	~ K	K ⊃ L	~ L
T	T	F	T	F
T	F	F	F	T
F	T	T	T	F
F	F	T	T	T

On row 3 both premisses are true while the conclusion is false. The argument, therefore, is truth-functionally invalid.

The first example of an argument given in this section will turn out to be truth-functionally valid:

A
_____

A ∨ B

The argument is checked by putting the single premiss and the conclusion on a truth table:

A	B	A	A ∨ B
T	T	T	T
T	F	T	T
F	T	F	T
F	F	F	F

The only rows on which the premiss is true are rows 1 and 2. On these rows the conclusion is also true, so the argument is truth-functionally valid.

A more complicated argument is tested next:

J

K

K ⊃ (L ∨ ~ J)
_____

(L ∨ J) ∧ K

As before, the argument is checked by putting the premisses and the conclusion on a truth table:

J	K	L	J	K	K ⊃ (L v ~ J)			(L v J) ∧ K	
T	T	T	T	T	T	T	F	T	T
T	T	F	T	T	F	F	F	T	T
T	F	T	T	F	T	T	F	T	F
T	F	F	T	F	T	F	F	T	F
F	T	T	F	T	T	T	T	T	T
F	T	F	F	T	T	T	T	F	F
F	F	T	F	F	T	T	T	T	F
F	F	F	F	F	T	T	T	F	F
					1	2	3	2	1

Row 1 is the only row on which all the premisses are true. On this row the conclusion is also true, so the argument is truth-functionally valid.

Any argument with a truth-functionally false premiss is truth-functionally valid because it is not possible for all the premisses to be true while the conclusion is false. The following argument will be shown to be truth-functionally valid on a truth table, notwithstanding the fact that the conclusion appears to be completely unrelated to the premiss:

A ∧ ~ A

Q

A	Q	A ∧ ~ A		Q
T	T	F	F	T
T	F	F	F	F
F	T	F	T	T
F	F	F	T	F
		1	2	

Any argument with a truth-functionally true conclusion is truth-functionally valid, no matter what premisses it has. Since the conclusion cannot be false, it is clear that it cannot be the case that the premisses are true while the conclusion is false. The following argument which has a truth-functionally true conclusion is shown to be truth-functionally valid on a truth table:

$$\frac{Q}{A \lor \sim A}$$

A	Q	Q	A	∨	∼	A
T	T	T	T		F	
T	F	F	T		F	
F	T	T	T		T	
F	F	F	T		T	
			1		2	

The truth-functional validity of any argument whatever in sentence logic can be checked on a truth table. It does not matter whether the premisses seem to be unrelated to the conclusions, as is the case with the two arguments just discussed. Similarly, it does not matter how complicated the argument is. As long as there is no row of the truth table on which all the premisses are true and the conclusion is false, the argument is truth-functionally valid.

§2.21: EXERCISES

For each of the following arguments, use a truth table to determine whether or not the argument is truth-functionally valid.

1. F ⊃ G
F

F ∧ G

2. ∼ (∼ K ⊃ ∼ L)

K ⊃ L

3. P ≡ ∼ Q
Q ∨ P

∼ P

4. M ⊃ (N ⊃ O)
M ⊃ N

M ⊃ O

5. (R ⊃ S) ∨ (S ⊃ N)
∼ N ⊃ (R ∧ S)

S ⊃ ∼ R

6 (P ∨ Q) ⊃ ~ R
  P ≡ ~ Q
  ─────────
  Q ⊃ P

7 R ≡ S
  ─────────
  R ⊃ (S ∨ T)

8 L ⊃ ~ K
  ~ M
  K ⊃ (L ∨ M)
  ─────────
  ~ K

9 F ⊃ G
  F ∨ ~ G
  ─────────
  F ≡ G

10 F ⊃ ~ G
   F ⊃ G
   ─────────
   ~ F

11 (B ∧ C) ∨ (B ∧ D)
   ─────────
   B

12 (P ⊃ W) ∨ (P ∧ ~ W)
   ─────────
   P

13 K ∨ L
   L ≡ J
   ~ K ∧ J
   ─────────
   ~ J ∨ ~ L

14 (R ∨ S) ⊃ T
   T ⊃ (R ∧ S)
   ─────────
   (R ∨ S) ⊃ (R ∧ S)

15 ~ K ∧ V
   K ∨ ~ M
   T ⊃ ~ V
   ─────────
   M ∧ ~ T

§2.22: TRANSLATING ARGUMENTS

Translating arguments from English into the symbolic language can often be difficult, but the essential principles are straightforward. A sentence letter should be assigned to every English sentence or clause which is capable of having a truth value, the meaning of each sentence letter being stated clearly. The appropriate symbols should replace English expressions such as 'and', 'or' and 'if ... then'. The argument should then be written out, with the premisses followed by a line and the conclusion.

The importance of using as many simple sentences as possible can be seen from consideration of the following argument:

> If the coolant leaks, the oil overheats and the oil pressure drops.
> If the oil pressure drops, the bearings may be damaged. Thus, if
> the coolant leaks, the bearings may be damaged.

The correct way to translate this argument is as follows:

> L: The coolant leaks.
> O: The oil overheats.
> D: The oil pressure drops.
> B: The bearings may be damaged.

$$L \supset (O \wedge D)$$
$$D \supset B$$
$$\overline{L \supset B}$$

The truth-functional validity of the argument when translated in this way can easily be shown on a truth table.

An incorrect translation of this argument follows:

> L: The coolant leaks.
> O: The oil overheats and the oil pressure drops. †††
> D: The oil pressure drops.
> B: The bearings may be damaged.

$$L \supset O$$
$$D \supset B$$
$$\overline{L \supset B}$$

A truth-table check on the argument translated in this way will show it to be truth-functionally invalid; using a single sentence letter for 'The oil overheats and the oil pressure drops' and another sentence letter for 'The oil pressure drops' has hidden the logical relationship between these two sentences.

A slightly different version of the argument about the coolant and bearing damage follows:

> If the coolant leaks, the oil overheats and the oil pressure drops.
> If the oil overheats and the oil pressure drops, the bearings may be damaged. Thus, if the coolant leaks, the bearings may be damaged.

Translated as follows, the argument can be shown to be truth-functionally valid on a truth table:

> L: The coolant leaks.
> O: The oil overheats.
> D: The oil pressure drops.
> B: The bearings may be damaged.

$$L \supset (O \land D)$$
$$(O \land D) \supset B$$
$$\overline{L \supset B}$$

It can be seen that neither 'O' nor 'D' occurs except in the conjunction 'O ∧ D', and that therefore the logical role played by 'O ∧ D' could be played by a single sentence letter. Accordingly, the argument, for purposes of checking truth-functional validity on a truth table, could as well be translated as:

> L: The coolant leaks.
> O: The oil overheats and the oil pressure drops.   †††
> B: The bearings may be damaged.

$$L \supset O$$
$$O \supset B$$
$$\overline{L \supset B}$$

This translation, although it serves the immediate purpose well enough, is presented as an example of what should not be done. There are at least two reasons why one should not try to translate an argument with the minimum complexity which preserves the necessary logical structure. First, it is often unclear just what the necessary logical structure is until the argument has been translated. One advantage of using a symbolic language rather than English is that many aspects of the logical structure of sentences and arguments are often more apparent in the symbolic language than they are in English, and this advantage can be lost when the argument is simplified before it is translated. Second, there can be reasons for translating an argument other than allowing a truth-table check of truth-functional validity. For example, one may want to see whether the argument would still be truth-functionally valid or truth-functionally invalid if it were changed in certain ways, and a translation which is adequate for a truth-table check of truth-functional validity may not be adequate for this purpose. As a general rule, then, one should break up every English sentence into as many simple sentences as possible.

In dealing with a passage of argumentative English prose, the first step is to determine how many arguments there are. There are often several different arguments in one short piece of English, and these arguments must be distinguished before beginning the process of translation. There are no mechanical procedures to follow; what is required is careful attention to the sense of the passage. In some cases, it may be unclear how many arguments are being presented, or even what the conclusions of the arguments are. In all cases, one needs to use a little common sense and the **principle of charity**. This principle enjoins one to put the most reasonable interpretation on what an author says. In other words, if a passage can be interpreted in two ways, one interpretation being sensible and the other interpretation being silly or false, it should be interpreted in the former way. One should be careful, however, not to distort the meaning of what is given simply because one thinks that it is ridiculous or false; the principle of charity does not require the pretence that people never make false statements or construct bad arguments.

It is important to understand that statements in themselves are neither premises nor conclusions. What makes a statement a premiss or makes it a conclusion is the part it plays in the argument. If a statement serves as a basis for believing another statement, it serves as a premiss. If a statement is offered as being supported by one or more other statements, it serves as a conclusion. In the following argument, 'Bill has not studied logic' is the conclusion:

> Alice has not studied logic. Bill studied logic only if Alice did.
> Therefore, Bill has not studied logic.

However, the sentence, 'Bill has not studied logic', is a premiss in the next argument:

> Bill has not studied logic. Alice studied logic only if Bill did.
> Therefore, Alice has not studied logic.

Another difficulty in dealing with argumentative English prose is that the conclusion does not always appear at the end of a passage. In the following three passages, the same conclusion appears in three different places.

> The streets are not wet. If it were raining, the streets would be wet. Therefore, it is not raining.

> It is not raining because the streets are not wet and they would be wet if it were raining.

> Since the streets are not wet, it is not raining, because the streets would be wet if it were raining,

Having identified an argument, one can turn to the business of translating the premisses and the conclusion. Sometimes, premisses are marked by words such as 'because', 'since' and 'as'. Similarly, conclusions are sometimes marked by words such as 'thus', 'hence' and 'consequently'. Such **premiss-indicators** and **conclusion-indicators** should be dropped. They are not parts of the premisses or conclusions, but 'flags' which indicate how a statement is to be taken. For example, in the sentence 'Thus, Mary will buy the car', 'thus' is doing metalinguistic work, pointing out that the sentence 'Mary will buy the car' is the conclusion of an argument.

One must be careful not to assume that a term that can serve as a premiss-indicator is in fact serving that purpose. The following sentence is an example: 'I have not had a cold since I wrote my finals.' Here, the word 'since' is to be taken in a temporal sense; the sentence certainly is not an argument having 'I wrote my finals' as a premiss and 'I have not had a cold' as the conclusion. Similarly, 'He is late because his car broke down' is most naturally taken as an explanation; 'because' does not indicate that 'His car broke down' is to be taken as a premiss.

The warning just given about premiss-indicators applies also to conclusion-indicators. For example, 'He lived for years on a poor diet, and consequently his teeth are bad' is an explanation and not an argument. It is not claimed in this sentence that 'His teeth are bad' follows from 'He lived for years on a poor diet'; the sentence claims that the state of his teeth is caused by malnutrition rather than by something else.

In general, each English sentence in an argument should be translated as a single formula. The exception is the case in which a premiss and the conclusion are stated as a single sentence. In such cases, the English sentence should be divided and translated as two formulas. An example of correct translation follows:

Francesca will marry James if he is rich. Since James is rich, she will
marry him.

F: Francesca will marry James.

J: James is rich.

$$J \supset F$$
$$J$$
$$\overline{}$$
$$F$$

If one included 'Since James is rich' in the conclusion, the conclusion would
be 'J ⊃ F', exactly the same formula as the first premiss. Moreover, this
inclusion distorts the sense of the English. 'Since James is rich, she will marry
him' asserts that James is rich and asserts that Francesca will marry him; it
does not merely assert that her marrying him depends upon his wealth.
Another example should make the distinction clear. One can truly say to
anyone, 'If you are the first person to walk on the moon, you'll go down in
history.' By contrast, there is only one person to whom one can truly say,
'Since you are the first person to walk on the moon, you'll go down in
history.'

The following is another example of correct translation:

> If I were guilty, I would have been in New York at the time of the
> crime. If that were true, my passport would show that I have
> entered the United States recently. Since this isn't so, it follows
> that I am not guilty.
>
> G: I am guilty.
>
> N: I was in New York at the time of the crime.
>
> P: My passport shows that I have entered the United States
> recently.

$$G \supset N$$
$$N \supset P$$
$$\sim P$$
$$\overline{}$$
$$\sim G$$

The translation reflects the fact that 'If that were true ...' is to be taken as 'If
I were in New York at the time of the crime ...' and '... this isn't so ...' is to
be taken as the denial of 'My passport shows that I have entered the United
States recently.'

Translating arguments is much like translating single sentences except
that one has to consider the ways in which the different sentences are related
to each other. Even very complicated arguments can usually be translated
without serious difficulty. Occasionally, one comes across passages of what
seem to be argumentative prose in which there is no recognizable logical

structure. Such 'arguments' cannot be translated, but they are usually not worth serious attention.

§2.23: EXERCISES

Translate the following arguments into symbols. Provide a clear indication of the meaning of each sentence letter. Separate the conclusions from the premises as was done in §2.22.

1   If the chairman were a fool, he would have fired the manager. He is not a fool, since he did not fire the manager.

2   Either the fingerprints are those of the criminal or the criminal wore gloves. The fingerprints are not those of the criminal. Therefore, the criminal wore gloves.

3   The author is either a charlatan or a fool. If he is a charlatan and I take him seriously, I am gullible. If he is a fool, I am gullible if I take him seriously. So, if I take him seriously, I am gullible.

4   Danny has not gone out, unless he has gone out and left the lights on by mistake. So, if Danny did not leave the lights on by mistake, he has not gone out.

5   I can accept the principle that I may break the law on grounds of conscience only if I can accept the principle that anyone may break the law on grounds of conscience. Since I cannot accept the latter principle, I cannot accept the former.

6   The food poisoning can be traced to the rhubarb pie unless the shellfish was bad. The food poisoning can be traced to the rhubarb pie only if the cafeteria staff were at fault. Since the cafeteria staff were at fault if the shellfish was bad, it follows that the cafeteria staff were at fault.

7   John has been charged and will be either convicted or acquitted. If John is acquitted, the police have made a serious mistake; and, if this is so, the witness lied. John will be convicted, since the witness did not lie.

8   The meaning of a word is not an image in the mind. If it were, I would not know what you mean by a word unless I could look into your mind. I cannot do that, but I do know what you mean by a word.

9   Neither Jane nor Mary has taken a logic course. William has taken a logic course if Sam has not. Paul has taken a a logic course only if Sam has not. Since either Mary has taken a logic course or William has not, Paul has not taken a logic course.

10   If God were all-powerful and perfectly good, there would be no evil in the world. There is evil in the world. Hence, God is not all-powerful or not perfectly good.

11 If I am right, you are confused. If you are right, I am confused. I am right if and only if you are not right. Either you are right or I am right, and I am not confused. It follows that you are confused.

12 If neither Jack nor Carl has a spare key, then Mary has just come back from the track and has been locked out. Mary has been locked out only if she has just come back from the track. Since it is not the case that both Jack and Carl have spare keys, Mary has just come back from the track.

13 If the discount rate rises, stock prices fall; if investor confidence declines, new investors do not come into the market. If the discount rate does not rise and savings are not low, investor confidence declines and brokers lose money. Brokers are losing money but stock prices are not falling. Thus, if savings are low, investor confidence does not decline.

14 If either the alarm or the dog frightened the burglars, the police did not arrive at the scene. The burglars got away with the loot if either the police did not arrive at the scene or the night watchman did not frighten the burglars. The night watchman did frighten the burglars, but the night watchman did not frighten the burglars unless the alarm frightened them. Therefore, the burglars got away with the loot.

15 Potential criminals are deterred if and only if an act of punishment is inflicted on someone who is perceived to be guilty. If the town drunk is framed, an act of punishment is inflicted on someone who is perceived to be guilty. The criminal law is justified if and only if potential criminals are deterred. Therefore, if the town drunk is framed, the criminal law is justified.

§2.24: SUMMARY OF TOPICS

With a few possible exceptions to make the summary clearer, the topics appear in the order in which they appear in the text.

Truth value (See p. 7): The property of being true or false. The only sentences which are considered in this book are sentences having truth values.

Assign a truth value (See p. 8): To make an assumption about the truth or falsity of a sentence.

Truth function (See p. 8): A function that determines the truth value of a formula from the truth value of another formula (in the case of a negated formula) or the truth values of other formulas (in the case of other formulas).

Truth-functional operator (See p. 8): Many English words such as 'and' and 'or' serve as truth-functional operators. The symbolic truth-functional operators used in this book are: '~', '∨', '∧', '⊃' and '≡'.

Tilde (See p. 10): The word for the '~' symbol.

Caret (See p. 10): The word for the '∧' symbol.

Vel (See p. 10): The word for the '∨' symbol.

Horseshoe (See p. 10): The word for the '⊃' symbol.

Triplebar (See p. 10): The word for the '≡' symbol.

Object language (See p. 11): The language being discussed. In this book, the object language is the symbolic language being explained.

Metalanguage (See p. 11): The language used to discuss the object language.

Metatheory (See p. 12): Theory concerned with what can be shown about a logical system as opposed to what can be shown within a logical system.

Well-formed formula (See p. 12): A formula which conforms to the rules of the symbolic language. '(A ⊃ B)' is an example of a well-formed formula. In this book, outer brackets are often dropped, but it should be remembered that formulas like 'A ⊃ B' are not strictly speaking well formed.

WFF (See p. 12): Shorthand for 'well-formed formula'.

Atomic formula (See p. 12): A formula which contains no operators is an atomic formula. In sentence logic, the only atomic formulas are sentence letters.

Negation (See p. 12): A formula formed by placing a tilde before a WFF. '~ A' and '~ (A ∨ B)' are negations.

Main operator (See p. 13): Every well-formed formula has a main operator. The main operator of any formula in sentence logic can be determined by considering the way in which the WFF is built up from another formula in the case of the tilde or other formulas in the case of the other operators. The last operator which is added is the main operator. In creating a truth table, the column under the main operator is always the last column to be completed.

Conjunction (See p. 15): A formula formed by placing a caret between two WFFs. 'A ∧ B' and 'A ∧ (R ⊃ ~ B)' are conjunctions.

Conjuncts (See p. 15): The two formulas flanking a caret.

Disjunction (See p. 17): A formula formed by placing a vel between two WFFs. 'A ∨ B' and 'A ∨ (R ∧ B)' are disjunctions.

Disjuncts (See p. 17): The two formulas flanking a vel.

Exclusive sense of 'or' (See p. 17): 'Or' meaning 'either but not both'.

Inclusive sense of 'or' (See p. 17): 'Or' meaning 'either and perhaps both'.

Antecedent (See p. 18): The formula to the left of a horseshoe.

Consequent (See p. 18): The formula to the right of a horseshoe.

Truth table (See p. 26): A truth table is a table which shows all the possibilities of truth and falsity. A simple truth table follows:

A	B	~	(A ∧ B)
T	T	F	T
T	F	T	F
F	T	T	F
F	F	T	F
		1	2

Truth-functionally true (See p. 32): A formula which is true no matter what truth values are assigned to the atomic formulas which it contains.

Truth-functionally false (See p. 33): A formula which is false no matter what truth values are assigned to the atomic formulas which it contains.

Truth-functionally indeterminate (See p. 34): A formula which is either true or false depending on the truth values which are assigned to the atomic formulas which it contains.

Truth-functionally equivalent (See p. 35): Any two formulas of sentence logic, 'Φ' and 'Ψ', are truth-functionally equivalent if and only if 'Φ ≡ Ψ' can be shown to be truth-functionally true on a truth table.

Argument (See p. 39): A collection of statements consisting of one or more premises and a conclusion. In an argument, the premises are used to establish the conclusion.

Deductive (See p. 39): A deductive argument is one in which the truth of the premisses is supposed to guarantee the truth of the conclusion.

Premisses (See p. 39): The premisses of an argument are the sentences which are given as the justification for the conclusion.

Conclusion (See p. 39): The conclusion of an argument is a sentence which is or purports to be justified by the premisses

Valid (See p. 39): In a valid argument, the conclusion follows with certainty from the premisses.

Invalid (See p. 39): Not valid.

Truth-preserving (See p. 40): An informal way of describing valid arguments. Valid arguments 'preserve' truth in the sense that they cannot lead from true premisses to a false conclusion.

Truth-functional validity (See p. 40): Validity which can be shown on a truth table.

Truth-functionally invalid (See p. 40): Any argument which is not truth-functionally valid is truth-functionally invalid.

Principle of charity (See p. 47): The principle which directs one to put the most reasonable interpretation on what an author says.

Premiss-indicators (See p. 48): Words such as 'since' and 'because' which show that a sentence is to be taken as a premiss.

Conclusion-indicators (See p. 48): Words such as 'thus' and 'therefore' which show that a sentence is to be taken as a conclusion.

CHAPTER THREE

DERIVATIONS IN SENTENCE LOGIC

§3.1: WHAT A DERIVATION IS

In this chapter, derivations will be used to do two things. First, the conclusions of truth-functionally valid arguments will be derived from the premisses. Second, formulas which are truth-functional truths will be derived. Using the derivation rules of this chapter, the conclusions of arguments can be derived from their premisses if and only if those arguments can be shown to be truth-functionally valid on a truth table. Similarly, truth-functionally true formulas can be derived using the derivation rules of this chapter if and only if those formulas can be shown to be truth-functionally true on a truth table. This parallelism between derivations and truth tables can be demonstrated, but such a demonstration is a matter of metatheory which is not addressed in this book.

A **derivation** is simply a numbered sequence of formulas, each written against a vertical line which shows the extent or 'scope' of the derivation. This vertical line is a **scope line**. The occurrence of each formula is justified in one of four ways:

1 The formula is given as the premiss of an argument.

2 The formula is introduced as an assumption.

3 The formula is copied from an earlier stage of the derivation.

4 The formula is obtained by a rule of inference.

The following is a derivation:

1	F ∧ G	P
2	F	1, ∧E

The derivation has two lines. The 'P' at the right end of line 1 justifies the occurrence of 'F ∧ G' as the premiss of an argument. The '1, ∧E' at the right end of line 2 justifies the occurrence of 'F' by an appeal to line 1 and a rule of inference (∧E) which will be explained very shortly. The vertical line to the right of the line numbers is the **primary scope line,** which shows that the derivation extends from line 1 to line 2. Later on, derivations with more than one scope line will be discussed.

The derivation rules for sentence logic consist of two rules for each of the five sentence operators. In addition, there is a rule which allows one to introduce any formula as an assumption and a rule which allows one to reiterate a formula which has already occurred in the derivation. The rules for the sentence operators are of two kinds. For each operator, there is an **introduction rule** which serves to create a formula which has that operator as its main operator and an **elimination rule** which uses the main operator of a given formula to create a different formula.

Six of these rules can – and must – be used without a change of scope line. Accordingly, these six will be discussed first. The rules for adding and removing scope lines, together with the other rules, will then be considered. Of the six rules to be discussed first, two are introduction rules (conjunction introduction and disjunction introduction) and four are elimination rules (conjunction elimination, negation elimination, horseshoe elimination and triplebar elimination).

Each rule will be presented together with whatever explanation is necessary to provide an intuitive justification of the rule. In general, it is not hard to understand the rationale of the rules, and this means that they do not have to be learned by rote. As noted in Chapter 2, using truth tables is a purely mechanical procedure, simply a matter of mindlessly completing all the columns according to some very simple rules. The derivation rules, too, are very simple, but producing derivations is not mindless; there is room for a little flair and imagination.

§3.2: CONJUNCTION INTRODUCTION

If one knows that Dublin is the capital of Ireland and one also knows that Rome is the capital of Italy, then one certainly knows that Dublin is the capital of Ireland and Rome is the capital of Italy. Given any two sentences 'Φ' and 'Ψ', one can infer '$\Phi \wedge \Psi$'. The rule of **conjunction introduction**, '$\wedge$I', reflects this intuitively clear inference.

$\wedge$I
One can write the formula '$(\Phi \wedge \Psi)$' or the formula '$(\Psi \wedge \Phi)$' on any given scope line, provided that **both** of the following two conditions are met: 1 The formula 'Φ' is already on the same scope line. 2 The formula 'Ψ' is already on the same scope line. The justification for the new line consists of an appeal to the number of the line where 'Φ' occurs, the number of the line where 'Ψ' occurs and the rule, '$\wedge$I'.

The formal statement of the rule includes outer brackets in the formula, although this requirement is ignored in what follows.

The following argument is obviously truth-functionally valid:

> A
> B
> ———
> A $\wedge$ B

The conclusion can be derived from the premisses in three steps:

1	A	P
2	B	P
3	A $\wedge$ B	1, 2, $\wedge$I

'B $\wedge$ A' can be derived from the same two premisses.

1	A	P
2	B	P
3	B $\wedge$ A	1, 2, $\wedge$I

It should be noted that the formulas appealed to by $\wedge$I do not have to be distinct. Accordingly, the derivation of 'A $\wedge$ A' from 'A' immediately below is completely in order.

| 1 | A | P |
| 2 | A $\wedge$ A | 1, 1, $\wedge$I |

The formulas appealed to by the rule of ∧I do not have to be on consecutive lines, nor do they have to be atomic formulas. The following derivation which works from six premisses to any of five conclusions is completely in order:

1	R	P
2	A	P
3	F ⊃ G	P
4	R ∨ S	P
5	B	P
6	S ∧ Q	P
7	A ∧ B	2, 5, ∧I
8	B ∧ R	1, 5, ∧I
9	(F ⊃ G) ∧ R	1, 3, ∧I
10	B ∧ (R ∨ S)	4, 5, ∧I
11	(S ∧ Q) ∧ B	5, 6, ∧I

∧I can be used repeatedly to create increasingly complex formulas. In the following derivation, the conclusion of this argument is derived from the premisses:

$$F$$
$$G$$
$$H$$
$$\overline{(F \wedge G) \wedge H}$$

1	F	P
2	G	P
3	H	P
4	F ∧ G	1, 2, ∧I
5	(F ∧ G) ∧ H	3, 4, ∧I

It should be noted that this derivation requires two applications of ∧I. Every appeal to ∧I involves an appeal to just two lines. Accordingly, the following is incorrect:

1	F	P
2	G	P
3	H	P
4	(F ∧ G) ∧ H †††	1, 2, 3, ∧I

When a conjunctive formula which contains more than one occurrence of '∧' is needed, one must be careful to determine which caret of the needed formula is the main operator. This point is ignored in what follows:

```
1 │ F                                         P
2 │ G                                         P
3 │ H                                         P
4 │ G ∧ H                                     2, 3, ∧I
5 │ (F ∧ G) ∧ H  †††                          1, 4, ∧I
```

Line 5 is mistaken because the main operator of '(F ∧ G) ∧ H' is the second caret, and not the first. To obtain '(F ∧ G) ∧ H' by ∧I, one needs 'F ∧ G' and 'H'.

It is not necessary to memorize many examples of the correct uses of ∧I. Taking care that the formulas are well formed and that the rule introduces the main operator of the new formula will ensure that one does not make mistakes.

§3.3: CONJUNCTION ELIMINATION

If one knows that roses are red and violets are blue, one knows that roses are red and one knows that violets are blue. Given any sentence 'Φ ∧ Ψ', one can infer either 'Φ' or 'Ψ' (or both). **Conjunction elimination**, '∧E', is just as intuitively clear as ∧I.

∧E

One can write the formula 'Φ' or the formula 'Ψ' on any given scope line, provided that the following condition is met:

The formula '(Φ ∧ Ψ)' is already on the same scope line.

The justification for the new line consists of an appeal to the number of the line where '(Φ ∧ Ψ)' occurs and the rule, '∧E'.

The formal statement of the rule includes outer brackets in the formula, although this requirement is ignored in what follows.

The following argument is clearly truth-functionally valid:

$$\frac{A \wedge B}{A}$$

The conclusion is derived from the premiss in two steps:

```
1 │ A ∧ B                                     P
2 │ A                                         1, ∧E
```

Either of the conjuncts can be eliminated, so the following is also correct:

```
1 | A ∧ B                              P
2 | B                                  1, ∧E
```

∧E can be used repeatedly in a derivation to break up complex formulas. The following derivation is correct:

```
1 | ((F ∧ G) ∧ H) ∧ I                 P
2 | (F ∧ G) ∧ H                       1, ∧E
3 | F ∧ G                             2, ∧E
4 | F                                 3, ∧E
```

∧E can be applied only to the main operator of a complex formula, so the following is incorrect:

```
1 | (F ∧ G) ∧ H                       P
2 | F  †††                            1, ∧E
```

Line 2 is mistaken because the main operator of the formula on line 1 is the second caret and not the first.

∧E and ∧I are used in the following derivation to obtain 'B ∧ (C ∧ D)' from '(B ∧ C) ∧ D':

```
1 | (B ∧ C) ∧ D                       P
2 | B ∧ C                             1, ∧E
3 | B                                 2, ∧E
4 | C                                 2, ∧E
5 | D                                 1, ∧E
6 | C ∧ D                             4, 5, ∧I
7 | B ∧ (C ∧ D)                       3, 6, ∧I
```

It is easy to remember and use the rule of ∧E. Care must be taken that the rule is applied only to the main operator of a formula and that the formula which results from using the rule is itself well formed.

§3.4: NEGATION ELIMINATION

If one knows that it is false that John is not a fool, then one knows that John is a fool. Given any sentence '~ ~ Φ', one can infer 'Φ'. The rule of **negation elimination**, '~E', reflects the propriety of such inferences.

~E
One can write the formula 'Φ' on any given scope line, provided that the following condition is met: The formula '~ ~ Φ' is already on the same scope line. The justification for the new line consists of an appeal to the number of the line where '~ ~ Φ' occurs and the rule, '~E'.

The following derivation uses the rule of ~E:

```
1 | ~ ~ G                              P
2 | G                                  1, ~E
```

The formula which results from using ~E need not be an atomic formula. The following derivation is perfectly in order:

```
1 | ~ ~ ((F ⊃ R) ∨ (S ∧ ~ Q))         P
2 | (F ⊃ R) ∨ (S ∧ ~ Q)               1, ~E
```

Once the two tildes are removed from '~ ~ ((F ⊃ R) ∨ (S ∧ ~ Q))', the outer brackets are dropped since they are no longer necessary.

   ~E can be used only on a formula whose main operator is a '~' which is immediately followed by another '~'. The following is incorrect:

```
1 | F ∧ ~ ~ G                         P
2 | F ∧ G  †††                        1, ~E
```

Line 2 is mistaken because the main operator of the formula on line 1 is a caret, and not a tilde immediately followed by another tilde.

   To obtain 'F ∧ G' from 'F ∧ ~ ~ G', one needs to obtain 'F' and 'G' in order to use ∧I. 'F' can be obtained simply by ∧E. To obtain 'G', one needs to get '~ ~ G' and use ~E. One can then use ∧I to obtain 'F ∧ G'. The derivation follows:

```
1 | F ∧ ~ ~ G                         P
2 | F                                 1, ∧E
3 | ~ ~ G                             1, ∧E
4 | G                                 3, ~E
5 | F ∧ G                             2, 4, ∧I
```

Two and only two consecutive tildes can be removed at one time. In the event that one needs to remove four tildes, one needs to apply ~E twice, as in the following derivation:

```
1 | ~ ~ ~ ~ G                           P
2 | ~ ~ G                               1, ~E
3 | G                                   2, ~E
```

~E is an easy rule to understand and apply. There are two important points to remember. First, two and only two tildes can be removed by a single application of this rule. Second, the first of the two consecutive tildes which are removed must be the main operator of the formula on which ~E is applied.

§3.5: DISJUNCTION INTRODUCTION

If one knows that Peter is the captain of the team, then one is entitled to make the weaker claim that either Peter is the captain of the team or John is the captain of the team. Given any sentence 'Φ', one can infer '$\Phi \vee \psi$'. The rule of **disjunction introduction**, '$\vee$I', reflects the fact that a disjunctive formula can never be stronger – can never say more – than either of its disjuncts.

$\vee$I
One can write the formula '$(\Phi \vee \psi)$' on any given scope line, provided that **either** one of the following conditions is met:
1 The formula 'Φ' is already on the same scope line.
2 The formula 'ψ' is already on the same scope line.
The justification for the new line consists of an appeal to the number of the line where 'Φ' or 'ψ' occurs and the rule, '$\vee$I'.

The formal statement of the rule includes outer brackets in the formula, although this requirement is ignored in what follows.

This argument is truth-functionally valid:

$$\frac{M}{(N \vee M) \vee O}$$

The derivation of the conclusion from the premiss consists of three steps:

```
1 | M                                   P
2 | N ∨ M                               1, ∨I
3 | (N ∨ M) ∨ O                         2, ∨I
```

The vel which results from using ∨I must be the main operator of the new formula. ∨I can be applied only to an entire formula, not to a part of a formula. Although 'R ⊃ (S ∨ T)' can be derived from 'R ⊃ S', it cannot be derived just by applying ∨I. (A way of deriving the former from the latter will be given before the end of the chapter.) The following attempt to derive 'R ⊃ (S ∨ T)' from 'R ⊃ S' is incorrect:

```
1 | R ⊃ S                                       P
2 | R ⊃ (S ∨ T)  †††                            1, ∨I
```

The next derivation, however, is completely in order, because ∨I is applied to an entire formula:

```
1 | R ⊃ S                                       P
2 | (R ⊃ S) ∨ T                                 1, ∨I
```

The two following special cases should be noted. Both derivations are correct:

```
1 | A                                           P
2 | A ∨ A                                        1, ∨I
```

```
1 | A                                           P
2 | A ∨ ~ A                                      1, ∨I
```

In using ∨I, one need not introduce only atomic formulas, and the rule can be used repeatedly to create formulas of increasing complexity. All of the uses of ∨I in the next derivation are correct:

```
1 | F                                                   P
2 | (G ∧ H) ∨ F                                         1, ∨I
3 | (P ⊃ Q) ∨ ((G ∧ H) ∨ F)                             2, ∨I
4 | ((P ⊃ Q) ∨ ((G ∧ H) ∨ F)) ∨ (A ≡ B)                 3, ∨I
```

At this point, it may not seem that ∨I is a very useful rule, and indeed it is true that one rarely wants to derive a conclusion which is simply a disjunction having a premiss as one of its disjuncts. However, the rule will be extremely useful in the course of complex derivations. It is important in applying the rule that ∨I introduces the main operator of the new formula. Care must be taken that ∨I is applied only to an entire formula and not to a part of a formula, and that the formula which results from applying ∨I is well formed.

§3.6: HORSESHOE ELIMINATION

If one knows that Sam will be elected if he runs and one knows that Sam will run, one certainly knows that Sam will be elected. Given any two sentences 'Φ' and 'Φ ⊃ Ψ', one can infer 'Ψ'. The rule of **horseshoe elimination, '⊃E',** is as intuitively obvious as the inference concerning Sam's election.

⊃E

One can write the formula 'Ψ' on any given scope line, provided that **both** of the following conditions are met:

1 The formula 'Φ' is already on the same scope line.

2 The formula '(Φ ⊃ Ψ)' is already on the same scope line.

The justification for the new line consists of an appeal to the number of the line where 'Φ' occurs, the number of the line where '(Φ ⊃ Ψ)' occurs and the rule, '⊃E'.

The formal statement of the rule includes outer brackets in the formula, although this requirement is ignored in what follows.

The following derivation illustrates some uses of ⊃E:

1	F	P
2	G	P
3	F ⊃ (G ⊃ R)	P
4	G ⊃ R	1, 3, ⊃E
5	R	2, 4, ⊃E

One very common mistake in using ⊃E follows:

1	V	P
2	F ⊃ V	P
3	F †††	1, 2, ⊃E

The mistake is obvious in English. From the fact that I would be old enough to vote if I were forty and the fact that I am old enough to vote, it does not follow that I am forty.

In order to use ⊃E, one must have a formula whose main operator is a horseshoe. The following argument is truth-functionally valid:

N
~ ~ (N ⊃ R)
―――――――――
R

However, the following attempt to derive the conclusion from the premisses is illegitimate:

```
1 | N                              P
2 | ~ ~ (N ⊃ R)                    P
3 | R  †††                         1, 2, ⊃E
```

The move at line 3 is wrong because the main operator of the formula on line 2 is not a horseshoe. The following is the correct derivation of the conclusion from the premisses:

```
1 | N                              P
2 | ~ ~ (N ⊃ R)                    P
3 | N ⊃ R                          2, ~E
4 | R                              1, 3, ⊃E
```

When ⊃E is applied to complex formulas, care must be taken to ensure that the rule is applied to the main operator of the formula in question. The following two derivations are completely in order:

```
1 | A                              P
2 | B                              P
3 | C                              P
4 | A ⊃ (B ⊃ (C ⊃ D))              P
5 | B ⊃ (C ⊃ D)                    1, 4, ⊃E
6 | C ⊃ D                          2, 5, ⊃E
7 | D                              3, 6, ⊃E
```

```
1 | R                              P
2 | K ⊃ (R ⊃ S)                    P
3 | R ⊃ K                          P
4 | (R ⊃ S) ⊃ ((M ∧ N) ≡ O)        P
5 | K                              1, 3, ⊃E
6 | R ⊃ S                          2, 5, ⊃E
7 | (M ∧ N) ≡ O                    4, 6, ⊃E
```

The rule of ⊃E is easy to remember and to apply. Care must be taken to ensure that one has both a formula whose main operator is a horseshoe and the antecedent of that formula. The consequent of that formula is the result of applying ⊃E.

§3.7: TRIPLEBAR ELIMINATION

Suppose that one knows that stock market averages will rise if and only if interest rates fall. Then, if one knows that stock market averages will rise, one knows that interest rates will fall. Likewise, given this background information, if one knows that interest rates will fall, one knows that stock market averages will rise. Given any two sentences 'Φ' and '$\Phi \equiv \psi$', one can infer 'ψ'. In just the same way, given any two sentences 'ψ' and '$\Phi \equiv \psi$', one can infer 'Φ'. The rule of **triplebar elimination**, '$\equiv$E', is as intuitively clear as the two inferences concerning interest rates and stock market averages.

$\equiv$E

One can write the formula 'ψ' on any given scope line, provided that **both** of the following conditions are met:
 	
  1 The formula 'Φ' is already on the same scope line.
 	
  2 The formula '$(\Phi \equiv \psi)$' is already on the same scope line.
 	
The justification for the new line consists of an appeal to the number of the line where 'Φ' occurs, the number of the line where '$(\Phi \equiv \psi)$' occurs and the rule, '$\equiv$E'.
 	
Similarly, one can write the formula 'Φ' on any given scope line, provided that **both** of the following conditions are met:
 	
  1 The formula 'ψ' is already on the same scope line.
 	
  2 The formula '$(\Phi \equiv \psi)$' is already on the same scope line.
 	
The justification for the new line consists of an appeal to the number of the line where 'ψ' occurs, the number of the line where '$(\Phi \equiv \psi)$' occurs and the rule, '$\equiv$E'.

The formal statement of the rule includes outer brackets in the formula, although this requirement is ignored in what follows.

The following two derivations illustrate the rule:

```
1 | K                        P
2 | K ≡ R                    P
3 | R                        1, 2, ≡E
```

```
1 | R                        P
2 | K ≡ R                    P
3 | K                        1, 2, ≡E
```

All the uses of $\equiv$E in the following derivation are correct:

1	F	P
2	G	P
3	R ≡ F	P
4	R ≡ (G ≡ H)	P
5	R	1, 3, ≡E
6	G ≡ H	4, 5, ≡E
7	H	2, 6, ≡E

Care must be taken to ensure that ≡E is applied only to the main operator of a formula. Thus, the following is mistaken:

1	M	P
2	(M ≡ N) ≡ O	P
3	N ≡ O †††	1, 2, ≡E

It is easy to avoid mistakes in using ≡E if one takes care to apply the rule only to the triplebar which is the main operator of a formula.

§ 3.8: EXERCISES

Each of the following derivations has several justifications missing. Supply the justifications, giving the name of the rule and the line numbers which justify the use of the rule.

Question 1

1	A	P
2	~ ~ G	P
3	G	?
4	A ∧ G	?
5	(A ∧ G) ∨ ~ G	?

Question 2

1	R ≡ S	P
2	Q	P
3	(Q ∨ P) ⊃ (M ∧ N)	P
4	N ⊃ S	P
5	Q ∨ P	?
6	M ∧ N	?
7	N	?
8	S	?
9	R	?

Question 3

1	A	P
2	R	P
3	A ⊃ (R ≡ B)	P
4	B ⊃ ((R ⊃ Q) ∧ (B ⊃ C))	P
5	R ≡ B	?
6	B	?
7	(R ⊃ Q) ∧ (B ⊃ C)	?
8	R ⊃ Q	?
9	B ⊃ C	?
10	Q	?
11	C	?
12	Q ∧ C	?
13	(Q ∧ C) ∨ (F ∧ L)	?

§3.9: CONSTRUCTING DERIVATIONS

Following a given derivation and seeing how each step is justified is simple once one has learned the rules. Creating a derivation from scratch is a very different thing. No one becomes adept at producing derivations without much practice and without making many mistakes. However, unless one has some strategy in mind, it is impossible to begin to practise constructing derivations and to learn from one's mistakes; nothing is learned by staring at the page in complete bewilderment. Those who are very good at constructing derivations seem to make the right move at every point, but to someone learning there seems to be no way of deciding ahead of time what the right move is. One can, of course, just apply a rule to a given formula and hope that something useful turns up, but this is hardly a rational procedure. In this section a strategy will be applied and discussed in dealing with various examples.

Ignoring 'categorical derivations' (which will be discussed at the end of this chapter), the problem in a derivation is to get from the premiss or premisses to the conclusion by a series of legitimate moves. The problem is analogous to the problem of getting from one place to another; there is no point in deciding what one's first step is going to be until one has decided where one is trying to go and how one is trying to get there. For example, in travelling from Chicago to Rome, one can fly to New York and take a direct flight from there. One can also fly to Paris and continue on another flight from Paris to Rome. In addition, one can take a circuitous route, going from Chicago to Tokyo and then from Tokyo to Rome. No rational decision about the first step of a journey is possible without consideration of the other steps of the journey. In constructing derivations, as in travelling, there are usually many options. Sometimes some of these options are obviously absurd, and sometimes one option looks to be far more promising than any other.

The following argument is truth-functionally valid, as a check on a truth table will show. The conclusion can be derived from the premisses, using only the rules discussed thus far in this chapter.

$$Q$$
$$C \equiv D$$
$$\underline{Q \supset \sim \sim D}$$
$$C$$

The problem is to construct a derivation which begins with the premisses and ends with the conclusion. How many lines long the derivation will be is not known, so one can start the derivation by numbering the premiss lines and calling the last line 'Z' as follows:

1	Q	P
2	C ≡ D	P
3	Q ⊃ ~ ~ D	P
Z	C	?

The question is: how can one get 'C'? The only line on which 'C' appears is line 2, where it is in 'C ≡ D'. If one had 'D', one could use ≡E to get 'C'. Thus, there is a new problem of getting 'D'. To keep track of what one is doing, the outline of the derivation is changed, with the addition of line Y and a justification for line Z:

1	Q	P
2	C ≡ D	P
3	Q ⊃ ~ ~ D	P
Y	D	?
Z	C	2, Y, ≡E

'D', of course, is available at line 2, but to get it from 'C ≡ D' would require one to get 'C', which is what one is trying to do by getting 'D'. To return to the travelling analogy, getting 'D' from line 2 when one is trying to get 'C' from line 2 is like trying to get to Rome in order to take a flight from Rome to Naples so as to take a flight from Naples to Rome. As an example of a useless strategy, an attempt to obtain 'D' from 'C ≡ D' follows:

```
1 | Q                                        P
2 | C ≡ D                                    P
3 | Q ⊃ ~ ~ D                                P
  :
W | D                                        ?
X | C                                        2, W, ≡E
Y | D                                        2, X, ≡E
Z | C                                        2, Y, ≡E
```

If one could obtain 'D' at line W, one would have 'C' at line X. Lines Y and
Z would then be unnecessary. Obviously, trying to get 'D' by getting 'C' and
using line 2 is pointless. One must go back and consider another strategy.

The only other formula in which 'D' appears is 'Q ⊃ ~ ~ D' on line 3.
If one could obtain '~ ~ D', it would be easy to obtain 'D' by ~E. This looks
far more promising:

```
1 | Q                                        P
2 | C ≡ D                                    P
3 | Q ⊃ ~ ~ D                                P
  :
X | ~ ~ D                                    ?
Y | D                                        X, ~E
Z | C                                        2, Y, ≡E
```

'~ ~ D' can be obtained by ⊃E from 'Q ⊃ ~ ~ D' provided one has 'Q',
and 'Q' is available at line 1. Accordingly, the derivation can be completed.
The lines can now be properly numbered and the justifications can refer to
lines by their numbers:

```
1 | Q                                        P
2 | C ≡ D                                    P
3 | Q ⊃ ~ ~ D                                P
4 | ~ ~ D                                    1, 3, ⊃E
5 | D                                        4, ~E
6 | C                                        2, 5, ≡E
```

The following argument is somewhat more complex, and the derivation will
be longer. However, the complexity is no cause for alarm. At any point in
the derivation, there is only one immediate problem: there are certain
formulas available and another formula is needed. To return to the travel
analogy, at any point in a journey there is only one immediate problem:
getting to one's next destination. That this leg of the journey is only one leg
among many need not and should not prevent one from concentrating on

the immediate problem. Similarly, in constructing derivations, one should concentrate on one problem at a time. Doing this will ensure that one is not completely baffled merely by the fact that a straightforward problem requires many steps for its solution.

> A
> F ⊃ (R ∧ G)
> (A ∧ M) ⊃ F
> A ⊃ ~ ~ M
> (A ∧ (R ∨ B)) ⊃ K
> _____
> K

The first step in producing the derivation is straightforward. As in the previous example, one lists the premisses and notes the conclusion:

1	A	P
2	F ⊃ (R ∧ G)	P
3	(A ∧ M) ⊃ F	P
4	A ⊃ ~ ~ M	P
5	(A ∧ (R ∨ B)) ⊃ K	P
Z	K	?

'K' could be obtained from '(A ∧ (R ∨ B)) ⊃ K' by ⊃E if one had 'A ∧ (R ∨ B)'. Hence, a sensible strategy would be to try to obtain 'A ∧ (R ∨ B)'. The sketch of the derivation is developed, with a justification for line Z:

1	A	P
2	F ⊃ (R ∧ G)	P
3	(A ∧ M) ⊃ F	P
4	A ⊃ ~ ~ M	P
5	(A ∧ (R ∨ B)) ⊃ K	P
Y	A ∧ (R ∨ B)	?
Z	K	5, Y, ⊃E

There is now a new problem, the problem of obtaining 'A ∧ (R ∨ B)'. This formula appears in '(A ∧ (R ∨ B)) ⊃ K', but since it is on the left side of a horseshoe, one cannot use ⊃E to derive it. Since one cannot use an elimination rule to derive 'A ∧ (R ∨ B)' from an available formula, one must consider an introduction rule. The main operator of 'A ∧ (R ∨ B)' is '∧', so the introduction rule must be ∧I. To obtain 'A ∧ (R ∨ B)' by ∧I, one needs 'A' and 'R ∨ B'. 'A' is one of the premisses; the only problem at this point is obtaining 'R ∨ B'. The new sketch of the derivation follows:

1	A	P
2	F ⊃ (R ∧ G)	P
3	(A ∧ M) ⊃ F	P
4	A ⊃ ~ ~ M	P
5	(A ∧ (R ∨ B)) ⊃ K	P
X	R ∨ B	?
Y	A ∧ (R ∨ B)	1, X, ∧I
Z	K	5, Y, ⊃E

'R ∨ B' appears at line 5. If one could obtain 'A ∧ (R ∨ B)', one could use ∧E to obtain 'R ∨ B'. However, 'A ∧ (R ∨ B)' is the very formula one is trying to obtain at line Y. Trying to obtain 'A ∧ (R ∨ B)' in order to obtain 'R ∨ B' so that one can obtain 'A ∧ (R ∨ B)' is plainly a pointless strategy. Accordingly, one is again forced to use an introduction rule. To obtain 'R ∨ B' by ∨I one needs either 'R' or 'B'. There is no apparent way to get 'B', but one could use ∧E to get 'R' from 'R ∧ G' which appears as part of a formula on line 2. Taking things one step at a time, the sketch of the derivation is changed:

1	A	P
2	F ⊃ (R ∧ G)	P
3	(A ∧ M) ⊃ F	P
4	A ⊃ ~ ~ M	P
5	(A ∧ (R ∨ B)) ⊃ K	P
W	R	?
X	R ∨ B	W, ∨I
Y	A ∧ (R ∨ B)	1, X, ∧I
Z	K	5, Y, ⊃E

The strategy is to get 'R' from 'R ∧ G' by ∧E. Accordingly, the new problem is to obtain 'R ∧ G':

1	A	P
2	F ⊃ (R ∧ G)	P
3	(A ∧ M) ⊃ F	P
4	A ⊃ ~ ~ M	P
5	(A ∧ (R ∨ B)) ⊃ K	P
V	R ∧ G	?
W	R	V, ∧E
X	R ∨ B	W, ∨I
Y	A ∧ (R ∨ B)	1, X, ∧I
Z	K	5, Y, ⊃E

'R ∧ G' could be obtained by ⊃E from 'F ⊃ (R ∧ G)' if one had 'F'. Accordingly, the next problem is to obtain 'F':

1	A	P
2	F ⊃ (R ∧ G)	P
3	(A ∧ M) ⊃ F	P
4	A ⊃ ~ ~ M	P
5	(A ∧ (R ∨ B)) ⊃ K	P
U	F	?
V	R ∧ G	2, U, ⊃E
W	R	V, ∧E
X	R ∨ B	W, ∨I
Y	A ∧ (R ∨ B)	1, X, ∧I
Z	K	5, Y, ⊃E

It should be noted that as each new problem is introduced the justification for a subsequent line is provided. Although the derivation is now looking quite complicated, there is still only one question mark at any one time – there is only one problem to be solved at any one time. Returning to the derivation, the current problem is obtaining 'F'. This formula appears on line 2, but since it is on the left side of a horseshoe, it cannot be obtained by ⊃E. However, 'F' could be obtained by ⊃E from '(A ∧ M) ⊃ F' which appears on line 3. Thus, the new problem is obtaining 'A ∧ M':

1	A	P
2	F ⊃ (R ∧ G)	P
3	(A ∧ M) ⊃ F	P
4	A ⊃ ~ ~ M	P
5	(A ∧ (R ∨ B)) ⊃ K	P
T	A ∧ M	?
U	F	3, T, ⊃E
V	R ∧ G	2, U, ⊃E
W	R	V, ∧E
X	R ∨ B	W, ∨I
Y	A ∧ (R ∨ B)	1, X, ∧I
Z	K	5, Y, ⊃E

'A ∧ M' cannot be obtained by an elimination rule, so one needs to use the appropriate introduction rule, ∧I. To obtain 'A ∧ M' by ∧I, one needs both 'A' and 'M'. 'A' is a premiss on line 1; the problem now is to obtain 'M'. The revised outline of the derivation shows the new problem:

1	A	P
2	F ⊃ (R ∧ G)	P
3	(A ∧ M) ⊃ F	P
4	A ⊃ ~ ~ M	P
5	(A ∧ (R ∨ B)) ⊃ K	P
S	M	?
T	A ∧ M	1, S, ∧I
U	F	3, T, ⊃E
V	R ∧ G	2, U, ⊃E
W	R	V, ∧E
X	R ∨ B	W, ∨I
Y	A ∧ (R ∨ B)	1, X, ∧I
Z	K	5, Y, ⊃E

'M' appears on line 3 in the formula '(A ∧ M) ⊃ F', but since 'A ∧ M' is on the left side of the horseshoe and is thus not accessible, one cannot use ∧E to get 'M' from 'A ∧ M'. Moreover, 'A ∧ M' is the very formula one is trying to obtain at line T. However, 'M' also appears in the formula 'A ⊃ ~ ~ M' on line 4. If one could obtain '~ ~ M', it would be easy to obtain 'M' by ~E. The new problem, therefore, is to obtain '~ ~ M', and the derivation is revised to show this:

1	A	P
2	F ⊃ (R ∧ G)	P
3	(A ∧ M) ⊃ F	P
4	A ⊃ ~ ~ M	P
5	(A ∧ (R ∨ B)) ⊃ K	P
R	~ ~ M	?
S	M	R, ~E
T	A ∧ M	1, S, ∧I
U	F	3, T, ⊃E
V	R ∧ G	2, U, ⊃E
W	R	V, ∧E
X	R ∨ B	W, ∨I
Y	A ∧ (R ∨ B)	1, X, ∧I
Z	K	5, Y, ⊃E

The solution to this problem is easy. '~ ~ M' appears on line 4 in the formula 'A ⊃ ~ ~ M'. To obtain '~ ~ M', one needs 'A', and 'A' is a premiss on line 1. Accordingly, the derivation can be completed, with the temporary alphabetic line names being replaced by numbers and the justifications being appropriately amended:

1	A	P
2	F ⊃ (R ∧ G)	P
3	(A ∧ M) ⊃ F	P
4	A ⊃ ~ ~ M	P
5	(A ∧ (R ∨ B)) ⊃ K	P
6	~ ~ M	1, 4, ⊃E
7	M	6, ~E
8	A ∧ M	1, 7, ∧I
9	F	3, 8, ⊃E
10	R ∧ G	2, 9, ⊃E
11	R	10, ∧E
12	R ∨ B	11, ∨I
13	A ∧ (R ∨ B)	1, 12, ∧I
14	K	5, 13, ⊃E

In the two derivations which have been discussed in this section, whenever two formulas were needed, one of the formulas was immediately available. The result was that there was never more than one formula which one needed to look for at any one time. Sometimes things are a little more complicated, but the general strategy of dealing with one problem at a time remains the only sensible approach. This is demonstrated in solving the problem of deriving the conclusion of the following argument from the premisses:

$$R$$
$$R \supset \sim \sim Q$$
$$Q \supset F$$
$$R \supset G$$
$$(F \wedge G) \supset M$$
$$\overline{}$$
$$M$$

The first step in producing the derivation is the same as in the other examples; one lists the premisses and notes the conclusion:

1	R	P
2	R ⊃ ~ ~ Q	P
3	Q ⊃ F	P
4	R ⊃ G	P
5	(F ∧ G) ⊃ M	P
Z	M	?

In what follows, to save the space required for showing the development of the derivation, the more obvious steps will not be discussed separately. To get 'M' from line 5, one needs 'F ∧ G'. This formula can be obtained only by using ∧I, which requires both 'F' and 'G'. Thus, there are two problems in the following outline of the derivation:

1	R	P
2	R ⊃ ~ ~ Q	P
3	Q ⊃ F	P
4	R ⊃ G	P
5	(F ∧ G) ⊃ M	P
W	F	?
X	G	?
Y	F ∧ G	W, X, ∧I
Z	M	5, Y, ⊃E

There are two problems: obtaining 'F' and obtaining 'G'. Which problem is tackled first does not matter. As an arbitrary choice, one can approach the problems in alphabetical order. Hence, the immediate problem is obtaining 'F'. This formula can be obtained from 'Q ⊃ F' by ⊃E:

1	R	P
2	R ⊃ ~ ~ Q	P
3	Q ⊃ F	P
4	R ⊃ G	P
5	(F ∧ G) ⊃ M	P
V	Q	?
W	F	3, V, ⊃E
X	G	?
Y	F ∧ G	W, X, ∧I
Z	M	5, Y, ⊃E

The obvious candidate for obtaining 'Q' is 'R ⊃ ~ ~ Q' on line 2. One should obtain '~ ~ Q' by ⊃E and use ~E to obtain 'Q'. A glance at the formula on line 2 shows that the next formula needed is 'R', and this is available at line 1. The sketch of the derivation is amended:

1	R	P
2	R ⊃ ~ ~ Q	P
3	Q ⊃ F	P
4	R ⊃ G	P
5	(F ∧ G) ⊃ M	P
6	~ ~ Q	1, 2, ⊃E
7	Q	6, ~E
8	F	3, 7, ⊃E
X	G	?
Y	F ∧ G	8, X, ∧I
Z	M	5, Y, ⊃E

The first problem, that of obtaining 'F', has been solved. There remains the problem of obtaining 'G'. This is easily solved. 'G' appears on line 4 in 'R ⊃ G', and 'R' is available on line 1. The derivation can now be completed. Dealing with the two problems separately allowed one to concentrate on a single manageable problem at each step of the derivation. The completed derivation follows:

1	R	P
2	R ⊃ ~ ~ Q	P
3	Q ⊃ F	P
4	R ⊃ G	P
5	(F ∧ G) ⊃ M	P
6	~ ~ Q	1, 2, ⊃E
7	Q	6, ~E
8	F	3, 7, ⊃E
9	G	1, 4, ⊃E
10	F ∧ G	8, 9, ∧I
11	M	5, 10, ⊃E

The various steps in working out the derivations in this section have been deliberately shown in excessive detail with a degree of neatness hardly to be expected in the course of actually solving a problem. In practice, there would be a lot of erasing or scratching out, and probably use of some sort of 'shorthand'. As a practical matter, it is important to keep rough work neat enough to read. In the course of a long derivation, one can easily become confused, even forgetting what formula one is trying to obtain at a particular point. In dealing with complex derivations, there are often several equally good ways of getting to the conclusion, and without some written record it is easy to lose track of the overall strategy.

In §3.10 there are exercises that require the construction of derivations. In dealing with these exercises, the following advice should be kept in mind:

1 One should not try to produce a final copy straight away. There should be a rough copy of the derivation on a separate sheet. This need not be neat, but it must be legible, since in all probability it will be needed for reference.

2 One should deal with one problem at a time.

3 One should not try to complete a derivation by bending the rules a bit to obtain what is needed. A problem half solved by legitimate use of the rules is better than a problem 'solved' by cheating.

§3.10: EXERCISES

For each of the following arguments, derive the conclusion from the premiss(es).

1 A
   B
   $A \supset \sim \sim (B \supset \sim \sim C)$

   C

2 B
   $B \equiv \sim \sim A$
   $(A \wedge B) \supset R$

   R

3 B
   $B \equiv \sim \sim A$
   $(A \vee S) \supset R$

   R

4 $A \wedge B$

   $(B \vee C) \wedge A$

5 A
   $A \supset G$
   $B \equiv R$
   $B \supset S$
   $G \equiv \sim \sim I$
   $((F \vee G) \wedge (H \vee I)) \supset R$

   $A \wedge S$

6 P
   $P \supset \sim \sim \sim S$
   $A \equiv (R \vee S)$
   $(A \vee B) \equiv (P \wedge Q)$
   $\sim S \supset F$
   $F \supset R$

   $(P \wedge Q) \wedge R$

§3.11: ASSUMPTIONS

In arguing for a conclusion, it is often useful to assume something in order
to see what follows from the assumption. This is a legitimate move in
derivations. It is, of course, necessary to keep in mind that anything one
assumes is only an assumption, and in a derivation this is done by keeping
the assumption to the right of a new scope line. Every scope line except the
primary scope line which is drawn against the line numbers is a **secondary
scope line**. Every secondary scope line of a derivation in sentence logic
begins with an **assumption**. By the end of a derivation, one wants to be back
against the primary scope line; that is, what one has established should not
depend upon the truth of assumptions which have been introduced
provisionally. Later in this chapter there will be rules for justifying formulas
on the primary scope line by appeal to information which is on secondary
scope lines. For the moment, however, the important point to remember is
that the secondary scope line serves to keep information away from other
scope lines; it is a reminder that the information on the secondary scope line
is dependent on the assumption with which that secondary scope line began.

In the following derivation, 'S ⊃ R' is derived from 'R'. In addition to
the rule of assumption, the derivation uses two rules – R and ⊃I – which
have not yet been discussed. For the moment, appeals to these rules can be
ignored; what matters at present is the way the new scope line is begun.

1	Q	P
2	S	A
3	Q	1, R
4	S ⊃ Q	2–3, ⊃I

It is possible to make one assumption and then go on to make another
assumption. There are no limits to the number of assumptions which can be
made in a derivation. In the following derivation, four assumptions are
made, each assumption beginning a new scope line:

1	D	P
2	B ⊃ C	P
3	K ∧ B	A
4	B	3, ∧E
5	B ⊃ C	2, R
6	C	4, 5, ⊃E
7	D	1, R
8	C ∧ D	6, 7, ∧I
9	(K ∧ B) ⊃ (C ∧ D)	3–8, ⊃I
10	F	A
11	G	A
12	H	A
13	D	1, R
14	H ⊃ D	12–13, ⊃I
15	G ⊃ (H ⊃ D)	11–14, ⊃I
16	F ⊃ (G ⊃ (H ⊃ D))	10–15, ⊃I
17	((K ∧ B) ⊃ (C ∧ D)) ∧ (F ⊃ (G ⊃ (H ⊃ D)))	9, 16, ∧I

Again, appeals to R and ⊃I can be ignored for the moment. These rules will be discussed later in this chapter.

The derivation just considered has four **subderivations**. Lines 3–8 and 10–15 are subderivations of the main derivation. Lines 11–14 are a subderivation of the main derivation as well as a subderivation of the subderivation which consists of lines 10–15. Similarly, lines 12–13 are a subderivation of the main derivation, a subderivation of the subderivation which consists of lines 10–15, and a subderivation of the subderivation which consists of lines 11–14. Secondary scope lines show the extent of subderivations just as primary scope lines show the extent of complete derivations.

Assumptions, once made, need not be maintained for ever. When an assumption is no longer needed, for any reason whatever, the scope line which began with that assumption is ended. The rules for ending scope lines will be discussed shortly. These rules will allow one to make use of assumptions and the formulas which appear in the subderivations. When a scope line is ended, any new formula and any new scope line should be placed as far left as possible. It should be noted that ⊃E, ∧E and ∧I work in exactly the same way on secondary scope lines as they do on primary scope lines. The other familiar rules – ∨I, ≡E and ~E – can also be used on secondary scope lines in exactly the same way in which they are used on primary scope lines.

The formal statement of the rule of assumption follows:

A
At any point in a derivation, one can introduce any well-formed formula as an assumption, provided that the following condition is met: The formula is written at the beginning of a new scope line. The formula which is assumed should be followed by a short horizontal line to distinguish it from other formulas which may appear on the new scope line. The justification for the new line is simply the rule, 'A'.

There are two crucial points which require care in using the rule of assumption. First, what is assumed must be a well-formed formula, but of course unnecessary outer brackets can be dropped. Second, every assumption must be the first formula on a new scope line.

§3.12: REITERATION

If one knows something, that piece of knowledge is usable no matter what else one knows and no matter what assumptions one makes. For example, if one knows that John is married, then, if one assumes that John is an accountant, one still knows that John is married. This is obvious, and the rule of **reiteration** is equally obvious.

R
At any point on a scope line, one can copy any formula which already appears in the derivation onto the scope line, provided that the following condition is met: The scope line from which the formula is copied has not been ended. The justification for the new line consists of an appeal to the number of the line from which the formula is reiterated and the rule, 'R'.

In dealing with predicate logic, some restrictions will be placed on the rule of reiteration. However, for purposes of doing sentence logic, the rule of reiteration as just stated is completely adequate.

Some examples of proper uses of the rule of reiteration appeared in §3.11. There are more examples in the following derivation which uses some rules which have not yet been discussed. The details of these rules can be ignored for the moment; the derivation is presented to provide examples of reiteration.

```
 1 | D ∨ B                          P
 2 | D ⊃ C                          P
 3 | B ⊃ (M ⊃ (F ⊃ C))              P
 4 |   | D                          A
 5 |   |   | M                      A
 6 |   |   | D                      4, R
 7 |   |   | D ⊃ C                  2, R
 8 |   |   | C                      6, 7, ⊃E
 9 |   |   |   | F                  A
10 |   |   |   | C                  8, R
11 |   |   | F ⊃ C                  9–10, ⊃I
12 |   | M ⊃ (F ⊃ C)               5–11, ⊃I
13 |   | B                          A
14 |   | B ⊃ (M ⊃ (F ⊃ C))          3, R
15 |   | M ⊃ (F ⊃ C)               13, 14, ⊃E
16 | M ⊃ (F ⊃ C)                   1, 4–12, 13–15, ∨E
```

In the following derivation, some common mistakes in reiteration are shown:

```
 1 | M ∧ N                          P
 2 | F ⊃ K                          P
 3 |   | F                          A
 4 |   | M †††                      1, R
 5 |   | F ⊃ K                      2, R
 6 |   | F                          3, R
 7 |   | K                          3, 5, ⊃E
 8 | K †††                          7, R
 9 |   | G                          A
10 |   | F †††                      3, R
11 | F †††                          10, R
12 | F ∧ K                          8, 11, ∧I
```

The reiteration at line 6 is in order. However, since 'F' is already on the scope line, no purpose is served by its repetition. The reiteration at line 4 is incorrect because only part of a formula is reiterated. All three of the reiterations at lines 8, 10 and 11 are wrong because in each case the formula is reiterated from a scope line which has ended. This is by far the most common mistake made in reiteration.

§3.13: HORSESHOE INTRODUCTION

The way the horseshoe is defined on the truth table guarantees that any formula '$\Phi \supset \Psi$' is true if 'Ψ' is true, no matter what the truth value of 'Φ' may be. Given any sentence 'Ψ', one is entitled to infer '$\Phi \supset \Psi$'. Inferences of this sort sometimes have odd consequences. From the fact that Shakespeare is the author of *Hamlet,* it follows that, if today is Tuesday, then Shakespeare is the author of *Hamlet* – a claim that would strike most people as very strange. However, the inference is licensed by the truth-table definition of the horseshoe, and such inferences are reflected in the rule of **horseshoe introduction, '$\supset$I'**.

$\supset$I

One can end any subderivation and write the formula '$(\Phi \supset \Psi)$' on the scope line immediately to the left of the ended subderivation, provided that **both** of the following conditions are met:

1 The subderivation begins with the assumption 'Φ'.

2 The formula 'Ψ' appears in the subderivation.

The justification for the new line consists of an appeal to the range of numbers in the ended subderivation of 'Ψ' from 'Φ' and the rule, '$\supset$I'.

The formal statement of the rule includes outer brackets in the formula, although this requirement is ignored in what follows.

Some examples of correct uses of $\supset$I follow:

1	A	P
2	B	P
3	C	P
4	D	A
5	A	1, R
6	B	2, R
7	C	3, R
8	D $\supset$ A	4–5, $\supset$I
9	D $\supset$ B	4–6, $\supset$I
10	D $\supset$ C	4–7, $\supset$I

The formulas involved need not be atomic formulas. $\supset$I can be used several times in the same derivation to obtain increasingly complex formulas.

Nothing in the rule requires that the two formulas joined by the horseshoe be distinct, so formulas such as 'A ⊃ A' can be introduced by use of ⊃I. The following derivation exemplifies these points:

```
 1 │ ((S ⊃ L) ⊃ M) ⊃ R                          P
 2 │    S                                        A
 3 │       L                                     A
 4 │          M                                  A
 5 │             S ⊃ L                           A
 6 │             M                               4, R
 7 │          (S ⊃ L) ⊃ M                        5–6, ⊃I
 8 │          ((S ⊃ L) ⊃ M) ⊃ R                  1, R
 9 │          R                                  7, 8, ⊃E
10 │       M ⊃ R                                 4–9, ⊃I
11 │    L ⊃ (M ⊃ R)                              3–10, ⊃I
12 │ S ⊃ (L ⊃ (M ⊃ R))                          2–11, ⊃I
13 │    P                                        A
14 │ P ⊃ P                                       13–13, ⊃I
15 │ (P ⊃ P) ∧ (S ⊃ (L ⊃ (M ⊃ R)))              12, 14, ∧I
```

Line 13 and line 14 of this derivation may seem a little strange. The scope line which began with the assumption at line 13 was ended at line 13. This provides a one-line subderivation, which is appealed to at line 14. It would be correct, but unnecessary, to reiterate 'P', providing a two-line subderivation. The derivation would then be slightly longer:

1	$((S \supset L) \supset M) \supset R$	P
2	S	A
3	L	A
4	M	A
5	$S \supset L$	A
6	M	4, R
7	$(S \supset L) \supset M$	5–6, $\supset$I
8	$((S \supset L) \supset M) \supset R$	1, R
9	R	7, 8, $\supset$E
10	$M \supset R$	4–9, $\supset$I
11	$L \supset (M \supset R)$	3–10, $\supset$I
12	$S \supset (L \supset (M \supset R))$	2–11, $\supset$I
13	P	A
14	P	13, R
15	$P \supset P$	13–14, $\supset$I
16	$(P \supset P) \wedge (S \supset (L \supset (M \supset R)))$	12, 15, $\wedge$I

In using $\supset$I, it is important that only the scope line on which the assumption is introduced be ended and that the new formula be written against the scope line immediately to the left of the ended scope line. If moves such as the mistaken one in the following attempt at a derivation were allowed, one could 'derive' anything whatever from any premiss:

1	A	P
2	B	A
3	A	A
4	B	2, R
5	$A \supset B$ †††	3–4, $\supset$I
6	B	1, 5, $\supset$E

'B' was properly introduced as an assumption at line 2 with a new scope line. That scope line serves to show that anything derived after line 2 may depend on 'B', a formula which has been only assumed. In ending the two scope lines simultaneously at line 5, the fact that 'B' was only an assumption has been completely ignored.

It is important to remember that ⊃I introduces a horseshoe as the main operator of a new formula. With this rule, as with others, it is necessary to pay attention to brackets, to avoid mistakes such as the following:

1	(B ⊃ C) ⊃ R	P
2	B ⊃ C	A
3	(B ⊃ C) ⊃ R	1, R
4	R	2, 3, ⊃E
5	B ⊃ (C ⊃ R) †††	2–4, ⊃I

The correct way to derive 'B ⊃ (C ⊃ R)' from '(B ⊃ C) ⊃ R' follows:

1	(B ⊃ C) ⊃ R	P
2	B	A
3	C	A
4	B	A
5	C	3, R
6	B ⊃ C	4–5, ⊃I
7	(B ⊃ C) ⊃ R	1, R
8	R	6, 7, ⊃E
9	C ⊃ R	3–8, ⊃I
10	B ⊃ (C ⊃ R)	2–9, ⊃I

It should be noted that 'B' occurs at line 4 as an assumption and is not reiterated from line 2. The fact that a formula appears earlier in a derivation does not mean that it cannot be assumed at the beginning of a new scope line.

If one pays attention to brackets and is careful to end only one scope line at a time, it is easy to avoid mistakes in using ⊃I.

§3.14: TRIPLEBAR INTRODUCTION

'$\Phi \equiv \Psi$' is truth-functionally equivalent to '$(\Phi \supset \Psi) \wedge (\Psi \supset \Phi)$'. Accordingly, if one can derive 'Ψ' from 'Φ' and derive 'Φ' from 'Ψ', one should be able to derive '$\Phi \equiv \Psi$'. It is not surprising, therefore, that the rule of **triplebar introduction**, '$\equiv$I', is very similar to two applications of horseshoe introduction.

$\equiv$I

One can write the formula '$(\Phi \equiv \Psi)$' or the formula '$(\Psi \equiv \Phi)$' on any scope line, provided that **both** of the following conditions are met:

1 On a scope line immediately to the right of the given scope line, there is a subderivation of 'Ψ' from 'Φ'.

2 On a scope line immediately to the right of the given scope line, there is a subderivation of 'Φ' from 'Ψ'.

The justification for the new line consists of an appeal to the range of numbers of the subderivation of 'Ψ' from 'Φ', the range of numbers of the subderivation of 'Φ' from 'Ψ' and the rule, '$\equiv$I'.

The formal statement of the rule includes outer brackets in the formula, although this requirement is ignored in what follows.

The following derivation shows some legitimate uses of $\equiv$I:

1	A ⊃ B	P
2	B ⊃ A	P
3	A	A
4	A ⊃ B	1, R
5	B	3, 4, ⊃E
6	B	A
7	B ⊃ A	2, R
8	A	6, 7, ⊃E
9	A ≡ B	3–5, 6–8, ≡I
10	B ≡ A	3–5, 6–8, ≡I

The following derivation provides another example of the correct use of ≡I:

```
 1 | M                                              P
 2 | (~ R v M) ⊃ ((F ∧ G) ∧ ~ S)                    P
 3 | F ⊃ (~ S ⊃ ~ R)                                P
 4 |   | ~ R                                        A
 5 |   | ~ R v M                                    4, vI
 6 |   | (~ R v M) ⊃ ((F ∧ G) ∧ ~ S)               2, R
 7 |   | (F ∧ G) ∧ ~ S                              5, 6, ⊃E
 8 |   | F ∧ G                                      7, ∧E
 9 |   | ~ S                                        7, ∧E
10 |   | F                                          8, ∧E
11 |   | F ∧ ~ S                                    9, 10, ∧I
12 |   | ~ R                                        A
13 |   | M                                          1, R
14 | ~ R ⊃ M                                        12–13, ⊃I
15 |   | F ∧ ~ S                                    A
16 |   | F                                          15, ∧E
17 |   | F ⊃ (~ S ⊃ ~ R)                            3, R
18 |   | ~ S ⊃ ~ R                                  16, 17, ⊃E
19 |   | ~ S                                        15, ∧E
20 |   | ~ R                                        18, 19, ⊃E
21 | ~ R ≡ (F ∧ ~ S)                                4–11, 15–20, ≡I
22 | (~ R ≡ (F ∧ ~ S)) ∧ (~ R ⊃ M)                  14, 21, ∧I
```

It should be noted that the use of ≡I at line 21 is completely in order, notwithstanding the fact that the two subderivations which are appealed to are separated by the derivation of '~ R ⊃ M' which extends from line 12 to line 14.

Some common mistakes involving ≡I are made in the following attempt to derive 'A ≡ B' from 'A ⊃ B'. As in this example, mistakes are often made not in applying the rule of triplebar introduction but in illegitimate moves before the ≡I step.

1	A ⊃ B	P
2	A	A
3	A ⊃ B	1, R
4	B	2, 3, ⊃E
5	B	A
6	A	A
7	B	A
8	A	6, R
9	B ⊃ A †††	7–8, ⊃I
10	A †††	2, R
11	A †††	6, R
12	A	5, 9, ⊃E
13	A ≡ B †††	2–4, 7–8, ≡I
14	A ≡ B	2–4, 5–10, ≡I
15	A ≡ B	2–4, 5–11, ≡I
16	A ≡ B	2–4, 5–12, ≡I

Lines 14, 15, and 16 are not in themselves wrong, but each of them relies on an occurrence of 'A' which was obtained illegitimately earlier in the derivation. The mistake at line 9 is a mistake in ⊃I. The scope line which begins at line 6 and the assumption 'A' are simply ignored. The reiteration at line 10 is illegitimate because 'A' was reiterated from a scope line which has been ended. The reiteration at line 11 is illegitimate for the same reason. Line 13 is incorrect because the subderivation of 'A' from 'B' is not immediately to the right of the scope line on which 'A ≡ B' appears.

To use triplebar introduction, one has to derive one formula from another and then derive the latter from the former. If both of these formulas are legitimately derived on scope lines immediately to the right of the scope line on which one introduces the formula whose main operator is a triplebar, it is hard to go wrong in using ≡I.

§3.15: NEGATION INTRODUCTION

If one knows that Peter cannot see, one knows that the assumption that Peter saw the accident is false. The assumption leads to a flat contradiction, such as that Peter is both blind and not blind. Similarly, given the premises 'Φ' and '$\Phi \supset \sim \psi$', the assumption of 'ψ' leads to a contradiction: 'ψ' and '$\sim \psi$'. The rule of **negation introduction**, '$\sim$I', allows one to derive '$\sim \Phi$' when the assumption of 'Φ' leads to a contradiction.

$\sim$I

One can write the formula '$\sim \Phi$' on any scope line, provided that **both** of the following conditions are met:

1 On a scope line immediately to the right of the given scope line, there is a subderivation which begins with the assumption 'Φ'.

2 On the scope line which begins with the assumption 'Φ' there appear two formulas which form a contradiction: 'ψ' and '$\sim \psi$'.

The justification for the new line consists of an appeal to the number of the line where the assumption 'Φ' is introduced, the number of the line where 'ψ' occurs, the number of the line where '$\sim \psi$' occurs and the rule, '$\sim$I'.

The following derivation illustrates some correct uses of $\sim$I:

1	$\sim$ (A $\vee$ B)	P
2	A	A
3	A $\vee$ B	2, $\vee$I
4	$\sim$ (A $\vee$ B)	1, R
5	$\sim$ A	2, 3, 4, $\sim$I
6	B	A
7	A $\vee$ B	6, $\vee$I
8	$\sim$ (A $\vee$ B)	1, R
9	$\sim$ B	6, 7, 8, $\sim$I
10	$\sim$ A $\wedge$ $\sim$ B	5, 9, $\wedge$I

It should be noted that the pair of formulas on lines 3 and 4 and on lines 7 and 8 are a genuine contradictory pair, even though no brackets are written around 'A $\vee$ B'. Strictly speaking, the contradictory pair consists of '(A $\vee$ B)' and '$\sim$ (A $\vee$ B)'.

The assumption itself can be one of the contradictory pair of formulas, so the following derivation is also correct:

```
1 | B                                    P
2 |    |— ~ B                            A
3 |    |  B                              1, R
4 | ~ ~ B                                2, 2, 3, ~I
```

In the following derivation, '~ G ⊃ ~ F' is derived from 'F ⊃ G':

```
1 | F ⊃ G                                P
2 |    | ~ G                             A
3 |    |   | F                           A
4 |    |   | F ⊃ G                       1, R
5 |    |   | G                           3, 4, ⊃E
6 |    |   | ~ G                         2, R
7 |    | ~ F                             3, 5, 6, ~I
8 | ~ G ⊃ ~ F                            2–7, ⊃I
```

The formula derived by ~I must be the formula which results from adding a tilde to the assumption. If the assumption is a negated formula, it is incorrect simply to remove the tilde; a tilde must be added. It is, of course, legitimate to remove the two tildes by ~E in a subsequent step. The following is an incorrect use of ~I:

```
1 | P                                    P
2 | ~ N ⊃ ~ P                            P
3 |    | ~ N                             A
4 |    | ~ N ⊃ ~ P                       2, R
5 |    | ~ P                             3, 4, ⊃E
6 |    | P                               1, R
7 | N  †††                               3, 5, 6, ~I
```

The proper way to derive 'N' from 'P' and '~ N ⊃ ~ P' follows:

```
1 | P                                    P
2 | ~ N ⊃ ~ P                            P
3 |   | ~ N                              A
4 |   | ~ N ⊃ ~ P                        2, R
5 |   | ~ P                              3, 4, ⊃E
6 |   | P                                1, R
7 | ~ ~ N                                3, 5, 6, ~I
8 | N                                    7, ~E
```

In using ~I, one must pay careful attention to brackets. The following derivation illustrates this point:

```
1 | ~ A                                  P
2 |   | A ∧ B                            A
3 |   | A                                2, ∧E
4 |   | ~ A                              1, R
5 | ~ A ∧ B  †††                         2, 3, 4, ~I
```

The rule of ~I allows one to obtain the negation of an assumption, not the negation of part of an assumption. Line 5 is mistaken because the entire assumption is not negated. '~ A ∧ B' cannot be legitimately derived from '~ A', although '~ (A ∧ B)' can. This is done in the following derivation:

```
1 | ~ A                                  P
2 |   | A ∧ B                            A
3 |   | A                                2, ∧E
4 |   | ~ A                              1, R
5 | ~ (A ∧ B)                            2, 3, 4, ~I
```

It should be noted that in this derivation the tilde negates the entire formula which is assumed on line 2.

In using ~I, one must take care to ensure that one really has a contradictory pair. Most mistakes in using this rule involve mistakes about the contradictory pair of formulas. To illustrate this sort of mistake, three mistaken attempts to derive '~ C' are exemplified in what follows. In each case, what is appealed to as a contradictory pair is not a genuine contradictory pair.

1	P	P
2	Q	P
3	P ⊃ ~ Q	P
4	C	A
5	P	A
6	Q	2, R
7	P ⊃ Q	5–6, ⊃I
8	~ P	A
9	Q	2, R
10	~ P ⊃ Q	8–9, ⊃I
11	P ⊃ ~ Q	3, R
12	P	1, R
13	P ∨ R	12, ∨I
14	P ∨ ~ R	12, ∨I
15	~ C †††	4, 7, 10, ~I
16	~ C †††	4, 7, 11, ~I
17	~ C †††	4, 13, 14, ~I

The rule of negation introduction is very easy to use and remember, but care must be taken to ensure that one has a genuine contradictory pair under the assumption.

§3.16: DISJUNCTION ELIMINATION

If one knows that taxes will go up if Jones wins the election, that taxes will go up if Smith wins the election, and that either Jones or Smith will win the election, then one certainly knows that taxes will go up. Given any disjunctive formula '$\Phi \lor \Psi$', if one can derive some formula 'Ω' from 'Φ' and one can derive 'Ω' from 'Ψ' then one is entitled to infer 'Ω'. The rule of **disjunction elimination**, '$\lor$E', reflects the propriety of this sort of inference.

$\lor$E
One can write the formula 'Ω' on any scope line, provided that **all** of the following conditions are met: 1 There is a disjunctive formula '$(\Phi \lor \Psi)$' on the given scope line. 2 On a scope line immediately to the right of the given scope line there is a subderivation of the formula 'Ω' from 'Φ'. 3 On a scope line immediately to the right of the given scope line there is a subderivation of that same formula 'Ω' from 'Ψ'. The justification for the new line consists of an appeal to the number of the line on which the disjunctive formula '$(\Phi \lor \Psi)$' appears, the two ranges of numbers of the two subderivations and the rule, '$\lor$E'.

The formal statement of the rule includes outer brackets in the formula, although this requirement is ignored in what follows.

The following derivation shows the correct use of $\lor$E:

```
 1 │ A ∨ B                        P
 2 │ A ⊃ C                        P
 3 │ B ⊃ C                        P
 4 │  │ A                         A
 5 │  │ A ⊃ C                     2, R
 6 │  │ C                         4, 5, ⊃E
 7 │  │ B                         A
 8 │  │ B ⊃ C                     3, R
 9 │  │ C                         7, 8, ⊃E
10 │ C                           1, 4–6, 7–9, ∨E
```

$\lor$E is often used to obtain one of the disjuncts from a disjunctive formula. In the following derivation, 'F' is derived from 'F $\lor$ G' and '$\sim$ G':

1	F ∨ G	P
2	~ G	P
3	F	A
4	G	A
5	~ F	A
6	G	4, R
7	~ G	2, R
8	~ ~ F	5, 6, 7, ~I
9	F	8, ~E
10	F	1, 3–3, 4–9, ∨E

As with the other rules, ∨E can be used with complex formulas as well as atomic formulas. The sequence in which the disjunctive formula and the two subderivations appear does not matter. Sometimes there are disjunction eliminations within the subderivations. These points are exemplified in the following derivation:

1	~ M ⊃ R	P
2	~ K	P
3	~ L	P
4	(K ∨ L) ∨ (M ∧ R)	P
5	M ∧ R	A
6	R	5, ∧E
7	K ∨ L	A
8	K	A
9	M	A
10	K	8, R
11	~ K	2, R
12	~ M	9, 10, 11, ~I
13	L	A
14	M	A
15	L	13, R
16	~ L	3, R
17	~ M	14, 15, 16, ~I
18	~ M	7, 8–12, 13–17, ∨E
19	~ M ⊃ R	1, R
20	R	18, 19, ⊃E
21	R	4, 5–6, 7–20, ∨E

The most common mistake in using ∨E is trying to use it on a formula whose main operator is not a vel. It is only through failure to look carefully at the brackets that someone would think of applying ∨E to a formula such as 'P ⊃ (R ∨ S)'. The other mistakes in using ∨E are usually mistakes in the subderivations. The discussion of mistakes in using ≡I in § 3.14 illustrates the sort of mistake which is common.

Care must be taken to ensure that ∨E is applied to a disjunctive formula, that the subderivations are legitimate and that the subderivations are on scope lines immediately to the right of the disjunctive formula. If this is done, use of ∨E is completely straightforward.

§ 3.17: EXERCISES

Supply the missing justifications in the following derivations.

Question 1

1	G ⊃ (F ⊃ (H ⊃ I))	P
2	F	?
3	G	?
4	G ⊃ (F ⊃ (H ⊃ I))	?
5	F ⊃ (H ⊃ I)	?
6	F	?
7	H ⊃ I	?
8	G ⊃ (H ⊃ I)	?
9	F ⊃ (G ⊃ (H ⊃ I))	?

Question 2

1	K	P
2	K ⊃ R	?
3	K	?
4	K ⊃ R	?
5	R	?
6	R	?
7	K	?
8	K ≡ R	?
9	(K ⊃ R) ⊃ (K ≡ R)	?

Question 3

1	D ⊃ (R ⊃ M)	P
2	~ N ⊃ ~ M	P
3	D ⊃ R	?
4	D	?
5	~ N	?
6	~ N ⊃ ~ M	?
7	~ M	?
8	D	?
9	D ⊃ R	?
10	R	?
11	D ⊃ (R ⊃ M)	?
12	R ⊃ M	?
13	M	?
14	~ ~ N	?
15	N	?
16	D ⊃ N	?
17	(D ⊃ R) ⊃ (D ⊃ N)	?

Question 4

1	S ≡ T	P
2	S	?
3	S ≡ T	?
4	T	?
5	S ⊃ T	?
6	~ S	?
7	T	?
8	S ≡ T	?
9	S	?
10	~ S	?
11	~ T	?
12	~ S ⊃ ~ T	?
13	(S ⊃ T) ∧ (~ S ⊃ ~ T)	?

Question 5

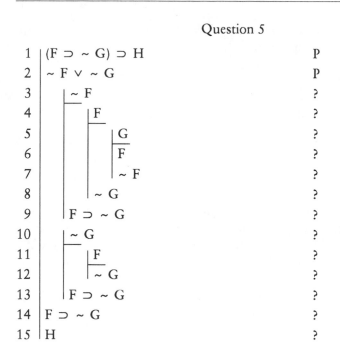

1	(F ⊃ ~ G) ⊃ H	P
2	~ F ∨ ~ G	P
3	~ F	?
4	F	?
5	G	?
6	F	?
7	~ F	?
8	~ G	?
9	F ⊃ ~ G	?
10	~ G	?
11	F	?
12	~ G	?
13	F ⊃ ~ G	?
14	F ⊃ ~ G	?
15	H	?

§3.18: MORE DERIVATION CONSTRUCTION

In the discussion of constructing derivations in §3.9, the general strategy was to try to use an elimination rule first. If that did not work, one turned to an introduction rule. This strategy will have to be changed somewhat, since there are now more rules to think about.

The first additional rule to be considered is reiteration. If a formula is needed and it can be reiterated onto the scope line on which one is working, the obvious thing to do is simply to reiterate it. As a general guide, then, when one wants a formula 'Φ', one should:

1 See if one can reiterate 'Φ'.

2 See if one can use an elimination rule to get 'Φ'. Usually, but by no means always, immediately using ∨E when a disjunctive formula is available results in a shorter derivation.

3 See if one can use an introduction rule to get 'Φ'. The introduction rule to use is determined by the main operator of 'Φ'. If 'Φ' has no main operator – if it is an atomic formula – there is, of course, no way in which one can get 'Φ' by an introduction rule.

The point of approaching problems in this order will become clearer as some derivations are constructed in this section.

Beginners at the business of producing derivations frequently make the mistake of immediately assuming what is needed. As a strategy for deriving

'R ⊃ (S ∨ T)' from 'R ⊃ S', introducing 'R ⊃ (S ∨ T)' as an assumption does nothing to solve the problem:

```
1 | R ⊃ S                                          P
2 |    | R ⊃ (S ∨ T)                               A
3 | (R ⊃ (S ∨ T)) ⊃ (R ⊃ (S ∨ T))                 2–2, ⊃I
```

'R ⊃ (S ∨ T)' must be derived against the primary scope line, but this formula is on a secondary scope line. '(R ⊃ (S ∨ T)) ⊃ (R ⊃ (S ∨ T))' was legitimately derived on the primary scope line by ⊃I, but that is not what is needed.

The above attempt at a derivation fails because the assumption was introduced for no good reason. In introducing an assumption and starting a new scope line, one should have a clear idea of why one is doing it and a clear idea of what rule is to be used to end the scope line. To derive 'R ⊃ (S ∨ T)' from 'R ⊃ S', one need only think a bit about possible strategies. The first thing to do is to lay out a plan of the derivation, showing what is available and what is wanted:

```
1 | R ⊃ S                                          P
  :
Z | R ⊃ (S ∨ T)                                    ?
```

There are no secondary scope lines, so the question of reiteration does not arise. 'R ⊃ (S ∨ T)' does not appear anywhere in what is available, and it seems clear that one cannot obtain it by an elimination rule. The main operator of 'R ⊃ (S ∨ T)' is a horseshoe, so the introduction rule to be used is ⊃I. One should assume the antecedent of the formula and try to obtain the consequent:

```
1 | R ⊃ S                                          P
2 |    | R                                         A
  :    :
Y |    | S ∨ T                                     ?
Z | R ⊃ (S ∨ T)                                    2–Y, ⊃I
```

The formula which is needed at line Y cannot be obtained by reiteration or an elimination rule. The main operator of 'S ∨ T' is a vel, so the appropriate introduction rule is ∨I. To obtain 'S ∨ T' by ∨I, one needs either 'S' or 'T'. There seems to be no way of obtaining 'T', but 'S' appears in 'R ⊃ S' on line 1. It seems plain that one should try to obtain 'S', and then go on to obtain 'S ∨ T' from 'S' by ∨I. The outline of the derivation is modified to show this:

1	R ⊃ S	P
2	R	A
X	S	?
Y	S ∨ T	X, ∨I
Z	R ⊃ (S ∨ T)	2–Y, ⊃I

To obtain 'S' from 'R ⊃ S' one needs 'R', and this formula is available at line 2. Once 'R ⊃ S' is reiterated onto the secondary scope line, it is clear where 'S' is to come from. It can simply be obtained by ⊃E. The derivation can thus be completed:

1	R ⊃ S	P
2	R	A
3	R ⊃ S	1, R
4	S	2, 3, ⊃E
5	S ∨ T	4, ∨I
6	R ⊃ (S ∨ T)	2–5, ⊃I

It should not be supposed that it is never a sensible strategy to assume what one needs. This is done in deriving the conclusion of the following argument:

(R ⊃ S) ⊃ R
S
_____
R

The derivation begins with the premisses and conclusion:

1	(R ⊃ S) ⊃ R	P
2	S	P
Z	R	?

The obvious strategy is to try to obtain 'R' by using ⊃E on line 1. To do this, one needs 'R ⊃ S':

1	(R ⊃ S) ⊃ R	P
2	S	P
Y	R ⊃ S	?
Z	R	1, Y, ⊃E

The only way to obtain 'R ⊃ S' is by ⊃I. One must assume 'R' and try to get 'S'. Since 'S' is available by reiteration from line 2, the derivation can be completed without difficulty:

1	(R ⊃ S) ⊃ R	P
2	S	P
3	R	A
4	S	2, R
5	R ⊃ S	3–4, ⊃I
6	R	1, 5, ⊃E

The point about the assumption of 'R' at line 3 is that it was assumed in order to obtain 'R ⊃ S' by ⊃I. The fact that 'R' is the conclusion of the argument which one was trying to obtain as the last line of the derivation is just a coincidence.

Another problem is deriving the conclusion from the premiss of the following argument:

$$(M \wedge O) \equiv (S \vee N)$$
$$\overline{S \supset (O \vee R)}$$

The derivation is begun by writing the premiss at line 1 and the conclusion at line Z:

1	(M ∧ O) ≡ (S ∨ N)	P
Z	S ⊃ (O ∨ R)	?

'S ⊃ (O ∨ R)' does not appear anywhere, and it is clear that it cannot be obtained by an elimination rule. The horseshoe is the main operator, so the appropriate introduction rule is ⊃I. The outline of the derivation is developed accordingly:

1	(M ∧ O) ≡ (S ∨ N)	P
2	S	A
Y	O ∨ R	?
Z	S ⊃ (O ∨ R)	2–Y, ⊃I

There seems to be no way to obtain what is needed at line Y by an elimination rule. To obtain 'O ∨ R' by ∨I, one needs either 'O' or 'R'. There is no easy way to obtain 'R', so the alternative is to obtain 'O'. The skeleton of the derivation reflects this:

1	(M ∧ O) ≡ (S ∨ N)	P
2	S	A
X	O	?
Y	O ∨ R	X, ∨I
Z	S ⊃ (O ∨ R)	2–Y, ⊃I

The only way to obtain 'O' seems to be by ∧E from 'M ∧ O' which appears on line 1 as part of '(M ∧ O) ≡ (S ∨ N)'. If one had 'S ∨ N', one could obtain 'M ∧ O' by ≡E. Accordingly, '(M ∧ O) ≡ (S ∨ N)' is reiterated and the derivation is developed:

1	(M ∧ O) ≡ (S ∨ N)	P
2	S	A
3	(M ∧ O) ≡ (S ∨ N)	1, R
V	S ∨ N	?
W	M ∧ O	3, V, ≡E
X	O	W, ∧E
Y	O ∨ R	X, ∨I
Z	S ⊃ (O ∨ R)	2–Y, ⊃I

'S ∨ N' cannot be obtained by an elimination rule, but it is easy to obtain 'S ∨ N' by using ∨I. To do this, one needs either 'S' or 'N', and 'S' is already on the present scope line at line 2. All that remains is to complete this step and number the lines and justifications of the derivation.

1	(M ∧ O) ≡ (S ∨ N)	P
2	S	A
3	(M ∧ O) ≡ (S ∨ N)	1, R
4	S ∨ N	2, ∨I
5	M ∧ O	3, 4, ≡E
6	O	5, ∧E
7	O ∨ R	6, ∨I
8	S ⊃ (O ∨ R)	2–7, ⊃I

A more difficult problem is that of obtaining the conclusion from the premises of the following argument:

$$(F \supset G) \supset (G \land I)$$
$$F \supset H$$

$$(H \supset G) \supset G$$

As before, the skeleton of the derivation is constructed from the premisses and the conclusion:

```
1 | (F ⊃ G) ⊃ (G ∧ I)           P
2 | F ⊃ H                        P
  ⋮
Z | (H ⊃ G) ⊃ G                  ?
```

Since there are no secondary scope lines, reiteration is not a possible strategy. The formula '(H ⊃ G) ⊃ G' does not appear as part of one of the premisses, and thus it cannot be obtained by any elimination rule. Turning to introduction rules, since the main operator of '(H ⊃ G) ⊃ G' is the second horseshoe, one should try to use ⊃I. One should assume what is to the left of the main operator, and try to obtain what is to the right. The outline of the derivation is altered to show this:

```
1 | (F ⊃ G) ⊃ (G ∧ I)           P
2 | F ⊃ H                        P
3 |   | H ⊃ G                    A
  ⋮
Y |   | G                        ?
Z | (H ⊃ G) ⊃ G                  3–Y, ⊃I
```

'G' cannot be reiterated. Turning to elimination rules, 'G' appears in '(F ⊃ G) ⊃ (G ∧ I)' and in the assumption 'H ⊃ G'. If one tried to get 'G' from 'H ⊃ G', one would need 'H':

```
1 | (F ⊃ G) ⊃ (G ∧ I)           P
2 | F ⊃ H                        P
3 |   | H ⊃ G                    A
  ⋮
X |   | H                        ?
Y |   | G                        3, X, ⊃E
Z | (H ⊃ G) ⊃ G                  3–Y, ⊃I
```

The only reasonable strategy here is to obtain 'H' from 'F ⊃ H', which can be reiterated from line 2. The sketch of the derivation is suitably amended:

1	(F ⊃ G) ⊃ (G ∧ I)	P
2	F ⊃ H	P
3	H ⊃ G	A
4	F ⊃ H	2, R
W	F	?
X	H	4, W, ⊃E
Y	G	3, X, ⊃E
Z	(H ⊃ G) ⊃ G	3–Y, ⊃I

The only places in which 'F' appears are on the left side of a horseshoe; in both places it is completely inaccessible. Plainly, some other strategy must be tried. When the problem of getting 'G' at line Y was first posed, there were two options: trying to get it from 'H ⊃ G' and trying to get it from '(F ⊃ G) ⊃ (G ∧ I)'. The first option has led nowhere, so one must try the second option. The step from 'G ∧ I' to 'G' is obvious, as is the step from 'F ⊃ G' and '(F ⊃ G) ⊃ (G ∧ I)' to 'G ∧ I', so the problem is obtaining 'F ⊃ G'. The sketch of the derivation is appropriately amended:

1	(F ⊃ G) ⊃ (G ∧ I)	P
2	F ⊃ H	P
3	H ⊃ G	A
4	(F ⊃ G) ⊃ (G ∧ I)	1, R
W	F ⊃ G	?
X	G ∧ I	4, W, ⊃E
Y	G	X, ∧E
Z	(H ⊃ G) ⊃ G	3–Y, ⊃I

It is impossible to reiterate 'F ⊃ G' and it cannot be obtained by an elimination rule. Accordingly, one must try the appropriate introduction rule, ⊃I. One should assume 'F' and try to obtain 'G'. The revised sketch of the derivation shows this:

```
1 | (F ⊃ G) ⊃ (G ∧ I)                    P
2 | F ⊃ H                                 P
3 |    H ⊃ G                              A
4 |      (F ⊃ G) ⊃ (G ∧ I)               1, R
5 |          F                            A
  :          :
V |          G                            ?
W |       F ⊃ G                           5–V, ⊃I
X |       G ∧ I                           4, W, ⊃E
Y |       G                               X, ∧E
Z | (H ⊃ G) ⊃ G                          3–Y, ⊃I
```

What one needs at line V is exactly the same as what one needed earlier at line Y. It might be supposed that, since one could not get 'G' from 'H ⊃ G' at line Y, one cannot get 'G' from 'H ⊃ G' now. This would be a mistake, but the mistake is worth exploring. If one cannot get 'G' from 'H ⊃ G', one must get it from 'G ∧ I' – and this is just what is being attempted now. Accordingly, the steps involved in getting 'G' from 'G ∧ I' will be similar to the steps one has already taken. The sketch of the derivation is revised to show this strategy:

```
1 | (F ⊃ G) ⊃ (G ∧ I)                    P
2 | F ⊃ H                                 P
3 |    H ⊃ G                              A
4 |      (F ⊃ G) ⊃ (G ∧ I)               1, R
5 |          F                            A
6 |            (F ⊃ G) ⊃ (G ∧ I)         1, R
7 |                F                      A
  :                :
S |                G                      ?
T |             F ⊃ G                     7–S, ⊃I
U |             G ∧ I                     6, T, ⊃E
V |             G                         U, ∧E
W |       F ⊃ G                           5–V, ⊃I
X |       G ∧ I                           4, W, ⊃E
Y |       G                               X, ∧E
Z | (H ⊃ G) ⊃ G                          3–Y, ⊃I
```

With the outline of the derivation on paper, it is clear why the present strategy is a mistake. One needs 'G' at line S, just as one needed 'G' at line V. At line S there is no more information available than there was when one first tried to get 'G' at line V; if there is a strategy which serves to obtain 'G' at line S, exactly the same strategy would have served to obtain 'G' at line V. It is time to back up a step:

1	(F ⊃ G) ⊃ (G ∧ I)	P
2	F ⊃ H	P
3	H ⊃ G	A
4	(F ⊃ G) ⊃ (G ∧ I)	1, R
5	F	A
V	G	?
W	F ⊃ G	5–V, ⊃I
X	G ∧ I	4, W, ⊃E
Y	G	X, ∧E
Z	(H ⊃ G) ⊃ G	3–Y, ⊃I

Although what one needs at line V is exactly the same as what one first needed at line Y, and although one could not get 'G' from 'H ⊃ G' at line Y, another attempt to get 'G' from 'H ⊃ G' is now a sensible move. The reason for this is that one has more information available at line V than one had previously. Whenever one introduces a new assumption, it is always possible that a strategy which did not previously work will now work with the new information available from the new assumption. To get 'G' from 'H ⊃ G', one needs 'H', and the sketch of the derivation is amended accordingly:

1	(F ⊃ G) ⊃ (G ∧ I)	P
2	F ⊃ H	P
3	H ⊃ G	A
4	(F ⊃ G) ⊃ (G ∧ I)	1, R
5	F	A
6	H ⊃ G	3, R
U	H	?
V	G	6, U, ⊃E
W	F ⊃ G	5–V, ⊃I
X	G ∧ I	4, W, ⊃E
Y	G	X, ∧E
Z	(H ⊃ G) ⊃ G	3–Y, ⊃I

The problem of obtaining 'H' is easily solved. A glance at what is available shows that 'H' is available from 'F ⊃ H' on line 2. To obtain 'H' from 'F ⊃ H' one needs 'F', and 'F' is the formula which was introduced as an assumption at line 5. All that is needed is to reiterate 'F ⊃ H' onto the present scope line and then use ⊃E. The derivation is completed in this way:

1	(F ⊃ G) ⊃ (G ∧ I)	P
2	F ⊃ H	P
3	H ⊃ G	A
4	(F ⊃ G) ⊃ (G ∧ I)	1, R
5	F	A
6	H ⊃ G	3, R
7	F ⊃ H	2, R
8	H	5, 7, ⊃E
9	G	6, 8, ⊃E
10	F ⊃ G	5–9, ⊃I
11	G ∧ I	4, 10, ⊃E
12	G	11, ∧E
13	(H ⊃ G) ⊃ G	3–12, ⊃I

The general strategy of trying an elimination rule before trying an introduction rule usually results in a shorter derivation. This is not always so, however, and there is often a good reason to start a derivation with an attempt to use an introduction rule. There are two perfectly sensible strategies in trying to obtain the conclusion from the premisses of the following argument:

$$M \supset G$$
$$N \supset G$$
$$M \lor N$$
$$\overline{S \supset G}$$

It does not take much logical insight to see that the disjunctive premiss is essential. Consequently, somewhere in the course of the derivation, one will have to use ∨E on the third premiss. A perfectly sensible approach is to start by assuming one of the disjuncts and obtaining the conclusion. One can then assume the other disjunct and obtain the conclusion. This approach is taken in the following derivation:

```
 1 | M ⊃ G                                    P
 2 | N ⊃ G                                    P
·3 | M ∨ N                                    P
 4 |   | M                                    A
 W |   ¦ S ⊃ G                                ?
 X |   | N                                    A
 Y |   ¦ S ⊃ G                                ?
 Z | S ⊃ G                                    3, 4–W, X–Y, ∨E
```

The two problems of obtaining 'S ⊃ G' at line W and at line Y are very similar. In neither case can 'S ⊃ G' be reiterated or obtained by use of an elimination rule. It follows that, in both cases, an introduction rule must be used. The sketch of the derivation shows the strategy:

```
 1 | M ⊃ G                                    P
 2 | N ⊃ G                                    P
 3 | M ∨ N                                    P
 4 |   | M                                    A
 5 |   |   | S                                A
 T |   |   ¦ G                                ?
 U |   | S ⊃ G                                5–T, ⊃I
 V |   | N                                    A
 W |   |   | S                                A
 X |   |   ¦ G                                ?
 Y |   | S ⊃ G                                W–X, ⊃I
 Z | S ⊃ G                                    3, 4–U, V–Y, ∨E
```

As might be expected, the two new subderivations are also very similar. In both cases one needs to get 'G' under the assumption 'S'. In neither case can one reiterate 'G', but in both cases a strategy with an elimination rule is evident. In the first new subderivation, one can reiterate 'M' and 'M ⊃ G'. In the second new subderivation, one can reiterate 'N' and 'N ⊃ G'. The derivation is completed according to this plan:

1	M ⊃ G	P
2	N ⊃ G	P
3	M ∨ N	P
4	M	A
5	S	A
6	M ⊃ G	1, R
7	M	4, R
8	G	6, 7, ⊃E
9	S ⊃ G	5–8, ⊃I
10	N	A
11	S	A
12	N ⊃ G	2, R
13	N	10, R
14	G	12, 13, ⊃E
15	S ⊃ G	11–14, ⊃I
16	S ⊃ G	3, 4–9, 10–15, ∨E

Since the main operator of 'S ⊃ G' is a horseshoe, another approach to the problem would be to start by trying to use horseshoe introduction. The derivation would then be developed as follows:

1	M ⊃ G	P
2	N ⊃ G	P
3	M ∨ N	P
4	S	A
Y	G	?
Z	S ⊃ G	4–Y, ⊃I

The problem of obtaining 'G' at line Y is similar to the problem of obtaining 'G' in the previous derivation. One cannot obtain what one needs either from 'M ⊃ G' or from 'N ⊃ G'. Thus, one needs to use ∨E on 'M ∨ N' once this has been reiterated:

1	M ⊃ G	P
2	N ⊃ G	P
3	M ∨ N	P
4	│ S	A
5	│ M ∨ N	3, R
6	│ │ M	A
V	│ │ G	?
W	│ │ N	A
X	│ │ G	?
Y	│ G	5, 6–V, W–X, ∨E
Z	S ⊃ G	4–Y, ⊃I

Obtaining 'G' in the two subderivations is a simple matter. 'G' can be derived under the assumption 'M' by reiterating 'M ⊃ G' and 'G' can be derived under the assumption 'N' by reiterating 'N ⊃ G'. The two reiterations and two applications of ⊃E are enough to complete the derivation:

1	M ⊃ G	P
2	N ⊃ G	P
3	M ∨ N	P
4	│ S	A
5	│ M ∨ N	3, R
6	│ │ M	A
7	│ │ M ⊃ G	1, R
8	│ │ G	6, 7, ⊃E
9	│ │ N	A
10	│ │ N ⊃ G	2, R
11	│ │ G	9, 10, ⊃E
12	│ G	5, 6–8, 9–11, ∨E
13	S ⊃ G	4–12, ⊃I

An important thing to remember in constructing derivations is that one should never do anything without some strategy in mind. In particular, one should never introduce an assumption without having a clear idea of how the new scope line which is introduced with the assumption is going to be ended.

§ 3.19: EXERCISES

For each of the following arguments, derive the conclusion from the premiss(es).

1 ~ (A ∨ B)
   _____
   ~ A

2 ~ A ∧ ~ B
   _____
   ~ (A ∧ B)

3 F
   _____
   D ⊃ (E ⊃ F)

4 A ⊃ (B ∧ C)
   ~ C
   _____
   ~ A

5 J ⊃ (K ⊃ L)
   J ⊃ K
   _____
   J ⊃ L

6 K ⊃ L
   _____
   (M ⊃ K) ⊃ (M ⊃ L)

7 (S ⊃ T) ⊃ T
   T ≡ U
   _____
   (S ⊃ U) ⊃ U

8 A ⊃ B
   B ⊃ C
   C ⊃ A
   _____
   A ≡ C

9 A ∨ D
   (~ B ∧ ~ C) ≡ D
   B ⊃ ~ (C ⊃ A)
   _____
   ~ B

10 K ⊃ (L ⊃ M)
    _____
    (K ∧ L) ⊃ M

11 N ⊃ O
    O ≡ P
    N ≡ S
    ─────
    S ⊃ P

12 (J ∨ K) ⊃ L
    ─────────
    J ⊃ L

13 (C ⊃ D) ∨ (C ⊃ E)
    C
    ────────────────
    D ∨ E

14 (~ F ∨ G) ⊃ (I ⊃ H)
    F ⊃ G
    ──────────────────
    F ⊃ (I ⊃ H)

15 A ≡ B
    A ∨ B
    ─────
    A ∧ B

§3.20: INDIRECT PROOF

The conclusion of the following argument can be obtained from the premisses:

    F ⊃ ~ G
    G
    ──────
    ~ F

The outline of the derivation looks like this:

1 | F ⊃ ~ G   P
2 | G   P
  ⋮
Z | ~ F   ?

'~ F' cannot be obtained by reiteration or by an elimination rule, so one must try ~I, the appropriate introduction rule:

```
1 | F ⊃ ~ G                              P
2 | G                                    P
3 |    | F                               A
X |    | Φ                               ?
Y |    | ~ Φ                             ?
Z | ~ F                                  3, X, Y, ~I
```

The problem now is to find a pair of contradictory formulas. Any pair whatever would serve. 'H' and '~ H' are a contradictory pair, but since neither appears anywhere in the derivation, it would be ridiculous to look for such a pair. A more promising approach would be to look for a formula which is readily available and its negation. The formulas which are readily available are 'F ⊃ ~ G', 'G' and 'F'. 'F' and '~ F' would be a contradictory pair, but since '~ F' is what one is looking for, this option is the least promising. 'G' and '~ G' are a contradictory pair. 'G' can be reiterated from line 2. '~ G' can be obtained from 'F ⊃ ~ G' provided one has 'F', and 'F' is on the present scope line. The most sensible strategy, then, is to complete the derivation using 'G' and '~ G' as the contradictory pair:

```
1 | F ⊃ ~ G                              P
2 | G                                    P
3 |    | F                               A
4 |    | G                               2, R
5 |    | F ⊃ ~ G                         1, R
6 |    | ~ G                             3, 5, ⊃E
7 | ~ F                                  3, 4, 6, ~I
```

The problem of obtaining the conclusion of the following argument is a little more complicated:

$$\frac{\sim (F \supset G)}{\sim G}$$

As before, the outline of the derivation is started:

```
1 | ~ (F ⊃ G)                            P
Z | ~ G                                  ?
```

The only way to obtain '~ G' is by ~I, so one should assume 'G' and look for a contradiction:

```
1 │ ~ (F ⊃ G)                    P
2 │   │ G                        A
X │   │ Φ                        ?
Y │   │ ~ Φ                      ?
Z │ ~ G                          2, X, Y, ~I
```

'G' and '~ G' are a contradictory pair, but the problem is the same as that encountered in the previous example; one member of this pair is what one is now trying to obtain. A better bet would be to try to get some other contradictory pair, one member of which is readily available. 'F ⊃ G' and '~ (F ⊃ G)' are such a pair. One should reiterate '~ (F ⊃ G)' and try to get 'F ⊃ G'. The sketch of the derivation shows this strategy:

```
1 │ ~ (F ⊃ G)                    P
2 │   │ G                        A
3 │   │ ~ (F ⊃ G)               1, R
Y │   │ F ⊃ G                    ?
Z │ ~ G                          2, 3, Y, ~I
```

'F ⊃ G' cannot be reiterated and it cannot be obtained by an elimination rule, so one must use ⊃I. One assumes 'F' and tries to obtain 'G'. This is easily done, since 'G' can be reiterated from line 2. The complete derivation follows:

```
1 │ ~ (F ⊃ G)                    P
2 │   │ G                        A
3 │   │ ~ (F ⊃ G)               1, R
4 │   │   │ F                    A
5 │   │   │ G                    2, R
6 │   │ F ⊃ G                    4–5, ⊃I
7 │ ~ G                          2, 3, 6, ~I
```

Proficiency in finding contradictory pairs increases with practice. This skill is extremely useful in constructing derivations whenever one needs a formula whose main operator is a tilde. The fact that every formula is truth-functionally equivalent to the negation of its negation, that 'Φ' is truth-functionally equivalent to '~ ~ Φ', suggests that negation introduction might be useful in some less obvious ways.

One of the most powerful strategies in constructing derivations is **indirect proof**. If one needs a formula 'Φ', and all the standard ways of obtaining it fail, it is always a possible strategy to try to obtain '~ ~ Φ' and use ~E to get 'Φ'. Since the main operator of '$\sim \sim \Phi$' is a tilde, the indirect proof strategy first uses ~I and then uses ~E. To obtain an unnegated formula 'Φ' by an indirect proof, one should assume '$\sim \Phi$' and try to obtain a contradictory pair of formulas. Any contradiction allows one to obtain '$\sim \sim \Phi$' by ~I. It is then a simple matter to use ~E in order to obtain 'Φ'. If the formula one needs is a negated formula '$\sim \Phi$', one should of course eliminate the ~E step by assuming 'Φ' rather than '$\sim \sim \Phi$'. In such a case, the negated formula is obtained by ~I directly and indirect proof is not used.

   Deriving the conclusion of the following argument is a good example of the use of indirect proof:

   $\sim (M \vee N) \equiv O$
   $M \wedge \sim P$
   _____

   $O \supset P$

The obvious strategy is to obtain '$O \supset P$' by $\supset$I, and the derivation is started accordingly:

1	$\sim (M \vee N) \equiv O$	P
2	$M \wedge \sim P$	P
3	O	A
Y	P	?
Z	$O \supset P$	3–Y, $\supset$I

'P' cannot be reiterated and it cannot be obtained by an elimination rule. Since 'P' is an atomic formula, no introduction rule can work. The only possible strategy is indirect proof. One should assume '$\sim$ P' and look for a contradictory pair:

1	$\sim (M \vee N) \equiv O$	P
2	$M \wedge \sim P$	P
3	O	A
4	$\sim P$	A
V	Φ	?
W	$\sim \Phi$	?
X	$\sim \sim P$	4, V, W, ~I
Y	P	X, ~E
Z	$O \supset P$	3–Y, $\supset$I

There are no obvious candidates for the contradictory pair of formulas to replace 'Φ' and '$\sim \Phi$'. One could start by looking for an atomic formula and its negation. It is pointless to look for 'P' and '~ P' since obtaining 'P' is the whole point of looking for a contradictory pair of formulas. Neither 'N' nor '~ N' appears as a complete formula anywhere in the derivation, and there seems to be no easy way to obtain either. 'O' and 'M' are easily obtained, but the only way to obtain either '~ O' or '~ M' is by an indirect proof. Obtaining either formula in this way would require finding a contradictory pair of formulas, and this is exactly the problem being addressed.

Accordingly, one must consider more complex formulas. One could reiterate the formula on line 1 and try to obtain '~ (~ (M ∨ N) ≡ O)'. The only way to obtain this formula is by ~I, and the problem of finding a contradictory pair of formulas seems just as baffling as it did when considering atomic formulas. One could reiterate the formula on line 2 and try to obtain '~ (M ∧ ~ P)', but once again the problem of finding a contradictory pair of formulas seems insurmountable. Using part of '~ (M ∨ N) ≡ O' seems to be the only strategy remaining. If one reiterated '~ (M ∨ N) ≡ O' and 'O', one could obtain '~ (M ∨ N)'. One would then need 'M ∨ N' to have a contradictory pair. This looks far more promising. 'M ∨ N' is a disjunctive formula which could be obtained by ∨I if one had either 'M' or 'N'. It is worth amending the outline of the derivation to pursue this strategy:

1	~ (M ∨ N) ≡ O	P
2	M ∧ ~ P	P
3	O	A
4	~ P	A
5	~ (M ∨ N) ≡ O	1, R
6	O	3, R
7	~ (M ∨ N)	5, 6, ≡E
W	M ∨ N	?
X	~ ~ P	4, 7, W, ~I
Y	P	X, ~E
Z	O ⊃ P	3–Y, ⊃I

To obtain 'M ∨ N' by ∨I at line W, one needs either 'M' or 'N'. There is no obvious way to obtain 'N', but 'M' can be obtained from 'M ∧ ~ P' by ∧E when 'M ∧ ~ P' is reiterated from line 2. The derivation can now be completed:

1	~ (M ∨ N) ≡ O	P
2	M ∧ ~ P	P
3	O	A
4	~ P	A
5	~ (M ∨ N) ≡ O	1, R
6	O	3, R
7	~ (M ∨ N)	5, 6, ≡E
8	M ∧ ~ P	2, R
9	M	8, ∧E
10	M ∨ N	9, ∨I
11	~ ~ P	4, 7, 10, ~I
12	P	11, ~E
13	O ⊃ P	3–12, ⊃I

Indirect proof is very useful when one needs a disjunctive formula but cannot obtain either of the disjuncts. For example, since '~ (~ A ∧ ~ B)' is truth-functionally equivalent to 'A ∨ B', it should be possible to derive the latter from the former:

1	~ (~ A ∧ ~ B)	P
Z	A ∨ B	?

It is impossible to derive either 'A' or 'B' from '~ (~ A ∧ ~ B)', so ∨I cannot be used to obtain 'A ∨ B'. Accordingly, one must use indirect proof. One assumes '~ (A ∨ B)' and looks for a contradiction:

1	~ (~ A ∧ ~ B)	P
2	~ (A ∨ B)	A
W	Φ	?
X	~ Φ	?
Y	~ ~ (A ∨ B)	2, W, X, ~I
Z	A ∨ B	Y, ~E

In considering what contradictory pair of formulas one could use instead of 'Φ' and '~ Φ', one must consider what formulas one can get onto the current scope line. In the present example, no atomic formulas can be obtained, and the only formulas available are the formulas on lines 1 and 2. The choices seem to be either the formula on line 1 and its negation or the formula on line 2 and its negation.

One possible strategy would be to look for the negation of the formula on line 2. Then one would want either 'A ∨ B' or '~ ~ (A ∨ B)'. There is no way of obtaining either formula except by indirect proof, and this would involve assuming '~ (A ∨ B)' and looking for a contradiction. The sketch of the derivation is appropriately amended:

1	~ (~ A ∧ ~ B)	P
2	~ (A ∨ B)	A
3	~ (A ∨ B)	A
V	Φ	?
W	~ Φ	?
X	~ ~ (A ∨ B)	3, V, W, ~I
Y	~ ~ (A ∨ B)	2, 2, X, ~I
Z	A ∨ B	Y, ~E

A glance at this outline is sufficient to show that the present strategy is hopeless. If one could obtain a contradiction on the scope line which begins at line 3, one could obtain exactly the same contradiction on the scope line which begins at line 2. Clearly, some other contradictory pair must be considered. The only other pair which looks at all promising is the formula on line 1 and '~ A ∧ ~ B'. Accordingly, the mistaken step is deleted from the sketch of the derivation and the new strategy is outlined:

1	~ (~ A ∧ ~ B)	P
2	~ (A ∨ B)	A
3	~ (~ A ∧ ~ B)	1, R
X	~ A ∧ ~ B	?
Y	~ ~ (A ∨ B)	2, 3, X, ~I
Z	A ∨ B	Y, ~E

The obvious way to obtain '~ A ∧ ~ B' is by ∧I from '~ A' and '~ B'. Neither of these formulas can be reiterated or obtained by an elimination rule, so in both cases one should try the appropriate introduction rule. One should assume 'A' and try to find a contradiction, and assume 'B' and try to find a contradiction. The contradiction under the assumption 'B' need not be the same as the contradiction under the assumption 'A', but of course it does not matter if it is. In the expanded sketch of the derivation, one contradictory pair is shown as 'Φ' and '~ Φ' and the other contradictory pair is shown as 'Ψ' and '~ Ψ', leaving open the possibility that 'Φ' and 'Ψ' may turn out to be identical formulas.

1	~ (~ A ∧ ~ B)	P
2	~ (A ∨ B)	A
3	~ (~ A ∧ ~ B)	1, R
4	A	A
Q	Φ	?
R	~ Φ	?
S	~ A	4, Q, R, ~I
T	B	A
U	ψ	?
V	~ ψ	?
W	~ B	T, U, V, ~I
X	~ A ∧ ~ B	S, W, ∧I
Y	~ ~ (A ∨ B)	2, 3, X, ~I
Z	A ∨ B	Y, ~E

The usefulness of ∨I is shown again at this point. One needs a contradictory pair under the assumption 'A' and a contradictory pair under the assumption 'B'. Since '~ (A ∨ B)' can be reiterated, it is easy to obtain the required contradictions. One can get 'A ∨ B' from 'A' by ∨I and one can get 'A ∨ B' from 'B' by ∨I. The derivation can now be completed:

1	~ (~ A ∧ ~ B)	P
2	~ (A ∨ B)	A
3	~ (~ A ∧ ~ B)	1, R
4	A	A
5	A ∨ B	4, ∨I
6	~ (A ∨ B)	2, R
7	~ A	4, 5, 6, ~I
8	B	A
9	A ∨ B	8, ∨I
10	~ (A ∨ B)	2, R
11	~ B	8, 9, 10, ~I
12	~ A ∧ ~ B	7, 11, ∧I
13	~ ~ (A ∨ B)	2, 3, 12, ~I
14	A ∨ B	13, ~E

It should be clear that if one contradictory pair of formulas can be obtained on a given scope line, any contradictory pair can be obtained simply by using indirect proof to obtain each member of the pair. However, using indirect proof twice to obtain an arbitrarily chosen contradictory pair is a poor strategy. When one needs a contradictory pair of formulas, one should spend some time in examining what is easily available before attempting to obtain a particular pair.

In producing derivations, it is not a good idea to try indirect proof too soon. In general, the following procedure will result in the shortest derivation. At each stage of a derivation, when one needs a formula 'Φ', one should go through these steps in order:

1 See if one can reiterate 'Φ'.

2 See if one can use an elimination rule to obtain 'Φ'. In most cases, if one has a disjunctive formula available, one should first try $\vee$E.

3 See if one can use an introduction rule to obtain 'Φ'.

4 See if one can obtain 'Φ' by an indirect proof.

§ 3.21: EXERCISES

For each of the following arguments, derive the conclusion from the premiss(es).

1 $F \supset \sim (G \vee H)$
   G

   ───────────

   $\sim F$

2 M

   ───────────

   $\sim M \supset O$

3 $M \supset (N \supset S)$
   $M \supset N$

   ───────────

   $\sim S \supset \sim M$

4 $F \supset (G \supset H)$
   $\sim H$

   ───────────

   $\sim (F \wedge G)$

5 $P \supset (Q \wedge \sim R)$
   $P \wedge (S \supset R)$

   ───────────

   $\sim S$

6 $\dfrac{F \supset (G \wedge H)}{(\sim G \vee \sim H) \supset \sim F}$

7 $F \vee G$
  $\dfrac{F \vee \sim G}{F}$

8 $A \supset (B \vee C)$
  $\dfrac{\sim C}{A \supset B}$

9 $(A \vee B) \supset C$
  $\dfrac{(\sim C \vee D) \wedge A}{D}$

10 $\sim ((P \vee Q) \wedge (R \vee S))$
   $\dfrac{\sim S \supset \sim Q}{\sim Q}$

11 $\sim A \supset \sim B$
   $A \supset G$
   $\dfrac{\sim (G \vee F)}{\sim B \vee F}$

12 A
   $(B \supset C) \supset D$
   $\dfrac{(C \supset A) \supset \sim D}{B}$

13 $\dfrac{\sim P \vee Q}{(S \supset P) \supset (S \supset Q)}$

14 $(A \vee B) \supset (C \vee D)$
   $C \supset \sim E$
   $D \supset \sim A$
   $\dfrac{A \wedge E}{\sim (C \vee D)}$

15 $M \supset R$
   $S \supset K$
   $\dfrac{\sim S \supset M}{\sim R \supset K}$

16 $\sim (A \lor B)$

$\overline{A \equiv B}$

17 K

$\sim Q \lor \sim S$

$(\sim K \lor S) \land Q$

$\overline{\sim Q}$

18 $(R \lor S) \supset F$

$\sim (F \land \sim G)$

$\sim R \supset M$

$\sim G$

$\overline{M}$

19 $\sim H \land G$

$F \supset ((G \land E) \supset (H \lor I))$

$E \land F$

$\overline{I}$

20 $R \equiv (S \lor T)$

$\sim S$

$\overline{T \equiv R}$

§3.22: CATEGORICAL DERIVATIONS

The most common sort of derivation starts with the premiss or premisses of an argument and ends with the conclusion. However, it is possible to derive certain formulas given no premisses whatever. A derivation of this sort is a **categorical derivation**.

A formula which is truth-functionally true does not depend on the truth of any other formula. In other words, given any information whatever, or no information at all, a truth-functionally true formula is bound to be true. Thus, it is possible to construct derivations having such formulas as their final steps without any premisses at the beginning.

Since one cannot appeal to a premiss for information in a categorical derivation, one cannot immediately use an elimination rule because there is no operator to eliminate. Every categorical derivation, therefore, must be based on some introduction rule. A few examples will make this clear.

One of the most obvious examples of a truth-functionally true formula is 'A $\supset$ A'. The derivation is very simple:

1   $\lfloor A$ A

2   $A \supset A$ 1–1, $\supset$I

The derivation of 'A ≡ A' is equally simple:

```
1 |   | A                          A
2 | A ≡ A                          1–1, 1–1, ≡I
```

Another example of a truth-functionally true formula is 'A ⊃ (B ⊃ A)'.
One can use ⊃I to obtain it:

```
1 |   | A                          A
2 |   |   | B                      A
3 |   |   | A                      1, R
4 |   | B ⊃ A                      2–3, ⊃I
5 | A ⊃ (B ⊃ A)                    1–4, ⊃I
```

The method of indirect proof is very useful in constructing categorical
derivations. It is used here to derive 'A ∨ ~ A':

```
1 |   | ~ (A ∨ ~ A)               A
2 |   |   | A                     A
3 |   |   | A ∨ ~ A               2, ∨I
4 |   |   | ~ (A ∨ ~ A)           1, R
5 |   | ~ A                       2, 3, 4, ~I
6 |   | A ∨ ~ A                   5, ∨I
7 | ~ ~ (A ∨ ~ A)                 1, 1, 6, ~I
8 | A ∨ ~ A                       7, ~E
```

The categorical derivation of '~ (F ∧ ~ F)' shows that 'F ∧ ~ F' is truth-
functionally false:

```
1 |   | F ∧ ~ F                   A
2 |   | F                         1, ∧E
3 |   | ~ F                       1, ∧E
4 | ~ (F ∧ ~ F)                   1, 2, 3, ~I
```

Categorical derivations are often used to demonstrate truth-functional equivalences. In each of the following three derivations, an intuitively clear truth-functional equivalence is shown:

1	A ∨ B	A
2	A	A
3	B ∨ A	2, ∨I
4	B	A
5	B ∨ A	4, ∨I
6	B ∨ A	1, 2–3, 4–5, ∨E
7	B ∨ A	A
8	A	A
9	A ∨ B	8, ∨I
10	B	A
11	A ∨ B	10, ∨I
12	A ∨ B	7, 8–9, 10–11, ∨E
13	(A ∨ B) ≡ (B ∨ A)	1–6, 7–12, ≡I

1	A ∧ B	A
2	A	1, ∧E
3	B	1, ∧E
4	B ∧ A	2, 3, ∧I
5	B ∧ A	A
6	A	5, ∧E
7	B	5, ∧E
8	A ∧ B	6, 7, ∧I
9	(A ∧ B) ≡ (B ∧ A)	1–4, 5–8, ≡I

1	A ⊃ B	A
2	~ B	A
3	A	A
4	A ⊃ B	1, R
5	B	3, 4, ⊃E
6	~ B	2, R
7	~ A	3, 5, 6, ~I
8	~ B ⊃ ~ A	2–7, ⊃I
9	~ B ⊃ ~ A	A
10	A	A
11	~ B	A
12	~ B ⊃ ~ A	9, R
13	~ A	11, 12, ⊃E
14	A	10, R
15	~ ~ B	11, 13, 14, ~I
16	B	15, ~E
17	A ⊃ B	10–16, ⊃I
18	(A ⊃ B) ≡ (~ B ⊃ ~ A)	1–8, 9–17, ≡I

§3.23: EXERCISES

Provide categorical derivations of the following formulas.

1 M ≡ (M ∧ M)

2 A ∨ (~ A ∨ B)

3 L ≡ (L ∨ L)

4 (R ⊃ S) ⊃ (R ⊃ (R ∧ S))

5 ((F ⊃ G) ⊃ R) ⊃ (G ⊃ R)

6 ((R ⊃ S) ∧ ~ S) ⊃ ~ R

7 ~ F ⊃ (F ⊃ G)

8 (A ∨ B) ⊃ ((A ⊃ B) ⊃ B)

9 (M ⊃ N) ⊃ (~ M ∨ N)

10 ~ ((F ∧ G) ∧ (~ F ∨ ~ G))

11 (~ M ∨ N) ⊃ (M ⊃ N)

12 G ∨ (G ⊃ H)

13 (F ⊃ G) ∨ (G ⊃ F)

14 (P ⊃ (Q ∧ R)) ⊃ ((~ Q ∨ ~ R) ⊃ ~ P)

15 ((P ∨ Q) ∨ R) ≡ (P ∨ (Q ∨ R))

§ 3.24: SUMMARY OF TOPICS

With a few possible exceptions to make the summary clearer, the topics appear in the order in which they appear in the text.

Derivation (See p. 55): A numbered sequence of formulas, each occurrence of a formula being justified.

Scope line (See p. 55): A vertical line which shows the extent ('scope') of a derivation or subderivation.

Primary scope line (See p. 56): The scope line which is furthest to the left in a derivation. See **Secondary scope line**.

Introduction rule (See p. 56): For every operator, there is an introduction rule which serves to create a formula which has that operator as its main operator.

Elimination rule (See p. 56): For every operator, there is an elimination rule which uses the main operator of a given formula to create a different formula.

Conjunction introduction (See p. 57): A rule, $\wedge I$, which serves to create a formula which has a caret as its main operator. Every use of conjunction introduction requires an appeal to exactly two lines. The general pattern of $\wedge I$ follows:

m | Φ

n | Ψ

o | $\Phi \wedge \Psi$ m, n, $\wedge I$

If 'Φ' and 'Ψ' are not distinct, if one is creating a formula such as '$\Phi \wedge \Phi$', the two lines which are appealed to would be identical. The appeal would look like 'm, m, $\wedge I$'.

Conjunction elimination (See p. 59): A rule, ∧E, which serves to obtain one of the conjuncts from a formula which has a caret as its main operator. Every use of conjunction elimination requires an appeal to exactly one line. The general pattern of ∧E follows:

m | Φ ∧ ψ

n | Φ   m, ∧E

    or

m | Φ ∧ ψ

n | ψ   m, ∧E

Negation elimination (See p. 61): A rule, ~E, which allows the removal of two consecutive tildes when the first of these tildes is the main operator. Every use of negation elimination requires an appeal to exactly one line. The general pattern of ~E follows:

m | ~ ~ Φ

n | Φ   m, ~E

Disjunction introduction (See p. 62): A rule, ∨I, which serves to create a formula which has a vel as its main operator. Every use of disjunction introduction requires an appeal to exactly one line. The general pattern of ∨I follows:

m | Φ

n | Φ ∨ ψ   m, ∨I

    or

m | Φ

n | ψ ∨ Φ   m, ∨I

Horseshoe elimination (See p. 64): A rule, ⊃E, which serves to obtain the consequent of a formula which has a horseshoe as its main operator. Every use of horseshoe elimination requires an appeal to exactly two lines. The general pattern of ⊃E follows:

```
m  | Φ ⊃ ψ
   |
n  | Φ
   |
o  | ψ                                    m, n, ⊃E
```

Triplebar elimination (See p. 66): A rule, ≡E, which serves to obtain one of the formulas flanking the '≡' in a formula which has a triplebar as its main operator. Every use of triplebar elimination requires an appeal to exactly two lines. The general pattern of ≡E follows:

```
m  | Φ ≡ ψ
   |
n  | Φ
   |
o  | ψ                                    m, n, ≡E
```

           or

```
m  | Φ ≡ ψ
   |
n  | ψ
   |
o  | Φ                                    m, n, ≡E
```

Secondary scope line (See p. 80): A scope line which serves to keep information which depends on an assumption away from the scope lines to the left of the secondary scope line.

Assumption (See p. 80): A formula which is assumed in order to produce another formula. Every assumption begins a new secondary scope line.

Subderivation (See p. 81): A derivation on a secondary scope line.

Reiteration (See p. 82): A rule which allows one to copy a formula from a scope line which has not ended onto a secondary scope line.

Horseshoe introduction (See p. 84): A rule, ⊃I, which serves to create a formula which has a horseshoe as its main operator. Every use of horseshoe introduction requires an appeal to exactly one range of lines. The general pattern of ⊃I follows:

```
m |   | Φ                              A
  |   |
  |   |
n |   | ψ
  |
  |
o | Φ ⊃ ψ                              m–n, ⊃I
```

If 'Φ' and 'ψ' are not distinct, if one is creating a formula such as 'Φ ⊃ Φ', the range can consist of a single line. The appeal would look like 'm–m, ⊃I'.

Triplebar introduction (See p. 88): A rule, ≡I, which serves to create a formula which has a triplebar as its main operator. Every use of triplebar introduction requires an appeal to exactly two ranges of lines. The general pattern of ≡I follows:

```
m |   | Φ                              A
  |   |
  |   |
n |   | ψ
  |
  |
o |   | ψ                              A
  |   |
  |   |
p |   | Φ
  |
  |
q | Φ ≡ ψ                              m–n, o–p, ≡I
```

If 'Φ' and 'ψ' are not distinct, if one is creating a formula such as 'Φ ≡ Φ', the two ranges together can consist of a single line. The appeal would look like 'm–m, m–m, ≡I'.

Negation introduction (See p. 91): A rule, ~I, which serves to create a
   formula which has a tilde as its main operator. Every use of negation
   introduction requires an appeal to exactly three lines, an assumption
   and a contradictory pair of formulas on the scope line which begins
   with the assumption. The general pattern of ~I follows:

```
m |    | Φ                               A


n |    | ψ


o |    | ~ ψ


p | ~ Φ                                  m, n, o, ~I
```

If 'Φ' and 'ψ' are not distinct, the appeal would look like 'm, m, n, ~I'.

Disjunction elimination (See p. 95): A rule, ∨E, which serves to create a
   new formula from a formula which has a vel as its main operator.
   Every use of disjunction elimination requires an appeal to exactly one
   line and exactly two ranges of lines, a disjunction and the new formula
   which is obtained from both of the disjuncts. It is important to
   remember that the identical formula must be obtained from both
   disjuncts. The general pattern of ∨E follows:

```
m | Φ ∨ ψ


n |    | Φ                               A


o |    | Ω


p |    | ψ                               A


q |    | Ω


r | Ω                                    m, n–o, p–q, ∨E
```

If the new formula is one of the disjuncts, one of the ranges would consist
   of a single line. The appeal would look like 'm, n–n, o–p, ∨E'.

Indirect proof (See p. 115): A way to derive a formula in two steps. The
first step is to obtain the desired formula, 'Φ', preceded by two tildes,
'$\sim \sim \Phi$'. The second step is to eliminate the two tildes. Every use of
indirect proof requires an appeal to exactly four lines, an assumption
which is the negation of the desired formula, a contradictory pair of
formulas on the scope line which begins with the assumption, and one
occurrence of negation elimination. The general pattern of indirect
proof follows:

m	$\mid\!\!-\ \sim \Phi$	A
n	ψ	
o	$\sim \psi$	
p	$\sim \sim \Omega$	m, n, o, ~I
q	Ω	p, ~E

As with ~I, 'Φ' and 'ψ' do not have to be distinct.

Categorical derivation (See p. 123): A categorical derivation is a derivation
which does not begin with premises. Categorical derivations in
sentence logic can be used to derive truth-functional truths. Every
categorical derivation in sentence logic begins with an assumption. A
simple categorical derivation follows:

1	$\mid\!\!-\ \Phi$	A
n	$\Phi \lor \psi$	1, $\lor$I
o	$\Phi \supset (\Phi \lor \psi)$	1–n, $\supset$I

CHAPTER FOUR

PREDICATE LOGIC

§4.1: INDIVIDUALS AND PREDICATES

There are some severe limitations to sentence logic. This can be seen from consideration of the following argument:

> Since all Frenchmen are Europeans and Pierre is a Frenchman, Pierre is a European.

The argument is obviously valid in some sense; if the premisses are true, the conclusion is bound to be true. However, when one represents each sentence by a sentence letter, all appearance of validity vanishes:

F: All Frenchmen are Europeans.
P: Pierre is a Frenchman.
E: Pierre is a European.

$$\frac{\begin{array}{c} F \\ P \end{array}}{E}$$

The argument as represented is truth-functionally invalid. The difficulty is that the original argument in English can be seen to be valid because of the internal structure of the sentences rather than because of truth-functional connections between sentences. Predicate logic is a way of dealing with such internal structure.

Ordinary English grammar texts make a distinction between the subject of a sentence and the predicate. In the sentence 'The book is expensive', 'the book' is the subject and 'is expensive' is the predicate. This simple example is sufficient to introduce two logical terms: 'the book' refers to an **individual** and 'is expensive' is a **predicate**.

An individual can be a person, a place, an idea or collection – virtually anything about which one can say something. Although mass nouns such as 'silver' and 'coal' are not normally thought of as referring to individuals, it is possible to say things about silver and coal. Accordingly, silver, coal, air and water are considered to be individuals in the logical sense of 'individual'. A predicate can deal with age, size, shape or complexity – virtually anything one can say about an individual. In all of the following sentences, the individuals are on the left of the dots and the predicates are on the right:

> John ... has won a medal.
> The new candidate ... will be elected.
> Oil ... is becoming more expensive.
> The price of oil ... is rising.
> That theory ... has been refuted.
> Sugar ... is soluble.
> Her husband ... turned out to be a creep.

The symbolic language can be expanded to reflect the internal structure of sentences. In addition to sentence letters and truth-functional operators, the expanded language includes symbols for individuals and symbols for predicates. Any of the lower-case Roman letters from 'a' to 't' can be used to stand for individuals. A letter standing for a particular individual is called a **constant**. Any upper-case Roman letter which is immediately followed by a constant can represent a predicate. Because a predicate letter is always immediately followed by a lower-case letter (which may be a constant or something else), it can never be confused with a sentence letter. As in the case of sentence letters, it is possible to increase the number of constants and predicate letters by use of subscripts, but the need will not arise in practice.

In translating English sentences into the expanded symbolic language, the meanings assigned to particular predicate letters and constants must be shown. Two simple translations follow:

> Peter is tired.
> p: Peter
> T __ : __ is tired
> Tp

That essay is short.
e: that essay
S __ : __ is short
Se

A predicate letter immediately followed by a constant is a sentence. The familiar sentence operators can be used to connect the sentences of predicate logic just as they are used in sentence logic. Using the same symbols, the sentences just translated can be combined in various ways, as in the following examples:

Peter is tired and that essay is short.
Tp ∧ Se

Peter is not tired but that essay is short.
~ Tp ∧ Se

If that essay is not short, Peter is tired.
~ Se ⊃ Tp

It is not often done, but there is no objection in principle to mixing sentence logic and predicate logic. Thus, the following is correct:

Greek is hard and French is easy.
G: Greek is hard.
f: French
E __ : __ is easy
G ∧ Ef

However, it would be more usual to use only predicate logic as follows:

Greek is hard and French is easy.
f: French
g: Greek
E __ : __ is easy
H __ : __ is hard
Hg ∧ Ef

There will be more later in this chapter about reasons for choosing among the various options which are possible in translation.

§4.2: ONE-PLACE AND MULTI-PLACE PREDICATES

In §4.1, the discussion dealt only with cases in which an individual has a certain property. All of the translations consisted of a predicate letter followed by a single constant. Thus, 'Peter is tired' was translated as 'Tp', using the **one-place predicate**, 'T __ '. Predicate logic, however, has also to deal with more complicated sentences. An example is 'Dick loves Jane.' This sentence asserts that there is a relation of loving between two individuals,

Dick and Jane. To reflect this relation between two individuals adequately, one needs a **multi-place predicate**. The sentence can be expressed symbolically by means of a two-place predicate as follows:

Dick loves Jane.

L_1_2: $\_1$ loves $\_2$

d: Dick

j: Jane

Ldj

Just as 'Dick loves Jane' does not have the same meaning as 'Jane loves Dick', so 'Ldj' does not have the same meaning as 'Ljd'. Of course, if the two-place predicate 'L_1_2' were defined differently, the formula 'Ldj' could be used to translate 'Jane loves Dick' as follows:

Jane loves Dick.

L_1_2: $\_1$ is loved by $\_2$

d: Dick

j: Jane

Ldj

The fact that the identical formula 'Ldj' can be used to express both 'Dick loves Jane' and 'Jane loves Dick' shows that attention must be paid to the order of places when one defines multi-place predicates. One can order the places in any way one likes. However, once a decision has been made, the order must be maintained or confusion will result.

There are three individuals mentioned in 'Bill gave the key to John', and this sentence can be translated by use of a three-place predicate:

Bill gave the key to John.

$G\_1\_2\_3$: $\_1$ gave $\_2$ to $\_3$

b: Bill

j: John

k: the key

Gbkj

In translating most English sentences, predicates having up to three places are usually sufficient. However, predicates with four or more places can be used on occasion. To assert that Tokyo is equidistant from Boston, Miami and Chicago, one can use a four-place predicate:

Tokyo is equidistant from Boston, Miami and Chicago.

$E\_1\_2\_3\_4$: $\_1$ is equidistant from $\_2$, $\_3$ and $\_4$

b: Boston

c: Chicago

m: Miami

t: Tokyo

Etbmc

Since it is false that Tokyo is equidistant from Boston, Miami and Chicago, '~ Etbmc' is true.

It is not required that the two or more individuals used with multi-place predicates be distinct. Thus, one can express 'Jack loves himself' as 'Ljj', 'Paul is as tall as Paul' as 'Tpp', and 'Jane despises herself if she is envious of Sally' as 'Ejs ⊃ Djj'.

When one uses the five sentence operators in predicate logic, it is important to bear in mind that these operators must be used only with sentences. 'John does not despise Mary' is properly translated as follows:

j: John
m: Mary
D__1__2: __1 despises __2
~ Djm

Both 'D ~ jm' ††† and 'Dj ~ m' ††† are mistaken because the tilde does not negate a sentence. Using the same symbolization, 'Mary despises John only if John despises Mary' can be translated as 'Dmj ⊃ Djm'. However, 'Dmj ⊃ jm' ††† is not a well-formed formula.

§4.3: CHOICES IN TRANSLATION

In predicate logic, to a much greater extent than in sentence logic, there are choices to be made in translation. There are many ways in which the sentence 'John sent the parcel to Kate' can be translated, including the following seven:

1 S: John sent the parcel to Kate.
   S

2 j: John
   S __ : __ sent the parcel to Kate
   Sj

3 k: Kate
   S __ : __ was sent the parcel by John
   Sk

4 p: the parcel
   S __ : John sent __ to Kate
   Sp

5 j: John
   k: Kate
   S __1__2: __1 sent the parcel to __2
   Sjk

6 j: John
   k: Kate
   p: the parcel
   S $\_1\_2\_3$: $\_1$ sent $\_2$ to $\_3$
   Sjpk

7 j: John
   k: Kate
   p: the parcel
   S $\_1\_2\_3$: $\_1$ was sent to $\_2$ by $\_3$
   Spkj

As a general principle, translations should be only as complex as is required in the context of argumentation and derivation. Without some knowledge of arguments in predicate logic (which will be discussed later in this chapter) and some knowledge of derivations in predicate logic (which will be discussed in Chapter 5), one often has no adequate basis for deciding how complex a translation is needed. However, there is no need for excessive caution. For example, if one needs to translate 'Catherine loves Michael and Catherine is loved by Peter', one should not use two predicates, one for 'loves' and one for 'is loved by'. Simple considerations of economy suggest that one should use a single predicate, either 'loves' or 'is loved by'. Moreover, the English sentence asserts that the same relation which holds between Catherine and Michael also holds between Peter and Catherine, and the translation should reflect this.

§4.4: EXERCISES

Translate each of the following sentences into symbols using the given predicates and constants.

   c: Carl
   p: Peter
   f: Frank
   A $\_1\_2$: $\_1$ annoyed $\_2$
   D $\_1\_2\_3$: $\_1$ discussed $\_2$ with $\_3$

1 Peter discussed Carl with Frank.

2 Peter was discussed by Frank with Carl.

3 Carl discussed Frank with Peter.

4 Carl annoyed Frank if he discussed Frank with Peter.

5 Carl discussed himself with Frank.

6 Carl discussed Peter with Frank but did not discuss Frank with Peter.

7 Carl discussed himself with Frank but not with Peter.

8 If Frank discussed himself with Peter, then Peter discussed Frank with Carl.

9 If Frank discussed Peter with Carl and Carl discussed Frank with Peter, then Frank discussed Carl with Peter.

10 Carl discussed himself with Frank and annoyed him.

11 Peter discussed himself with neither Frank nor Carl.

12 Peter did not discuss Frank with Carl unless Peter discussed himself with Frank.

13 Peter discussed himself with neither Frank nor Carl and annoyed both of them.

14 Assuming that Peter discussed Frank with Carl, then neither Frank nor Carl was annoyed by Peter.

15 Frank discussed himself with Carl only if either Peter or Carl discussed himself with Frank.

§4.5: QUANTIFIERS

In §4.1 it was pointed out that using a sentence letter to translate 'All Frenchmen are Europeans' made it impossible to state an obviously valid argument in terms of sentence logic in a way which maintains any appearance of validity. It is possible in principle to use sentence logic and still avoid the problem. There are a finite number of Frenchmen, and in principle it is possible to state that all Frenchmen are Europeans by using a finite number of sentences. Letting 'F_1' represent 'Frenchman number one is a European', 'F_2' represent 'Frenchman number two is a European' and so on, a conjunction of several million sentences will serve. Plainly, no human being could enumerate all Frenchmen in this way and no human being could write out such a conjunction, but in principle it is possible to do without the word 'all' in this case.

In much the same way, as long as there are a finite number of drunken fools, 'Some drunken fool is shouting in the street' can be thought of as a very long disjunction: '$((D_1 \lor D_2) \lor D_3) \lor \ldots D_n$'. In principle, it is possible to express 'some' in terms of a disjunction, but of course in practice this is often impossible. It should be remembered that the vel expresses the inclusive sense of 'or' and that the long disjunction leaves open the possibility that more than one drunken fool is shouting in the street.

When one is dealing with a small number of things, it is often easy to express 'all' and 'some' in sentence logic. If I have only three sisters, it is easy to use a conjunction to say that all my sisters are married. Similarly, if I have just four cousins it is easy to use a disjunction to say that at least one of my cousins plays golf. Problems arise when large numbers of things are involved or when one lacks knowledge. For example, even though I may not know very much about my local police force, I may well want to say that a policeman is on the scene. Similarly, I may want to say that none of the men on the field are tall, even though I may not know how many men there are on the field. As a practical matter, **quantifiers**, words like 'all', 'some' and 'no', are indispensable.

Aside from the practical need for quantifiers, there are theoretical reasons why quantifiers are needed. Many scientific claims are concerned with entities which cannot be enumerated. Much of mathematics involves infinities. One does not need to be a very sophisticated mathematician to understand sentences about all rational numbers, all multiples of 3 and all odd numbers. Quantifiers, therefore, are indispensable both in natural languages such as English and in the artificial languages which are used in symbolic logic.

§4.6: THE EXISTENTIAL QUANTIFIER

Using 'b' for 'this book' and 'R __ ' for ' __ is red', one can represent the claim that this book is red by 'Rb'. The claim that something is red can be represented by '$(\exists x)Rx$', which can be read as 'There is at least one thing which is R', or in rather stilted English as 'There is an x such that Rx.' The 'x' is not a constant because it does not name a particular individual; it is a **variable**. '$(\exists x)$' is an **existential quantifier**. '$(\exists y)$' and '$(\exists z)$' are also existential quantifiers because 'y' and 'z' are also variables. As with sentence letters and constants, the stock of variables can be increased by use of subscripts. Thus, 'x_1' and 'z_3' are also variables.

Using 'b' for 'this book', 'R __ ' for ' __ is red' and 'H __ ' for ' __ is heavy', one can represent the claim that this book is red and heavy by 'Rb ∧ Hb'. The claim that something is red and heavy can be represented by '$(\exists x)(Rx \wedge Hx)$', which can be read as 'There is an x which has properties R and H' or as 'There is an x such that Rx and Hx.'

'Rb' and 'Hb' are sentences and can be joined to form more complex sentences such as 'Rb ∧ Hb'. In the formula '$(\exists x)(Rx \wedge Hx)$', 'Rx' and 'Hx' are joined by a sentence operator, even though strictly speaking they are not sentences, no more than 'R __ ' and ' __ is red' are sentences. Such expressions are not sentences because they can be neither true nor false. However, it has become common to call such formulas 'open sentences'. An **open sentence** is a formula with this property: if all the variables in it were replaced by constants, the result would be a 'closed sentence'. A **closed sentence** which is the result of such a replacement is a genuine sentence capable of possessing a truth value. The legitimate use of sentence operators has been extended to allow these operators to be used with open sentences.

If '(∃x)Rx' represents 'Something is red', '~ (∃x)Rx' represents 'It is false that something is red', while '(∃x)~ Rx' represents 'There is something which is not red.' The difference between '~ (∃x)Rx' and '(∃x)~ Rx' can be seen by considering the real world. '~ (∃x)Rx' denies that there is something which is red, and that is manifestly false. By contrast, '(∃x)~ Rx' asserts that there is something which is not red, and that is manifestly true.

The claim that my dog is as large as Harry's dog can be represented by 'Lmh'. If my dog is as large as Harry's dog, something is as large as Harry's dog, which can be written as '(∃x)Lxh'. Similarly, if my dog is as large as Harry's dog, my dog is as large as something, which can be written as '(∃x)Lmx'. Finally, if my dog is as large as Harry's dog, something is as large as something. Because this claim involves two 'somethings', two existential quantifiers and two distinct variables must be used: '(∃x)(∃y)Lxy'. If one wrote '(∃x)(∃x)Lxx' †††, there would be no way of telling which quantifier goes with which variable.

The following two claims have completely different meanings. The first is a simple conjunction, while the second asserts that one and the same thing is both red and warm.

1 Something is red and something is warm.

2 Something is red and warm.

The former sentence can be expressed as '(∃x)Rx ∧ (∃x)Wx' or '(∃y)Ry ∧ (∃y)Wy', while the latter sentence can be expressed as '(∃x)(Rx ∧ Wx)' or '(∃z)(Rz ∧ Wz)'. Since 1 is a conjunction of two quantified formulas, each formula being capable of standing alone, it can also be expressed as '(∃x)Rx ∧ (∃y)Wy'. The claim that something is red and something is warm neither asserts nor denies that the red thing is identical to the warm thing, and this is reflected in every translation of 1 which has been given. Assertions of identity and non-identity will be discussed in §4.12.

To see why there is nothing to choose between '(∃x)Rx ∧ (∃x)Wx' and '(∃x)Rx ∧ (∃y)Wy', it is necessary to learn about the 'scope' of quantifiers. The **scope of a quantifier** determines what is governed by the quantifier. If one remembers how brackets extend what is negated by the tilde, it is a simple matter to determine the scope of a quantifier, since the two situations are analogous.

1 If a quantifier is followed by an unbracketed open sentence – something which would be a WFF if the variables were replaced by constants – the scope of the quantifier is that unbracketed open sentence.

2 If a quantifier is followed by a left bracket, the scope of the quantifier is that left bracket, its corresponding right bracket and what is between those two brackets.

3 If a quantifier is followed by a tilde, the scope of the quantifier is the
tilde and whatever the tilde negates.

There is no need to make an effort to memorize these four points. Working
through the examples in the next few sections will lead to an understanding
of the scope conventions.

§4.7: THE UNIVERSAL QUANTIFIER

One way to assert the manifestly false claim that everything is liquid is to say
that it is false that something is not liquid. One way to assert the manifestly
false claim that everything is non-liquid is by saying that it is false that
something is liquid. Similarly, one can deny that everything is liquid by
saying that something is non-liquid, and one can deny that everything is
non-liquid by saying that something is liquid. Thus, in English one could get
by without terms such as 'everything', and use negations and terms like
'something'. This would be cumbersome in English and it would be
cumbersome in the symbolic language. The difficulty is avoided by having a
universal quantifier. Using 'R __ ' to represent ' __ is red', one can represent
'Everything is red' by '$(\forall x)Rx$' or '$\sim (\exists x)\sim Rx$'. To deny that everything is
red, one can write either '$\sim (\forall x)Rx$' or '$(\exists x)\sim Rx$'.

Two translations of 'Everything is red' and two translations of its denial
have been given with an explanation of why there is nothing to choose
between them. '$(\forall x)Rx$' is **quantificationally equivalent** to '$\sim (\exists x)\sim Rx$',
just as '$\sim (\forall x)Rx$' is quantificationally equivalent to '$(\exists x)\sim Rx$'. In
Chapter 5 there are rules which allow one to derive quantificationally
equivalent formulas from each other.

A universally quantified formula should be understood as the rough
equivalent of an English sentence using 'all', 'any', 'each' or 'every'. Thus,
'$(\forall x)Bx$' should be read as 'For all x, x is B' or as 'For any x one picks,
x is B.' '$(\forall x)$', '$(\forall y)$', '$(\forall z)$', '$(\forall x_1)$' are all universal quantifiers. The scope
of the universal quantifier is determined in exactly the same way as that of
the existential quantifier.

Using '$S_{\_1\_2}$' to represent ' $\_1$ is the same size as $\_2$', '$(\forall x)Sxx$'
states the obvious truth that everything is the same size as itself: for any x
that one chooses, x is the same size as x. By contrast, '$(\forall x)(\forall y)Sxy$' asserts
the obvious falsehood that everything is the same size as everything: for any
x and any y that one chooses, x is the same size as y. As is the case with the
existential quantifier, the fact that two distinct quantifiers are used does not
preclude the possibility that the chosen x and the chosen y may be the same
thing.

'All dogs are brown' can be read as 'For any object one selects, if that
object is a dog, then that object is brown.' Using 'D __ ' to represent

'__ is a dog' and 'B __' to represent '__ is brown', the sentence can be written as '(∀x)(Dx ⊃ Bx)'. 'No dogs are reptiles' can be read as 'For any object one selects, if that object is a dog, then that object is not a reptile.' Using 'D __' to represent '__ is a dog' and 'R __' to represent '__ is a reptile', the sentence can be written as '(∀x)(Dx ⊃ ~ Rx)'.

Although in English a single word distinguishes 'Some dogs are brown' from 'All dogs are brown', the symbolic representation requires a change in the operator as well as a change in the quantifier. 'Some dogs are brown' asserts that there is at least one thing which is both a dog and brown and is properly translated as '(∃x)(Dx ∧ Bx)'. It should be noted that '(∃x)(Dx ⊃ Bx)' ††† is not a correct translation of this sentence, since it asserts that there is something such that if it is a dog then it is brown. It follows from the truth-table definition of the horseshoe that '(∃x)(Dx ⊃ Bx)' will be true if there is something in the universe which is not a dog. It should also be noted that '(∀x)(Dx ∧ Bx)' ††† is not a correct translation of 'All dogs are brown', since it asserts that everything is both a dog and brown.

Unlike the existential quantifier, the universal quantifier does not assert the existence of anything. '(∀x)(Dx ⊃ Bx)' neither asserts nor denies the existence of either dogs or brown things. It is natural to wonder why anyone would have anything serious to say about non-existent things. In fact, there are often occasions on which one makes true claims which turn out to be about non-existent entities. For example, there could be an award for anyone who develops a workable fusion reactor. One could then make the true claim that anyone with no knowledge of science or technology who develops a workable fusion reactor is eligible for an award, knowing full well that it is extremely unlikely that there is any such person.

Although the universally quantified formula '(∀x)(Px ⊃ Qx)' does not assert or deny the existence of anything which is P or anything which is Q, one can use the existential quantifier to do this. Thus, the two formulas '(∃x)Sx' and '(∀x)(Sx ⊃ Dx)' can be used to translate a sentence such as 'There are sharks and all sharks are dangerous.' Similarly, the two formulas '~ (∃x)Gx' and '(∀x)(Gx ⊃ Fx)' can be used to translate a sentence such as 'There are no ghosts, but all ghosts are frightening.'

Now that both quantifiers have been introduced, it is possible to explain what an **atomic formula** in predicate logic is. An atomic formula in predicate logic is any WFF which contain no operators, neither sentence operators nor quantifiers. Thus, 'Rc', 'Lms' and 'Gksd' are all atomic formulas.

§4.8: USING BOTH QUANTIFIERS

Many English sentences use both the existential and the universal quantifier. An example is 'Everything is larger than something.' This sentence means something quite different from 'Something is larger than everything', and one must be careful to maintain this difference in translations.

'Everything is larger than something' asserts that England is larger than something, that the moon is larger than something and so on. The claim that the moon is larger than something is the claim that there is something such that the moon is larger than it. This is easily translated as '$(\exists x)Lmx$'. The claim that everything is larger than something, however, is not a claim just about the moon. Accordingly, one should use a universal quantifier and replace 'm' with a variable which does not already appear in '$(\exists x)Lmx$': '$(\forall y)(\exists x)Lyx$'. It should be noted that the English sentence begins with a universal quantifier, as does its symbolic representation.

'Something is larger than everything' asserts that there is something which is larger than England, larger than the moon and so on. 'The moon is larger than everything' is easily translated '$(\forall x)Lmx$'. However, the claim that something is larger than everything is not a claim about the moon; it is a claim about an unspecified object. Accordingly, one should use an existential quantifier and replace 'm' with a variable which does not already appear in '$(\forall x)Lmx$': '$(\exists y)(\forall x)Lyx$'. It should be noted that the English sentence begins with an existential quantifier, as does its symbolic representation.

The position of quantifiers in English sentences cannot always be relied upon to ascertain the intended meaning. The shop advertising that it has a card for every occasion is not claiming that it has a single card which is suitable for birthdays, weddings and every other occasion. Likewise, it is not claiming that it has several cards, each of which is suitable for every occasion. It would be perverse to read the claim in any such way. Plainly, what it meant is that, for any occasion, the shop has at least one suitable card. In dealing with such sentences, one must consider the context and use some judgement as to what is intended.

Although the distinction between universal and existential quantification is important, there are contexts in which it makes little difference whether a sentence is considered as universally quantified or existentially quantified. If every street in a small town leads into the only square in the town, there is little to choose between 'Every street leads into a square' and 'There is a square into which every street leads.'

There are those who stoutly maintain that 'There is a card for every occasion' is ambiguous between the existential and universal readings. Others equally stoutly maintain that the universal reading is literally a misreading of a sloppy English sentence, that it is only the principle of charity which permits reading it as a universally quantified sentence. Such disputes about what something in a natural language 'really means' cannot easily be resolved. What is clear is that the principle of charity and a little common sense are always in order.

Notwithstanding the possibility of different readings of sentences in everyday English, the artificial examples found in the exercises of this book should always be treated as though the position of the quantifiers in English determines the meaning of the sentence. Exercises in textbooks generally do not provide a context which helps one to determine the intended meaning. Accordingly, any sentence which begins with an expression such as 'all' or 'no' should be translated into a universally quantified formula, while any sentence which begins with an expression such as 'there is', 'there are' or 'some' should be translated into an existentially quantified formula.

In many contexts, the differences between 'every', 'any' and 'all' are insignificant. For example, 'Every dog can be trained' is properly translated as '$(\forall x)(Dx \supset Tx)$', 'Any dog can be trained' is properly translated as '$(\forall x)(Dx \supset Tx)$' and 'All dogs can be trained' is properly translated as '$(\forall x)(Dx \supset Tx)$'. The differences between 'every', 'any' and 'all' become apparent in more complicated sentences. For instance, there is a world of difference between 'If you eat anything on the menu you will be sick' and 'If you eat everything on the menu you will be sick.' In translating such sentences, one must pay careful attention to the meaning and often use the principle of charity.

Although the universal quantifier is used to translate both 'every' and 'any' in the following two sentences, it is plain that 'Anything which is larger than everything is larger than itself' is true, whereas 'Anything which is larger than anything is larger than itself' is false. In learning how to translate such sentences, it is often helpful to think about what such sentences imply in particular cases.

'Anything which is larger than everything is larger than itself' makes a claim about everything. It asserts that if Spain is larger than everything then it is larger than itself, that if my car is larger than everything then it is larger than itself and so on. Using some obvious symbols, one can translate 'If Spain is larger than everything then it is larger than itself' as '$(\forall x)Lsx \supset Lss$'. The claim that anything which is larger than everything is larger than itself is not a claim just about Spain. Accordingly, one needs to add a universal quantifier. Before doing this, however, one needs to look carefully at the formula which is to be universally quantified. '$(\forall x)Lsx \supset Lss$' is not strictly speaking a WFF; before one can change the claim about Spain to a claim about everything, one needs to add brackets: '$((\forall x)Lsx \supset Lss)$'. Once this is done, the translation is straightforward; one simply prefaces the formula with a universal quantifier using a variable which does not already appear in '$((\forall x)Lsx \supset Lss)$'. A correct translation, therefore, of 'Anything which is larger than everything is larger than itself' is '$(\forall y)((\forall x)Lyx \supset Lyy)$'.

'Anything which is larger than anything is larger than itself' also makes a claim about everything. It asserts that if Spain is larger than Portugal then it is larger than itself, that if my car is larger than my briefcase then it is larger than itself and so on. One can translate 'If Spain is larger than Portugal then it is larger than itself' as '$Lsp \supset Lss$'. As the next step in translation, one can move to the claim that Spain is larger than itself if it is larger than anything, rather than just larger than Portugal. There are two ways in which this claim can be translated: '$(\forall x)(Lsx \supset Lss)$' or '$(\exists x)Lsx \supset Lss$'. It should be noted that the main operator of the former translation is a universal quantifier, while the main operator of the latter is a horseshoe. As with the translation in the previous paragraph, one needs to add a universal quantifier to make the translations reflect the fact that the claim makes an assertion about everything rather than just Spain. In addition, just as with the translation in the previous paragraph, one needs to be sure that there are no brackets missing. '$(\forall x)(Lsx \supset Lss)$' needs no attention, but brackets must be added to '$(\exists x)Lsx \supset Lss$' before the formula can be universally quantified. Accordingly, the sentence, 'Anything which is larger than anything is larger than itself' can be correctly translated as either '$(\forall y)(\forall x)(Lyx \supset Lyy)$' or '$(\forall y)((\exists x)Lyx \supset Lyy)$'.

The way in which brackets can alter meaning can be seen from consideration of the sentence 'If John becomes interested in anything, Mary will be happy.' One way to paraphrase this sentence is 'For anything one chooses, if John becomes interested in that thing, Mary will be happy.' Another way to paraphrase the sentence is 'If there is something in which John becomes interested, then Mary will be happy.' The first paraphrase is a universally quantified sentence, while the second is a conditional sentence. The sentence can be symbolized in either way, but the brackets must show whether the main operator is the existential quantifier or the horseshoe. The two translations of 'If John becomes interested in anything, Mary will be happy' follow:

Translation 1: $(\forall x)(Ijx \supset Hm)$

Translation 2: $(\exists x)Ijx \supset Hm$

To see the importance of bracketing, one can consider what would be asserted if one changed the brackets. Translation 1 would become:

Translation 1′: $(\forall x)Ijx \supset Hm$

Translation 1′ says that if John becomes interested in *everything*, then Mary will be happy, and this is not the meaning of the original sentence. Changing the brackets in Translation 2 also results in a radically changed meaning:

Translation 2′: (∃x)(Ijx ⊃ Hm)

Translation 2′ says that there is something such that, if John becomes interested in it, Mary will be happy. As long as there is something in the world in which John does not become interested, this claim will be trivially true. To see that this is so, suppose that John does not become interested in the history of shoelaces, which can be represented by the constant 's'. Then, since 'Ijs' is false, it follows from the definition of the horseshoe that 'Ijs ⊃ Hm' is true. Accordingly, if John does not become interested in the history of shoelaces, '(∃x)(Ijx ⊃ Hm)' will be trivially true.

§4.9: EXERCISES

Using the given notation, translate each of the following into symbols.

    e: the Empire State Building

    t: the Taj Mahal

    O __$_1$ __$_2$: __$_1$ is older than __$_2$

1 Something is older than something.

2 Everything is older than something.

3 Something is older than everything.

4 Nothing is older than everything.

5 Nothing is older than itself.

6 Nothing is older than the Taj Mahal.

7 Something is not older than itself.

8 Something is older than the Empire State Building.

9 Anything which is older than the Taj Mahal is older than something.

10 Something is older than the Empire State Building but not older than the Taj Mahal.

11 Everything which is older than the Taj Mahal is older than the Empire State Building.

12 Something is neither older than the Empire State Building nor older than the Taj Mahal.

13 Nothing which is not older than the Empire State Building is older than the Taj Mahal.

14 Anything which is older than everything is older than itself.

15 Anything which is older than itself is older than everything.

§4.10: PEOPLE AND THINGS

There is an additional point which requires care when one translates many English sentences. The English terms 'everybody' and 'somebody' are used to refer only to people, unlike 'everything' and 'something' which can refer to anything whatever. 'Everything' can be translated as '$(\forall x)$' and 'something' can be translated as '$(\exists x)$'.

'Everybody despises somebody' can be paraphrased as 'For any person one chooses, there is a person whom that person despises.' One can expand the paraphrase to 'For anything one chooses, if that thing is a person, there is a person whom that thing despises.' The paraphrase can be expanded yet again to 'For anything one chooses, if that thing is a person, there is something which is a person and which the first thing despises.' The final paraphrase, of course, is hardly an example of elegant English, but it does display the logic of the sentence in a way which suggests a proper translation.

'For anything one chooses, if that thing is a person, there is something which is a person and which the first thing despises' is a universally quantified sentence. It asserts that if Bill is a person, then there is something which is a person and which Bill despises and that if Nancy is a person, then there is something which is a person and which Nancy despises. Since Bill is a person, then according to this sentence there is a person whom Bill despises. However, the original sentence begins with 'For *anything* one chooses ...' Thus, it also makes the apparently bizarre assertion that if the Nile is a person, then there is something which is a person and which the Nile despises. Since the Nile is not a person, one is not forced to conclude that there is a person whom the Nile despises.

Using 'P __ ' for ' __ is a person' and 'D $_1$ __ $_2$' for ' __ $_1$ despises __ $_2$', one can begin the translation. It should be noted that this beginning is neither English nor the symbolic language; it is a concoction created purely for illustrative purposes.

$(\forall x)(Px \supset$ (there is something which is a person
        and which x despises))

'There is something which is a person and which Bill despises' can be translated as '$(\exists y)(Py \wedge Dby)$'. This formula would be true if Bill despises himself or if Bill despises someone else. Substituting 'x' for 'b', one can complete the translation:

$(\forall x)(Px \supset (\exists y)(Py \wedge Dxy))$

It should be noted that a variable other than 'x' was used with the existential quantifier. The use of different variables does not preclude the possibility that the person despising is the same person who is despised. If different variables had not been used, the result would not have been a WFF.

The following formula is not a WFF because there is no way of telling which variable is linked to which quantifier.

(∀x)(Px ⊃ (∃x)(Px ∧ Dxx)) †††

'Somebody despises everybody' is an existentially quantified sentence. It asserts that there is something which is a person and which despises everything which is a person. Expanding the paraphrase, the sentence asserts that there is something which is a person and, for anything one chooses, if that thing is a person, the first thing despises the second. Using the same symbols as before, one can begin the translation. Again it should be noted that this beginning is neither English nor the symbolic language.

(∃x)(Px ∧ (for anything one chooses, if that thing is a person
        then x despises that thing))

As before, one must use a different variable with the next quantifier. The person who despises everybody is, of course, bound to despise himself. However, if the world contains more than one person, there are other people whom he despises. 'Bill despises everybody' can be translated as '(∀y)(Py ⊃ Dby)'. Again substituting 'x' for 'b', one can complete the translation:

(∃x)(Px ∧ (∀y)(Py ⊃ Dxy))

It should be noted that brackets were added in the new formula, since '(∃x)Px ∧ (∀y)(Py ⊃ Dxy)' ††† is not a WFF because the 'x' in 'Dxy' is not within the scope of a quantifier.

§4.11: EXERCISES

Using the given notation, translate each of the following into symbols.

    c: the clock
    b: the book
    j: Jim
    k: Kate
    P __ : __ is a person
    S __₁ __₂ __₃: __₁ stole __₂ from __₃

1 Jim stole the book from Kate.

2 Kate stole the clock from Jim.

3 If Jim stole the clock from Kate, she stole the book from him.

4 Jim stole something from Kate.

5 Jim stole something from someone.

6 Someone stole something from Jim.

7 Everyone stole something from Jim.

8 Jim did not steal anything from Kate.

9 Jim did not steal anything from anyone.

10 Anyone who stole the clock from Jim stole the clock from someone.

§4.12: IDENTITY

Identity is a relation which can be expressed by a two-place predicate. English expressions such as 'is identical to', 'is the very same thing as' and often simply 'is' are used in doing such things as stating that the criminal who robbed a bank on Thursday is the same criminal who robbed a bank on Monday. It is useful to be able to translate such sentences. In addition, reference to identity is necessary in order to translate such phrases as 'only John', 'no one but John', 'only one' and 'at least two'.

Expressions of identity in the symbolic language have a unique notation. Instead of writing 'I$_{\_1\_2}$' for '$\_1$ is identical to $\_2$', the usual notation uses the familiar '=' sign. Thus, 'a is identical to b' is expressed as 'a = b'. Nevertheless, identity formulas are negated in just the same way as other formulas; the '≠' symbol is not used. Thus, 'a is not identical to b' is expressed as '~ a = b'.

A clarification of the use of constants can now be made. At the beginning of this chapter, constants were introduced as standing for individuals. Just as a single individual can have two names – 'Istanbul' and 'Constantinople', for example, refer to the same place – so different constants can represent the same individual. When one comes across two or more distinct constants, one should not assume that they refer to different individuals; the fact that more than one constant is used says nothing about whether or not the discussion involves one or more than one individual. To address that question, one needs to make an identity claim.

The simplest use of the identity predicate is in translating sentences which assert that two names refer to the same individual. Thus, using 'm' for 'Mark Twain' and 's' for 'Samuel Clemens', one can express the fact that these two names refer to the same person by the simple formula 'm = s'.

Expressions of identity are commonly used in translating sentences which claim that only one thing has some property. For example, to say that only Karen knows the solution is equivalent to saying that Karen knows the solution and no one but Karen knows the solution. Using 'k' for 'Karen' and 'S __' for '__ knows the solution', all three of the following formulas are correct translations of the sentence:

1 Sk ∧ (∀x)(Sx ⊃ x = k)

This formula says that Karen knows the solution and that anything which knows the solution is identical to Karen.

2 Sk ∧ ~ (∃x)(Sx ∧ ~ x = k)

This formula says that Karen knows the solution and that there is nothing which knows the solution which is not identical to Karen.

3 (∀x)(Sx ≡ x = k)

This formula says that, for anything one picks, that thing knows the solution if and only if that thing is identical to Karen.

As mentioned, identity expressions make possible the translation of such phrases as 'only one' and 'at least two'. An example is the statement that there is only one pope. Using 'P __ ' as '__ is a pope', the statement that there is a pope can be translated as:

(∃x)Px

However, this says that there is at least one pope; it leaves open the possibility that there is more than one pope. What is needed is the additional statement that there is at most one pope. Saying this amounts to saying that, for any x and any y, if x is a pope and y is a pope, then x and y are identical. This can be expressed as:

(∀x)(∀y)((Px ∧ Py) ⊃ x = y)

The statement that there is only one pope can be expressed by simply conjoining the two formulas:

(∃x)Px ∧ (∀x)(∀y)((Px ∧ Py) ⊃ x = y)

Another way of stating that there is only one pope is the following:

(∃x)(Px ∧ (∀y)(Py ⊃ x = y))

This formula says that there is something which is a pope and that anything which is a pope is identical to that something. This reading may be easier to follow if one replaces 'x = y' by 'y = x' and rewrites the formula as:

(∃x)(Px ∧ (∀y)(Py ⊃ y = x))

An even shorter way of making the same claim is:

(∃x)(∀y)(Py ≡ y = x)

This formula says that there is something such that for anything one chooses, the thing that one chooses is a pope if and only if it is identical to that something.

Some of these translations are far from intuitively obvious. Whether formulas are quantificationally equivalent or not quantificationally equivalent will become clearer after dealing with 'interpretations' at the end of this chapter and derivations in Chapter 5. This will make the translations seem less confusing. It will remain true, however, that predicate logic simply is more difficult than sentence logic; there frequently is no way to paraphrase an ordinary English sentence into unstilted English which mirrors the logical structure of a formula in predicate logic.

A statement of non-identity is used in translating 'James owns more than one piano.' Using 'j' for 'James', 'P __ ' for ' __ is a piano' and 'O __ ₁ __ ₂' for ' __ ₁ owns __ ₂', one can write:

$$(\exists x)(\exists y)(\sim x = y \land ((Px \land Py) \land (Ojx \land Ojy)))$$

This formula tells one that x and y are distinct, that they are pianos and that James owns both x and y.

It can be seen that the symbolic representation of some ordinary English sentences can become quite long and rather confusing, particularly when a specific number of things are involved. The claim that at least one thing has the property F is simply the claim that something is F, '$(\exists x)Fx$'. To say that at least two things have the property F, one can write:

$$(\exists x)(\exists y)(\sim x = y \land (Fx \land Fy))$$

This formula tells one that there are two distinct things and that each of them is F. It neither asserts nor denies that there are more than two such things.

The way to state that exactly one thing has a certain property has already been covered in the discussion of the statement that there is only one pope. To say that exactly two things have the property F, one can write:

$$(\exists x)(\exists y)((\sim x = y \land (Fx \land Fy)) \land (\forall z)(Fz \supset (z = x \lor z = y)))$$

This formula says that there are two distinct things having the property F and that anything which is F is identical to one or other of them.

As with the claim that there is exactly one pope, a shorter translation using the triplebar is possible:

$$(\exists x)(\exists y)(\sim x = y \land (\forall z)(Fz \equiv (z = x \lor z = y)))$$

This formula says that there are two distinct things and that anything one picks is F if and only if it is identical to one or other of them.

To say that at most two things have the property F is not to commit oneself to saying that anything is F; it is to say that there are not three distinct things which are F. One way to say this is to write:

$$\sim (\exists x)(\exists y)(\exists z)(((\sim x = y \land \sim x = z) \land \sim y = z) \land ((Fx \land Fy) \land Fz))$$

Another way to say that at most two things have the property F is to write:

$$(\forall x)(\forall y)(\forall z)(((Fx \land Fy) \land Fz) \supset ((z = x \lor z = y) \lor x = y))$$

This formula says that, for any x, y or z, if x is F and y is F and z is F, then x, y and z are not three distinct things.

When one needs to translate a sentence that specifically excludes some individual, one can do so by using the tilde and the '=' symbol. 'Every member of the club except Peter has a car' is such a sentence. Using 'p' for

'Peter', 'M __' as '__ is a member of the club' and 'C __' as '__ has a car', one can translate this sentence as:

$$(\forall x)((Mx \land \sim x = p) \supset Cx)$$

It would be odd to say 'Every member of the club except Peter has a car' when one knows that Peter has a car; one would simply say that every member of the club has a car. In an ordinary context, 'Every member of the club except Peter has a car' strongly suggests that Peter does not have a car. This can, of course, be added to the translation:

$$(\forall x)((Mx \land \sim x = p) \supset Cx) \land \sim Cp$$

Using the same symbols, 'Some member of the club other than Peter has a car' can be translated as:

$$(\exists x)((Mx \land \sim x = p) \land Cx)$$

Using the same symbols with the addition of 'f' to represent 'Frank', 'Some member of the club other than Peter and Frank has a car' can be translated as:

$$(\exists x)((Mx \land \sim (x = p \lor x = f)) \land Cx)$$

Much as the sentence 'Every member of the club except Peter has a car' suggests but does not assert that Peter does not have a car, sentences involving superlatives can sometimes be misleading. One can use the '=' symbol in translating superlative phrases such as 'the tallest', 'the poorest' and 'the slowest', but one must be careful to say neither more nor less than is required. The claim that Joseph is the tallest member of the family may suggest that Joseph is tall, but the family may consist entirely of short people. In the same way, the poorest person in an expensive restaurant may well be prosperous.

If the sentence 'Kate is the slowest runner on the team' is not taken to include the claim that Kate is a slow runner, it can be translated using 'k' for 'Kate', 'T __' for '__ is a runner on the team' and 'S $_1$ __$_2$' for '__$_1$ is slower than __$_2$':

$$(\forall x)((Tx \land \sim x = k) \supset Skx)$$

If the sentence is taken to include the claim that Kate is a slow runner, this claim can be added using 'R __' for '__ is slow':

$$Rk \land (\forall x)((Tx \land \sim x = k) \supset Skx)$$

In both of these translations the '$\sim x = k$' is necessary to avoid asserting that Kate is slower than herself.

If Kate is the slowest runner on the team, anything which is true of Kate is true of the slowest runner on the team. One can refer to Kate by a **definite description**. Another way of saying 'Kate has a brother' is to say 'The slowest runner of the team has a brother.' Some other examples of definite descriptions are: 'the oldest man in our town', 'the first person to swim the English Channel', 'the last house on this street' and 'the highest mountain in Canada'. Such phrases typically assert the existence of a unique individual with some property, and should be translated accordingly. For example, 'The man who just entered the room is a criminal' states that there is exactly one man who just entered the room and that he is a criminal. It can be translated using 'M __' as ' __ is a man', 'R __' as ' __ just entered the room' and 'C __' as ' __ is a criminal':

$$(\exists x)(((Mx \wedge Rx) \wedge (\forall y)((My \wedge Ry) \supset x = y)) \wedge Cx)$$

This formula says that there is exactly one man who just entered the room and that man is a criminal. An equivalent translation is:

$$(\exists x)(((Mx \wedge Rx) \wedge Cx) \wedge (\forall y)(((My \wedge Ry) \wedge Cy) \supset x = y))$$

This formula says that there is a man who just entered the room, that he is a criminal, and that any man who just entered the room and is a criminal is identical to that man.

As with the claim that there is only one Pope, a translation using the triplebar is also possible:

$$(\exists x)(\forall y)(((My \wedge Ry) \wedge Cy) \equiv x = y)$$

This formula says that there is something such that for anything one chooses, the thing that one chooses is a man who just entered the room and is a criminal if and only if it is identical to that something.

Sometimes a sentence which contains a phrase which looks like a definite description should be understood as a universally quantified sentence. For example, 'The next employee who smokes in the warehouse will be fired' contains the phrase 'the next employee who smokes in the warehouse'. This sentence does not assert the existence of anyone – indeed, its purpose is to prevent there being an employee who smokes in the warehouse. It should be translated as '$(\forall x)(Sx \supset Fx)$.

§4.13: TRANSLATION PROBLEMS AND DOMAINS

One problem which arises in translation is that sometimes use of either the universal or existential quantifier completely distorts the meaning of an English sentence. An example is 'John is searching for a way to cheat on his taxes without taking any risks.' Since there is no way in which John can cheat on his taxes without taking any risks, there is a problem about translating the sentence. Using 'j' for 'John', 'C __' for ' __ is a way in which John can cheat on his taxes without taking any risks' and '$S_{\_1 \_2}$' for ' $\_1$ is searching for $\_2$', one could try '$(\exists x)(Cx \wedge Sjx)$'. However, this commits one to the truth of '$(\exists x)Cx$', which is false although the original sentence about John may well be true. If one tried to use the universal quantifier, one would have '$(\forall x)(Cx \supset Sjx)$'. Given that nothing has the property C, '$(\forall x)(Cx \supset Sjx)$' is trivially true, no matter whether the sentence about John is true or not.

A similar problem arises with 'Mary is in terror of werewolves.' Using 'm' for 'Mary', 'T$\_\__1\_\__2$' for '$\_\__1$ is in terror of $\_\__2$' and 'W$\_\_$' for '$\_\_$ is a werewolf', one could try '$(\exists x)(Wx \wedge Tmx)$'. As in the example just discussed, using the existential quantifier commits one to an existence claim which is false, '$(\exists x)Wx$'. Use of the universal quantifier fails for the same reason as before; given that there are no werewolves, '$(\forall x)(Wx \supset Tmx)$' is trivially true.

The difficulty with examples like these is that they are sentences in which one talks about such things as the objects of people's hopes, fears and desires. Plainly, it is possible to fear, hope for, desire, search for or believe in things which do not exist. In cases in which the universal quantifier expresses a trivial truth and the existential quantifier makes an existence claim which is not made in the original sentence, the normal translation procedures of predicate logic will be inadequate. The best one can do in such circumstances is to use single-place predicates such 'C$\_\_$' to represent '$\_\_$ is searching for a way to cheat on his taxes without taking any risks' or 'T$\_\_$' to represent '$\_\_$ is in terror of werewolves'.

Another problem in translation is that the symbolic representation of an English sentence often requires more predicates than seem to be in the original. In real life, when people use words such as 'something' and 'everything', the context usually places a restriction on how their utterances are to be taken. For example, 'Everything has been checked' is not usually taken or meant to be taken as claiming that each thing in the universe has been checked. It is more naturally taken to mean that every important thing connected with the topic of conversation has been checked in the recent past. Similarly, 'Something is wrong with Sam's car' is naturally taken to mean that something in Sam's car which might be expected to work properly is no longer working properly. Of course, something is wrong with every car including Sam's, since no car is perfect, but this is not the sort of thing that is claimed when someone says 'Something is wrong with Sam's car.' In translating English into the symbolic language, one must often take account of such contextual considerations, and the final translation must state exactly what is necessary without relying on context.

This point was exemplified in some of the translations in previous sections of this chapter. These were complicated by the addition of the predicate 'is a person', which was added because the context or the use of words such as 'someone' rather than 'something' showed that it was necessary. Such complications can sometimes be avoided by specifying a **domain**, sometimes called a 'universe of discourse'. To specify a domain is to restrict the discussion by limiting it to include only certain things. One can specify a domain to include only people, left-handed people, dogs, anything which is either a person or a dog – whatever one wants.

Domains are **sets**. The words 'class' and 'collection' are often used to refer to sets. The standard notation in discussions of sets employs braces – the curly brackets: '{' and '}'. A particular set can be specified in two ways. First, one can list the members or **elements** of the set, as in '{a, b, c}', which can be read as 'the set consisting of a, b and c'. This is **list notation**. Depending on the context, the letters which are listed may either stand for letters or, as constants usually do, stand for individuals other than letters. Second, one can specify some property of the elements, as in '{X|X is green or X is blue}', which can be read as 'the set of all Xs which are green or blue'. This is **property notation**. It should be noted that the upper-case 'X' used in this notation has no connection at all with the lower-case 'x' used as a variable. Both types of notation are used in this book.

A domain can be used to simplify the translation of John's utterance, 'Everything is closed', when John and Jim are looking for an open restaurant at three in the morning. Plainly, John means that all the restaurants in the vicinity are closed. Using 'R __ ' to represent ' __ is a restaurant in the vicinity' and 'C __ ' to represent ' __ is closed', one can translate John's statement as:

$(\forall x)(Rx \supset Cx)$

Using the set of restaurants in the vicinity as a domain, John's statement can simply be translated as:

Domain: {X|X is a restaurant in the vicinity}
$(\forall x)Cx$

The saving here is hardly worth the trouble of specifying a domain, but in some cases translations are considerably shortened. An example is 'If everyone whom Mary loves loves Mary, and Mary loves John, then someone loves Mary.' Using some obvious symbols, one can translate the sentence as:

$((\forall x)((Px \wedge Lmx) \supset Lxm) \wedge Lmj) \supset (\exists x)(Px \wedge Lxm)$

A translation which is quantificationally equivalent is:

$((\forall x)(Px \supset (Lmx \supset Lxm)) \wedge Lmj) \supset (\exists x)(Px \wedge Lxm)$

The use of 'everyone', 'someone' and names which are normally used only for people shows that the domain is simply the set of people. Accordingly, a far simpler translation is possible:

Domain: {X|X is a person}
$((\forall x)(Lmx \supset Lxm) \wedge Lmj) \supset (\exists x)Lxm$

Whenever one can restrict the domain to one sort of entity, there is the possibility that translation can be simplified. It should be noted, however, that specifying a domain does not always eliminate the need to specify the kind of thing being discussed. 'Some French wines are appalling and no Frenchman drinks them' is a case in point. Without specifying a domain and using some obvious symbols, this can be translated as:

$(\exists x)(((Wx \wedge Fx) \wedge Ax) \wedge (\forall y)((My \wedge Fy) \supset \sim Dyx))$

Since everything under discussion is French, it is possible to specify a domain and dispense with the predicate 'is French':

Domain: {X|X is French}
$(\exists x)((Wx \wedge Ax) \wedge (\forall y)(My \supset \sim Dyx))$

Although this translation is simpler than the previous one, it is still necessary to distinguish between men and wines.

Restricting a domain restricts the predicates which can be used in the translation. 'Every Englishman loves all dogs' can be translated using 'E __ ' to represent 'is English' and 'L __ ' to represent 'loves all dogs':

Domain: {X|X is a man}
$(\forall x)(Ex \supset Lx)$

This sentence can also be translated without restricting the domain. Using 'E __ ' to represent 'is an Englishman', 'D __ ' to represent 'is a dog' and 'L __$_1$ __$_2$' to represent ' __$_1$ loves $_2$', the sentence can be translated as:

$(\forall x)(Ex \supset (\forall y)(Dy \supset Lxy))$

It would be a mistake, however, to use '$(\forall x)(Ex \supset (\forall y)(Dy \supset Lxy))$' while restricting the domain to men for the simple reason that dogs are not elements of the set of men. It would also be a mistake to restrict the domain to English things, because the claim that every Englishman loves all dogs is different from the claim that every Englishman loves all English dogs.

Many beginners, when faced with a translation problem, seem to decide first what quantifiers are needed and then go on to fill in the predicates. Thus, one sees a sentence such as 'Some French wines are appalling and no Frenchman drinks them' translated as:

Domain: {X|X is French}
$(\exists x)(\forall y)((Wx \wedge Ax) \wedge (My \supset \sim Dyx))$

In fact, this translation is quantificationally equivalent to the translation which was given earlier in this section. However, the beginner would do well to introduce the quantifiers as they are introduced in the English. Nothing is gained by forcing the quantifiers to the front of the formula, and it is very easy to make mistakes in doing this.

This point is shown even more clearly in the translation of 'Someone loves Carl and someone loves Jane, but no one loves them both.' This is simply a conjunction of three claims. Using the set of people as the domain and some obvious symbols, the sentence can be translated without any difficulty at all as:

Domain: {X|X is a person}
$((\exists x)Lxc \wedge (\exists x)Lxj) \wedge (\forall x)\sim (Lxc \wedge Lxj)$

The following translation is quantificationally equivalent to the previous one, but it has little to recommend it:

Domain: {X|X is a person}
$(\exists x)(\exists y)(\forall z)((Lxc \wedge Lyj) \wedge \sim (Lzc \wedge Lzj))$

In order to have all the quantifiers at the beginning of the formula, it is necessary to use different variables. The result is something far less clear than the first translation.

There are no mechanical procedures to follow in translation. For example, 'something' cannot always be treated as an existential quantifier. 'Something made of copper conducts electricity' must be read as a universally quantified sentence. Similarly, 'There is a serial number for every car which leaves the factory' should be read as a universally quantified sentence; it asserts that, for every car which leaves the factory, there is a serial number. Sometimes an English sentence contains no quantifier at all, as in 'He jests at scars, that never felt a wound.' Plainly, this is to be understood as 'Whoever jests at scars has never felt a wound.' In some cases, what is said in the English sentence cannot be taken at face value. A literal reading of 'All the monkeys aren't in the zoo' is that every monkey is out of the zoo, when plainly what is meant is that some monkeys are out of the zoo. The fact that people almost invariably expect what they hear and read to make something like good sense leads them to reinterpret the most bizarre sentences. A nice example is 'No head wound is too small to ignore.' People reading this sentence usually use the principle of charity without recognizing that they are doing so. The sentence is usually taken as a piece of sensible medical advice, when in fact it is no such thing. Any rational person using this sentence must mean something like 'No head wound is too small to treat' or 'No head wound is small enough to ignore.' Examples such as this show that there are cases in which one must do more than make a literal translation. However, caution is always in order; one should not assume that people never say things which are nonsensical or manifestly false.

§4.14: EXERCISES

§4.14 Part 1

Using the given notation, translate each of the following into symbols. For each example, use the set of people as the domain.

  f: Frank
  g: Gerald
  R __$_1$ __$_2$: __$_1$ recognized __$_2$

1 Someone recognized Frank but did not recognize Gerald.

2 Gerald recognized Frank but did not recognize anyone else.

3 No one recognized both Frank and Gerald.

4 Everyone recognized someone.

5 Gerald recognized Frank and at least one other person.

6 Gerald recognized Frank and exactly one other person.

7 Someone recognized himself, but no one recognized everybody.

8 At least two people recognized Frank.

9 At most two people recognized Gerald.

10 Only two people recognized Gerald.

11 Anyone who recognized Gerald recognized Frank.

12 Someone recognized someone other than himself, but recognized neither Frank nor Gerald.

§4.14 Part 2

Translate each of the following into symbols. Explain the meaning of each symbol. For each example, use the set of people as the domain.

1 No one who praises everyone is honest.

2 Francis Bacon is not the same person as Roger Bacon.

3 More than one person has walked on the moon.

4 Only one person has walked on the moon.

5 If Mad Max has blue eyes and Billy the Kid does not have blue eyes, then Mad Max is not the same person as Billy the Kid.

6 Sandra is intelligent; in fact, she is the most intelligent person in the class.

7 Some retired soldiers are richer than some soldiers who have not retired.

8 Jill has only two good friends.

9 Only the good die young.

10 Jane does not love Harry, but all the other girls do.

§4.15: ARGUMENTS IN PREDICATE LOGIC

Translating arguments in predicate logic is easy once one knows how to translate the sentences which make up the arguments. The same general points about separating premisses and conclusions apply to arguments in predicate logic as they do to arguments in sentence logic. The argument at the very beginning of this chapter is a case in point:

> Since all Frenchmen are Europeans and Pierre is a Frenchman, Pierre is a European.

p: Pierre
F __ : __ is a Frenchman
E __ : __ is a Europeans

$(\forall x)(Fx \supset Ex)$

$\underline{Fp}$

Ep

Sometimes arguments in predicate logic can be correctly translated using only formulas of sentence logic. An example follows:

> If Sally despises everybody, then someone despises Sally. If someone despises Sally, Peter does. Thus, if it is false that Peter despises Sally, it is false that Sally despises everybody.

Using 'D $\_{1}\_{2}$' to stand for '$\_{1}$ despises $\_{2}$', 'p' to stand for 'Peter', 's' to stand for 'Sally', and restricting the domain to the set of people, one can represent the argument as:

$(\forall x)Dsx \supset (\exists x)Dxs$

$\underline{(\exists x)Dxs \supset Dps}$

$\sim Dps \supset \sim (\forall x)Dsx$

It can be seen that the main operator of each premiss is the horseshoe and that the sense of the argument is preserved when it is expressed in terms of sentence logic:

D: Sally despises everybody.
S: Someone despises Sally.
P: Peter despises Sally.

$D \supset S$

$\underline{S \supset P}$

$\sim P \supset \sim D$

This argument is truth-functionally valid, as can be shown on a truth table. If an argument is truth-functionally valid, there is no need to complicate the translation. However, examples such as this one are relatively rare. If an argument is not truth-functionally valid, it may be **quantificationally valid,** and a translation which uses the necessary domain, constants, predicates and quantifiers will be required.

A sample translation of an argument follows:

> Since all Siamese cats are domestic animals, anyone who owns a Siamese cat owns a domestic animal.

There is no way in which the argument can be simplified by specifying a domain.

S __ : __ is a Siamese cat
D __ : __ is a domestic animal
P __ : __ is a person
O __$_1$ __$_2$: __$_1$ owns __$_2$

$$(\forall x)(Sx \supset Dx)$$
$$\overline{(\forall x)((Px \wedge (\exists y)(Sy \wedge Oxy)) \supset (\exists y)(Dy \wedge Oxy))}$$

The following argument can be translated using the same predicates:

> All Siamese cats are domestic animals. Therefore, if someone owns a Siamese cat someone owns a domestic animal.

$$(\forall x)(Sx \supset Dx)$$
$$\overline{(\exists x)(Px \wedge (\exists y)(Sy \wedge Oxy)) \supset (\exists x)(Px \wedge (\exists y)(Dy \wedge Oxy))}$$

The next argument is a little more complex.

> All classic cars are both prized and old. Classic cars in fine condition are rare. Nothing which is prized is a bargain and anything rare is hard to find. It follows that any classic car, if it is in fine condition, is no bargain and hard to find.

Several predicates are involved in this argument. Since things other than classic cars are discussed, there is no way in which restricting the domain can simplify matters without changing the sense of the passage. Accordingly, one must use all the predicates:

C __ : __ is a classic car
P __ : __ is prized
O __ : __ is old
F __ : __ is in fine condition
R __ : __ is rare
B __ : __ is a bargain
H __ : __ is hard to find

$(\forall x)(Cx \supset (Px \wedge Ox))$
$(\forall x)((Cx \wedge Fx) \supset Rx)$
$(\forall x)(Px \supset \sim Bx) \wedge (\forall x)(Rx \supset Hx)$
_____
$(\forall x)(Cx \supset (Fx \supset (\sim Bx \wedge Hx)))$

In the following argument, it is possible to make the translation simpler by restricting the domain to the set of people:

> Since Paul's father has the combination, he must be the bank manager. We know this because only one person has the combination.

Domain: {X|X is a person}
b: the bank manager
f: Paul's father
C __ : __ has the combination

Cf
$(\exists x)(\forall y)(Cy \equiv x = y)$
_____
f = b

Translation of the next argument can also be simplified by restricting the domain to the set of people:

> Every golfer is sillier than someone, but no golfer is sillier than everyone. Bob and Mike are golfers. Mike is not sillier than Bob. Therefore, Mike is sillier than someone other than Bob.

Domain: {X|X is a person}
b: Bob
m: Mike
G __ : __ is a golfer
S __₁__₂: __₁ is sillier than __₂

$(\forall x)(Gx \supset (\exists y)Sxy) \wedge \sim (\exists x)(Gx \wedge (\forall y)Sxy)$
$Gb \wedge Gm$
$\sim Smb$
_____
$(\exists x)(\sim x = b \wedge Smx)$

§4.16: EXERCISES

1   Translate the following argument into symbols. Use the given domain and notation.

Domain: {X|X is a person}
B __ : __ begs in the street
P __ : __ is a pensioner
R __ : __ is rich

Some pensioners are rich. Rich people do not beg in the street. It follows that some pensioners do not beg in the street.

2   Translate the following argument into symbols. Use the given notation. Use a completely unrestricted domain. Explain the meaning of any additional symbols which are needed.

S __ : __ is selfless
T __ : __ can be explained by economic theory

Some human actions are selfless. Selfless actions cannot be explained by economic theory. Consequently, some human actions cannot be explained by economic theory.

3   Translate the following argument into symbols. Use the given domain and notation. Explain the meaning of any additional symbols which are needed.

Domain: {X|X is an action}
S __ : __ is selfless
T __ : __ can be explained by economic theory

Some human actions are selfless. Selfless actions cannot be explained by economic theory. Consequently, some human actions cannot be explained by economic theory.

4   Translate the following argument into symbols. Use the given domain and notation.

Domain: {X|X is a human action}
S __ : __ is selfless
T __ : __ can be explained by economic theory

Some human actions are selfless. Selfless actions cannot be explained by economic theory. Consequently, some human actions cannot be explained by economic theory.

5   Translate the following argument into symbols. Use a completely unrestricted domain and explain the meaning of each symbol.

Someone stole the book and anyone who stole the book has a key to the library. Since anyone who stole anything is a thief, there is at least one thief with a key to the library.

6 Translate the following argument into symbols. Use the given notation. Use a completely unrestricted domain.

h: the book in my hand
s: the book on the shelf
N __ : __ is a novel
T __ : __ is a text
M __ ₁ __ ₂: __ ₁ is more interesting than __ ₂

The book on the shelf is a text and the book in my hand is a novel. The book in my hand is more interesting than the book on the shelf, since any novel is more interesting than any text.

7 Translate the following argument into symbols. Use the given domain and notation.

Domain: {X|X is a person}
p: Peter
H __ ₁ __ ₂: __ ₁ hates __ ₂

Peter hates no one but someone hates Peter. It follows that there is someone who is hated but hates no one.

8 Translate the following argument into symbols. Provide a suitable domain if that is helpful and explain the meaning of each symbol.

Frank laughs at all people in trouble and no one but people in trouble. When anyone laughs at anyone, the person being laughed at is annoyed with the person laughing. Paul is in trouble only if Mary is. Thus, Mary is annoyed with Frank if he laughs at Paul.

9 Translate the following argument into symbols. Use a completely unrestricted domain and explain the meaning of each symbol.

Everything is like itself. Something is not like anything else. Thus, it is false that a thing is like itself if and only if it is like something else.

10 Translate the following argument into symbols. Provide a suitable domain if that is helpful and explain the meaning of each symbol.

All of Anne's classmates are in physics or biology. Jane dislikes physics students and has contempt for biology students. Since neither Anne nor Jane dislikes or has contempt for any of her own classmates, Anne and Jane do not have a single classmate in common.

§4.17: SIMPLE INTERPRETATIONS

In the discussion of truth tables in Chapter 2, it was pointed out that a complete truth table covers all the possibilities of truth and falsehood. A formula such as 'P ⊃ (P ∨ Q)' is obviously truth-functionally true. In the unlikely event that one were in any doubt about this, it would be possible to check the formula on a truth table. It would turn out to be true on every row of the truth table. '(∀x)(Px ⊃ (Px ∨ Qx))' is a formula of predicate logic which says that anything whatever, if it is P, is also either P or Q. It is intuitively obvious that '(∀x)(Px ⊃ (Px ∨ Qx))' is **quantificationally true**. However, since one cannot inspect every item in the universe which is P to check whether it is also either P or Q, there is no way in which the quantificational truth of '(∀x)(Px ⊃ (Px ∨ Qx))' can be established by inspecting all the possibilities in the way that the truth-functional truth of 'P ⊃ (P ∨ Q)' can be established. Similarly, it is intuitively clear that the formula '(∃x)(Fx ∧ ~ Fx)' is **quantificationally false**, but it is impossible to check every item in the universe in order to see that it does not have the property of being both F and not F.

In sentence logic, the truth-functional equivalence of different formulas can be checked by examining all the possibilities on a truth table. Predicate logic differs from sentence logic in that all the possibilities cannot be arranged as they are on a truth table. A consequence of this is that one cannot check equivalence in predicate logic – quantificational equivalence – in anything like the way in which equivalence is checked in sentence logic.

The same sort of problem arises with validity. A truth-functionally valid argument is one in which there is no row of a truth table on which all the premisses are true and the conclusion is false. In predicate logic, since one cannot examine all the possibilities on a truth table, it follows that one cannot determine validity in predicate logic – quantificational validity – as one does in sentence logic.

In sentence logic, to show that a formula is truth-functionally indeterminate, it is sufficient to show a row of a truth table on which the formula is true and a row on which the formula is false. Something of the same sort can be done in predicate logic. To show that a formula is **quantificationally indeterminate**, it is sufficient to describe circumstances in which it is true and circumstances in which it is false.

In sentence logic, to show that two formulas are truth-functionally equivalent, it is enough to show on a truth table that the formulas have the same final columns. This cannot be done in predicate logic. However, one can show that two formulas are not quantificationally equivalent by describing circumstances in which one is true and the other is false.

Turning to validity, although the quantificational validity of an argument cannot be established in the way that truth-functional validity can be established, the **quantificational invalidity** of an argument in predicate logic can be demonstrated. To show that an argument in sentence logic is truth-functionally invalid, it is sufficient to show a row of a truth table on which all the premises are true and the conclusion is false. In predicate logic, to show that an argument is quantificationally invalid, it is sufficient to describe circumstances in which all the premises are true and the conclusion is false.

A simple way to specify a set of circumstances which is developed to show quantificational indeterminacy, quantificational non-equivalence or quantificational invalidity is to describe a world with the requisite features. Such a description is an **interpretation**. To deal with interpretations, one must understand that sets need not have elements. The set of unicorns is empty, as is the set of intelligent idiots. The symbol 'Ø' is often used to denote the **empty set**, but in this book two set brackets with nothing between them, '{   }', are used to represent the empty set.

The very simplest sort of interpretation requires two things:

1 A non-empty set of objects which is adequate for the purposes of the interpretation. This is the **domain of the interpretation**.

2 Lists of objects in the domain of which predicates are true. These are the **extensions of the predicates**.

What these requirements involve will become clearer as some interpretations are developed in what follows. A clarification must be made, however, before one can turn to the development of interpretations.

To keep things as simple as possible, the domains and the extensions of the predicates are specified by letters enclosed within set brackets, as follows:

Domain: {a, b, c}
Extension of G: {a}

It does not matter for some purposes what objects are in the sets, and in such cases the sets can be taken to consist of letters. However, in dealing with formulas which contain a constant, the constant which appears within the set brackets is to be taken as designating whatever the constant designates in the formula. Thus, if the formula 'Ga' is being considered and 'Ga' represents 'Albert is greedy', the 'a' in the domain is to be taken as designating the person rather than the first letter of the alphabet. Similarly, the extension of 'G' is to be taken as saying that Albert is an element of the set of greedy things, and not that the first letter of the alphabet is an element of that set.

When quantifiers were first discussed in §4.5, it was pointed out that in principle a conjunction could be used instead of a universally quantified formula and a disjunction could be used instead of an existentially quantified formula. The practical problems of dealing with a large or infinite number of items were noted. When using interpretations, these problems are avoided, since the domains are developed with a small number of elements to ensure that one can express quantified formulas as conjunctions or disjunctions. In dealing with interpretations, one should bear in mind that a universally quantified formula says something about every item in the domain, while an existentially quantified formula says something about some item or other in the domain.

The simple formula '$(\forall x)Fx$' will be considered first to show how an interpretation can be used. To show that this formula is quantificationally indeterminate, one needs to provide an interpretation on which it is true and provide an interpretation on which it is false. This is easily done:

Domain: {a}
Extension of F: {a}

'$(\forall x)Fx$' is true on this interpretation, since everything in the domain is F. One can now develop an interpretation on which '$(\forall x)Fx$' is false:

Domain: {a, b, c}
Extension of F: {a, c}

'$(\forall x)Fx$' is false on this interpretation, since there is something in the domain which is not F.

'$(\forall x)Fx$' would, of course, also be false if nothing were F. In the following interpretation the extension of 'F' is empty. On this interpretation '$(\forall x)Fx$' is false – as, incidentally, is '$(\exists x)Fx$':

Domain: {a}
Extension of F: {   }

In dealing with multi-place predicates, it is necessary to specify the order of the constants. For example, if Jack loves Sally but Sally does not love Jack, this must be shown in the extension of 'loves'. Order can be shown by use of the pointed brackets: '⟨' and '⟩'. Thus, if Jack loves Sally and Sally does not love Jack, the extension of 'loves' will be '{⟨j, s⟩}'. If, however, Jack's love is requited, the extension will be '{⟨j, s⟩, ⟨s, j⟩}'. The items between the pointed brackets are **ordered pairs**. It is possible to use the same pointed brackets to specify **ordered triples** and so on.

One further point about extensions needs explanation. In general, the extensions of the predicates must be complete but there is no need to make them redundant. It may sometimes happen that something falls within the extension of a predicate even though not all of its names are written out as being within the extension of that predicate. How this can come about can be seen from consideration of the following interpretation:

Domain: {a, b, c, d}
Extension of F: {a, d}
Extension of =: {⟨a, b⟩}

It would be correct, although pointless, to list the extensions as follows:

Domain: {a, b, c, d}
Extension of F: {a, b, d}
Extension of =: {⟨a, a⟩, ⟨b, b⟩, ⟨a, b⟩, ⟨b, a⟩}

The expanded extensions are no more informative than the original ones. The expanded extension of 'F' tells one nothing that could not be immediately inferred from the original extension of 'F' and the identity of a and b. Turning to the extension of identity, the addition of '⟨b, a⟩' is unnecessary because this follows immediately from '⟨a, b⟩'. That a = a and b = b is obvious, and the addition of '⟨a, a⟩' and '⟨b, b⟩' is unnecessary, as such identities are always within any extension of identity. When no information is provided about the extension of identity, it should be understood that only such obvious identities are within the extension. The extensions of the predicates can be incomplete in that they do not include such information, but in all other respects they must be complete in order to ensure that the interpretations really show what they purport to show.

'$(\forall x)(\forall y)(Rxya \supset (x = a \land y = b))$' is quantificationally indeterminate. To show this, one needs to produce two interpretations. On the following interpretation, '$(\forall x)(\forall y)(Rxya \supset (x = a \land y = b))$' is false:

Domain: {a, b}
Extension of R: {⟨b, b, a⟩}

Several strategies to develop an interpretation on which the formula is true are possible. One is to develop an interpretation which makes the formula true by making sure that 'R __ __ a' is false no matter which constants replace the blanks. This can be done by making the extension of 'R' empty:

Domain: {a, b}
Extension of R: {   }

'$(\forall x)(\forall y)(Rxya \supset (x = a \land y = b))$' is true on this interpretation. Another strategy is to ensure that '__ = a ∧ __ = b' is true no matter which constants replace the blanks. This is done in the following interpretation:

Domain: {a, b}
Extension of R: {⟨a, b, a⟩}
Extension of =: {⟨a, b⟩}

Since there is an interpretation on which the formula is false and an interpretation on which it is true, '$(\forall x)(\forall y)(Rxya \supset (x = a \land y = b))$' is quantificationally indeterminate.

So far in this section, claims about truth and falsity have been made with only the most off-hand sort of justification. In order to see the basis for these claims, the last interpretation will be considered again carefully. Since '$(\forall x)(\forall y)(Rxya \supset (x = a \land y = b))$' is a universally quantified formula, to show that it is true on the given interpretation, one must deal with every item in the domain. Since there are two items in the domain, '$(\forall x)(\forall y)(Rxya \supset (x = a \land y = b))$' can be understood as the conjunction of two formulas:

  1 $(\forall y)(Raya \supset (a = a \land y = b))$

     and

  2 $(\forall y)(Rbya \supset (b = a \land y = b))$

Both of these formulas, too, are universally quantified and can be expanded as conjunctions. 1 becomes the conjunction of:

1.1 $Raaa \supset (a = a \land a = b)$

     and

1.2 $Raba \supset (a = a \land b = b)$

When expanded, 2 becomes the conjunction of:

2.1 $Rbaa \supset (b = a \land a = b)$

     and

2.2 $Rbba \supset (b = a \land b = b)$

Since 'Raaa' is false and '$a = a \land a = b$' is true, 1.1 is true. Since 'Raba' is true and '$a = a \land b = b$' is true, 1.2 is true. Since 'Rbaa' is false and '$b = a \land a = b$' is true, 2.1 is true. Finally, since 'Rbba' is false and '$b = a \land b = b$' is true, 2.2 is true. Thus, 1.1, 1.2, 2.1 and 2.2 are all true. Because any conjunction of four true formulas is true, '$(\forall x)(\forall y)(Rxya \supset (x = a \land y = b))$' is true on the given interpretation.

Since in an interpretation, universally quantified formulas become conjunctions and existentially quantified formulas become conjunctions, one may wonder why truth tables are not used when dealing with interpretations. There are two reasons. The practical reason is that truth tables used for this purpose are messy and hard to construct. The theoretical reason is that truth tables give bizarre results when two or more items in the domain are identical. For example, when '$a = b$' and 'Fa' are both true, a complete truth table will have at least one row on which 'Fa' and 'Fb' have different truth values.

Although the quantificational equivalence of two formulas cannot be shown as simply as truth-functional equivalence, it is quite easy to use an interpretation to show that two formulas are not quantificationally equivalent. One need only provide an interpretation on which the formulas

have different truth values. An interpretation is used to demonstrate that
'(∃x)Gx ∧ (∃x)Hx' is not quantificationally equivalent to '(∃x)(Hx ∧ Gx)'
in the following example:

> Domain: {a, b}
> Extension of G: {a}
> Extension of H: {b}

On this interpretation, '(∃x)Hx ∧ (∃x)Gx' is true while '(∃x)(Hx ∧ Gx)' is
false.

As another example, an interpretation is used to demonstrate that
'(∃x)Rx ⊃ Ma' is not quantificationally equivalent to '(∃x)(Rx ⊃ Ma)':

> Domain: {a, b}
> Extension of M: {b}
> Extension of R: {a}

On this interpretation, '(∃x)Rx ⊃ Ma' is false while '(∃x)(Rx ⊃ Ma)' is
true, as can be seen by systematically substituting constants for variables.

As mentioned, quantificational validity cannot be shown in the simple
way that truth-functional validity can be shown. However, it is relatively
easy to use interpretations to show quantificational invalidity. If one can
produce an interpretation on which all the premises are true and the
conclusion is false, one can show that the argument is quantificationally
invalid. The quantificational invalidity of the following argument can be
shown by means of a simple interpretation:

> (∀x)(Fx ⊃ Gx)
> (∃x)~ Fx
> _____
> (∃x)~ Gx

To show that this argument is quantificationally invalid, an interpretation
with a domain consisting of two items suffices:

> Domain: {a, b}
> Extension of F: {a}
> Extension of G: {a, b}

On this interpretation, '(∀x)(Fx ⊃ Gx)' and '(∃x)~ Fx' are true, while
'(∃x)~ Gx' is false. The argument, therefore, is quantificationally invalid.

To show that the following argument is quantificationally invalid, one
again needs two items in the domain:

> (∃x)(Ax ∧ Bx)
> (∃x)(Bx ∧ Cx)
> _____
> (∃x)(Ax ∧ Cx)

The trick is to set up the extensions of 'A', 'B' and 'C' so that something is
both A and B, something is both B and C, and nothing is both A and C.

Setting up the extensions in this way allows all the premisses to be true while the conclusion is false:

Domain: {j, k}
Extension of A: {j}
Extension of B: {j, k}
Extension of C: {k}

In trying to develop an interpretation, one should first consider whether a domain with one object in it would be adequate. If not, the domain should be expanded only as necessary. With increasingly complex formulas requiring larger domains, the use of interpretations to show quantificational invalidity becomes impracticable.

The method of using interpretations discussed in this section is cumbersome, and it frequently requires much trial and error to arrive at the necessary domains and extensions. There are more sophisticated procedures. In fact, there are ways to use interpretations to do such things as show quantificational validity so long as one is dealing only with one-place predicates. However, these also are difficult to apply in practice, and a discussion of how interpretations can be used in such ways is beyond the scope of this book. Learning something about interpretations can be useful for seeing how the quantifiers work. However, as a technique to be methodically applied to problems, the use of interpretations has serious limitations.

§4.18: EXERCISES

§4.18 Part 1

Determine the truth value of each of the following formulas on the given interpretation.

Domain: {a, b, c, d}
Extension of F: {b}
Extension of G: {⟨b, a⟩, ⟨c, a⟩}
Extension of H: {⟨b, c, a⟩}
Extension of K: {   }
Extension of =: {⟨c, d⟩}

1 $(\exists x)\sim Fx$

2 $(\exists x)Fx$

3 $(\forall x)(\exists y)Gxy$

4 $(\forall x)\sim Kx$

5 $(\exists x)(Fx \lor Kx)$

6 $(\exists x)(\exists y)(\exists z)Hxyz$

7 $(\exists x)\sim x = b$

8 $(\forall x)x = c$

9 $(\exists x)(\forall y)Gxy$

10 $(\exists x)(\exists y)(\forall z)Hxyz$

§4.18 Part 2

For each of the following formulas, provide two interpretations to show that the formula is quantificationally indeterminate.

1 $(\forall x)(Fx \lor Gx)$

2 $(\exists x)(Fx \lor Gx)$

3 $(\exists x)Fx \supset (\forall x)Fx$

4 $(\exists x)(Fx \land Gx)$

5 $(\exists x)(Fx \land a = b) \land (\exists x)\sim Fx$

6 $(\forall x)((Fx \land Gx) \supset a = b)$

7 $(\exists x)(Fx \land Gx) \land (\exists x)\sim (Fx \lor Gx)$

8 $(\forall x)(\forall y)(Lxy \equiv Lyx)$

9 $(\forall x)Rx \supset (\forall x)\sim Rx$

10 $(\forall x)(\exists y)(\exists z)(Kxy \lor Kxz)$

§4.18 Part 3

For each of the following pairs of formulas, provide an interpretation to show that the formulas in each pair are not quantificationally equivalent.

1 $(\forall x)Fx$
   $(\exists x)Fx$

2 $(\forall x)Fx \supset (\forall x)Gx$
   $(\forall x)Gx \supset (\forall x)Fx$

3 $(\forall x)Fx \supset (\forall y)Gy$
   $(\forall x)(Fx \supset (\forall y)Gy)$

4 $(\forall x)(Fx \lor Gx)$
   $(\forall x)Fx \lor (\forall x)Gx$

5 $(\exists x)Fx \equiv (\exists x)Gx$
   $(\forall x)(Fx \equiv Gx)$

6 $(\exists x)Fx \supset (\exists y)Gy$
   $(\exists x)(Fx \supset (\exists y)Gy)$

7 $(\exists x)(Mx \lor Ra)$
   $(\exists x)(Mx \lor Rb)$

8 $((\exists x)Fx \lor (\exists x)Gx) \supset (\forall y)Ry$
   $(\exists x)Fx \lor ((\exists x)Gx \supset (\forall y)Ry)$

9 $(\forall x)(Qx \supset (\forall y)Rxy)$
   $(\exists x)(Qx \wedge (\forall y)Rxy)$

10 $(\forall x)(\exists y)(\exists z)Rxyz$
   $(\exists x)(\exists y)(\forall z)Rxyz$

§4.18 Part 4

For each of the following arguments, provide an interpretation to show that
the argument is quantificationally invalid.

1 $\sim a = b$
   $\underline{\sim b = c}$
   $\sim a = c$

2 $(\forall x)(Fx \supset Gx)$
   $\underline{\sim Fa}$
   $\sim Ga$

3 $\underline{(\forall y)(\exists x)Kxy}$
   $(\exists x)(\forall y)Kxy$

4 $(\forall x)(Fx \supset Gx)$
   $\underline{(\forall x)\sim Fx}$
   $(\forall x)\sim Gx$

5 $\underline{(\forall x)Fx \supset (\exists y)Gy}$
   $Fa \supset (\exists y)Gy$

6 $\underline{(\exists x)(Fx \supset Gx)}$
   $(\forall x)(Fx \supset Gx)$

7 $\underline{(\forall x)(Fx \supset (x = a \vee x = b))}$
   $Fa \vee Fb$

8 $(\forall x)(Kx \supset Mx)$
   $\underline{(\exists x)(Fx \wedge \sim Kx)}$
   $(\exists x)(Fx \wedge \sim Mx)$

9 $(\exists x)Rxa$
   $\underline{(\forall x)Rxa \supset (\exists x)Rax}$
   $(\exists x)Rax$

10 $(\forall x)(Hx \supset Fx)$
   $\underline{(\exists x)(Fx \wedge \sim Gx)}$
   $(\forall x)(Hx \supset \sim Gx)$

§4.19: SUMMARY OF TOPICS

With a few possible exceptions to make the summary clearer, the topics appear in the order in which they appear in the text.

Individual (See p. 134): An individual can be a person, a place, an idea or collection. Mass nouns such as 'water' and 'sugar' should be treated as individuals.

Predicate (See p. 134): A predicate can deal with age, size, shape or complexity – anything one can say about an individual. It is represented by an upper-case letter distinguished from a sentence letter by being immediately followed by a lower-case letter.

Constant (See p. 134): A constant is a lower-case letter which names a particular individual and follows a predicate letter. All the lower-case letters from a to t can serve as constants. In the formulas, 'Gb' and 'Mdhk', 'b', 'd', 'h' and 'k' are constants.

One-place predicate (See p. 135): A predicate which is represented by a predicate letter followed by a single lower-case letter. 'Fa' and 'Rc' are examples of one-place predicates.

Multi-place predicate (See p. 136): A predicate which is represented by a predicate letter followed by more than one lower-case letter. 'Fac', 'Hejk', 'Mekk' are examples of multi-place predicates.

Quantifiers (See p. 140): Words such as 'each', 'all', 'some' and 'no' are quantifiers.

Variable (See p. 140): A single lower-case letter which does not name a particular individual as a constant does. 'x', 'y' and 'z' (with subscripts if needed) are the only variables used in this book. In a WFF, every variable is within the scope of a quantifier.

Existential quantifier (See p. 140): Expressions like '$(\exists x)$' and '$(\exists y)$' are used to represent quantifiers such as 'some'.

Open sentence (See p. 140): An open sentence is not a WFF. If all the variables in it were replaced by constants, the result would be a WFF. 'Hx' and 'Rxy' and examples of open sentences.

Closed sentence (See p. 140): A closed sentence is a WFF. 'Ha' and 'Rdg' are examples of closed sentences.

Scope of a quantifier (See p. 141): The scope of a quantifier determines what is governed by the quantifier. Brackets extend the scope of a quantifier in much the same way as brackets extend what is negated by the tilde.

Universal quantifier (See p. 142): Expressions like '$(\forall x)$' and '$(\forall y)$' are used to represent quantifiers such as 'all' and 'every'.

Quantificationally equivalent (See p. 142): '$\sim (\exists x)Fx$' and '$(\forall x)\sim Fx$' can easily be seen to be quantificationally equivalent. In Chapter 5 there are rules which allow the derivation of one member of a pair of quantificationally equivalent formulas from the other.

Atomic formula (See p. 143): An atomic formula in predicate logic is any WFF which contain no operators (sentence operators or quantifiers). 'Ma', 'Qba' and 'Pdek' are all atomic formulas.

Identity (See p. 150): Expressions of identity use the familiar '=' sign. Thus, 'a is identical to b' is expressed as '$a = b$'. Nevertheless, identity formulas are negated in just the same way as other formulas; the '$\neq$' symbol is not used. Thus, 'a is not identical to b' is expressed as '$\sim a = b$'. Expressions of identity are necessary to translate such phrases as 'no one but Paul', 'only Paul', 'only one' and 'at least two'.

Definite descriptions (See p. 153): Expressions such as 'the smartest thief of the gang' and 'the youngest student at the college' are typical definite descriptions.

Sets (See p. 156): Sets are collections of elements.

Elements (See p. 156): Elements are the members which constitute sets.

List notation (See p. 156): Listing the elements of a set between set brackets as in '{a, b, c}'. The elements in this notation are separated by commas.

Property notation (See p. 156): Specifying some property of the elements, as in '{X|X is green or X is blue}', which can be read as 'the set of all Xs which are green or blue'.

Domain (See p. 155): To specify a domain is to restrict the discussion by limiting it to include only certain things. This is done by specifying a set which constitutes the domain.

Quantificationally valid (See p. 161): An argument in predicate logic is quantificationally valid if the conclusion can be derived from the premisses using the rules of Chapter 5.

Quantificationally true (See p. 165): A formula in predicate logic is quantificationally true if it can be derived in a categorical derivation using the rules of Chapter 5.

Quantificationally false (See p. 165): A formula in predicate logic is quantificationally false if its negation can be derived in a categorical derivation using the rules of Chapter 5.

Interpretation (See p. 166): An interpretation uses a domain to show that a formula is quantificationally indeterminate or that an argument is quantificationally invalid.

Empty set (See p. 166): The set having no elements.

Domain of the interpretation (See p. 166): The domain of the interpretation is a non-empty set which is appealed to in determining the truth or falsity of formulas in the interpretation. Every interpretation has a single domain.

Extensions of the predicates (See p. 166): A list of what predicates are true of what items in an interpretation.

Ordered pairs (See p. 167): In an interpretation, order is shown in the extensions of predicates by the pointed brackets: '⟨' and '⟩'. Thus, if 'Rab' is true and 'Rba' is false, the extension of 'R' is '{⟨a, b⟩}'. If 'Rab' and 'Rba' are both true, the extension of 'R' is '{⟨a, b⟩, ⟨b, a⟩}'.

Ordered triples (See p. 167): Ordered triples are just like ordered pairs but are used with three-place predicates. '{⟨a, b, c⟩, ⟨b, b, a⟩}' is an example of an extension including ordered triples.

Quantificationally indeterminate (See p. 165): A formula in predicate logic is quantificationally indeterminate if it is possible to provide both an interpretation on which it is true and an interpretation on which it is false.

Quantificational invalidity (See p. 166): The quantificational invalidity of an argument can be shown by providing an interpretation on which the premisses are true and the conclusion is false.

CHAPTER FIVE

DERIVATIONS IN PREDICATE LOGIC

§5.1: PREDICATE LOGIC DERIVATIONS

Derivations in predicate logic can be used to derive the conclusions of quantificationally valid arguments and to derive quantificationally true formulas categorically. Since the negation of a quantificationally true formula is quantificationally false, derivations in predicate logic can also be used to show quantificational falsehood. Using the derivation rules from Chapter 3 together with the rules which will be presented in this chapter, one can derive the conclusions of all quantificationally valid arguments and only quantificationally valid arguments from their premisses. In addition, the rules will allow the categorical derivation of all quantificationally true formulas and only quantificationally true formulas. That the rules are logically respectable in this way can be demonstrated, but such a demonstration is a matter of metatheory. Derivations in predicate logic make use of six rules in addition to the derivation rules of sentence logic. The new rules are introduction and elimination rules for the existential quantifier, the universal quantifier and identity.

   Interpretations can often be developed by trial and error to show that an argument is quantificationally invalid. Interpretations can also be used to show that a formula is quantificationally indeterminate, and thus neither quantificationally true nor quantificationally false. However, the method of interpretations does not provide a mechanical procedure to determine such things in the way that a check on a truth table does. One may not know that an argument is quantificationally invalid or that a formula is quantificationally indeterminate simply because one has not developed the necessary interpretation. Accordingly, there is an important difference between derivations in sentence logic and derivations in predicate logic. In sentence logic, if one is trying without success to derive a formula, it is always possible to refer to a truth table to make sure that the formula is in fact derivable. In predicate logic, it is possible in principle to work for a lifetime on a derivation with no way of determining with certainty whether the formula one is trying to derive is in fact derivable. In practice, working seriously at a derivation usually leads either to success or to an understanding of why the formula one has been trying to derive cannot be derived. All the derivation exercises in this book have been checked to ensure that the required derivations are of a reasonable length.

§ 5.2: EXISTENTIAL QUANTIFIER INTRODUCTION

If one knows that grass is green, one knows that something is green. Given any constant 'τ' and any predicate 'Φ' in a sentence 'Φτ', one can infer '(∃x)Φx'. Similarly, if one knows that something is behind the house, one knows that something is behind something. Given any constant 'τ' and any predicate 'Φ' in a sentence '(∃x)Φxτ', one can infer '(∃y)(∃x)Φxy'. The rule of **existential quantifier introduction**, '∃I', reflects the propriety of such inferences.

Before stating the rule for introducing the existential quantifier, it is necessary to look ahead a little bit. Some of the rules which will be discussed later in this chapter will use dummy names, much as the name 'John Doe' is often used. These dummy names are called 'parameters' and their use will be explained in the appropriate place. For the moment, it is sufficient to recognize that one will have to deal with two kinds of names, constants and parameters. In what follows, the word 'term' will be used to refer to both constants and parameters.

Although using existential quantifier introduction is really quite easy, the formal statement of the rule is somewhat forbidding.

∃I

One can write an existentially quantified formula 'Φ' on any given scope line, provided that **all** of the following conditions are met:

1 A formula which contains one or more occurrences of the term 'τ' appears on that scope line.

2 The variable 'χ' does not appear in this original formula.

3 The existentially quantified formula 'Φ' is formed by replacing one or more occurrences of the term 'τ' in the original formula by the variable 'χ' and writing '$(\exists\chi)$' in front of the result of the replacement.

The justification for the new line consists of an appeal to the number of the line where the original formula containing 'τ' appears and the rule, '∃I'.

This may seem difficult to follow, but a few examples will make matters clear. All uses of ∃I in the following derivation are correct:

1	Rab	P
2	Fc	P
3	$(\exists z)Fz \supset Qj$	P
4	$(\exists z)Fz$	2, ∃I
5	Qj	3, 4, $\supset$E
6	$(\exists x)Qx$	5, ∃I
7	$(\exists y)Ryb$	1, ∃I
8	$(\exists x)(\exists y)Ryx$	7, ∃I
9	$(\exists x)(\exists y)Ryx \wedge (\exists x)Qx$	6, 8, $\wedge$I
10	$(\exists x)((\exists z)Fz \supset Qx)$	3, ∃I

It should be noted that the brackets were added to '$(\exists z)Fz \supset Qj$' when ∃I was used at line 10. Strictly speaking, ∃I was used on '$((\exists z)Fz \supset Qj)$'. If this had not been done, the appeal to ∃I at line 10 would have been illegitimate, since the 'x' in 'Qx' would not have been within the scope of a quantifier.

In using ∃I, one can replace as many occurrences of the same term as one likes. All of the following uses of ∃I are correct:

1	Raaa	P
2	(∃x)Rxaa	1, ∃I
3	(∃x)Raxa	1, ∃I
4	(∃x)Raax	1, ∃I
5	(∃x)Rxxa	1, ∃I
6	(∃x)Rxxx	1, ∃I
7	(∃y)(∃x)Rxya	2, ∃I
8	(∃z)(∃y)(∃x)Rxyz	7, ∃I

There are three important points to remember in connection with ∃I. First, the new variable must not already occur in the formula which is to be quantified. Second, one cannot replace different terms with the same variable. Third, the existential quantifier which is introduced must quantify the entire formula. This means that any outer brackets which have not been included must be added before the existential quantifier is introduced. Some common mistakes in using ∃I are exemplified below:

1	~ Ma	P
2	(∃x)Fx ⊃ Gb	P
3	Jmn	P
4	Ha ⊃ Hb	P
5	(∃x)Kx ∧ Lm	P
6	~ (∃x)Mx †††	1, ∃I
7	(∃x)Jxx †††	3, ∃I
8	(∃x)((∃x)Kx ∧ Lx) †††	5, ∃I
9	(∃x)Hx ⊃ Hb †††	4, ∃I
10	(∃x)Fx ⊃ (∃y)Gy †††	2, ∃I

Line 6 is completely mistaken. It is possible to obtain '(∃x)~ Mx' from '~ Ma' by ∃I but not '~ (∃x)Mx'. The error in line 7 is that two distinct terms, 'm' and 'n', are replaced by a single variable. This error would be obvious in English: letting 'Jmn' represent 'Michael played a joke on Norman', it certainly does not follow that Michael or anyone else played a joke on himself. Line 8 is mistaken because the variable which is used in the new quantified formula has already been used in the formula which is to be quantified. The result is not a WFF. Line 9 is mistaken because the complete formula is not quantified. It is possible to obtain '(∃x)(Hx ⊃ Hb)' from 'Ha ⊃ Hb' but not '(∃x)Hx ⊃ Hb'. This error, too, would be obvious in English. From the fact that Bill is happy if Ann is happy, it does not follow that Bill is happy if somebody is happy. Line 10 is mistaken because only part of a formula is quantified. '$(\exists x)Fx \supset (\exists y)Gy$' is obtained legitimately from '$(\exists x)Fx \supset Gb$' in the following derivation:

1	$(\exists x)Fx \supset Gb$	P
2	$(\exists x)Fx$	A
3	$(\exists x)Fx \supset Gb$	1, R
4	Gb	2, 3, $\supset$E
5	$(\exists y)Gy$	4, $\exists$I
6	$(\exists x)Fx \supset (\exists y)Gy$	2–5, $\supset$I

The rule of existential quantifier introduction is easy to remember and use. In introducing the existential quantifier, one must remember that the scope of the quantifier is the entire formula. Therefore, the formulas which are going to be existentially quantified must be properly bracketed. It is then a simple matter to avoid mistakes in using this rule.

§5.3: UNIVERSAL QUANTIFIER ELIMINATION

The rule of **universal quantifier elimination**, '$\forall$E', is even easier to understand than $\exists$I. From the claim that everyone is sick, one can infer that John is sick. Likewise, if one knows that anything which is water is H_2O, one knows that the water in this glass is H_2O. Given any universally quantified formula '$(\forall \chi)\Phi\chi$' and any parameter or constant 'τ', one can infer '$\Phi\tau$'.

$\forall$E

One can write the formula '$\Phi\tau$' on any given scope line, provided that **both** of the following conditions are met:

1 A universally quantified formula '$(\forall\chi)\Phi\chi$' is already on the same scope line.

2 '$\Phi\tau$' is the result of removing the universal quantifier '$(\forall\chi)$' from '$(\forall\chi)\Phi\chi$' and the replacement of **every** occurrence of the variable 'χ' in '$(\forall\chi)\Phi\chi$' by the **same** term 'τ'.

The justification for the new line consists of an appeal to the number of the line where '$(\forall\chi)\Phi\chi$' appears and the rule, '$\forall$E'.

The following derivation shows some correct uses of $\forall$E. It should be noted that in each case $\forall$E is applied to the universal quantifier which is the main operator of the formula.

1	$(\forall x)(\forall y)(\forall z)(Rxy \supset Pzy)$	P
2	$(\forall y)(\forall z)(Ray \supset Pzy)$	1, $\forall$E
3	$(\forall z)(Rab \supset Pzb)$	2, $\forall$E
4	$Rab \supset Pcb$	3, $\forall$E

The constants or parameters which replace the different variables do not have to be different. The next derivation is just like the previous one, except that the constant 'k' is used in each application of $\forall$E:

1	$(\forall x)(\forall y)(\forall z)(Rxy \supset Pzy)$	P
2	$(\forall y)(\forall z)(Rky \supset Pzy)$	1, $\forall$E
3	$(\forall z)(Rkk \supset Pzk)$	2, $\forall$E
4	$Rkk \supset Pkk$	3, $\forall$E

$\forall$E and $\exists$I are used to derive '$(\exists x)Gx$' from '$(\forall x)(Fx \supset Gx)$' and 'Fa' in the following derivation:

1	$(\forall x)(Fx \supset Gx)$	P
2	Fa	P
3	$Fa \supset Ga$	1, $\forall$E
4	Ga	2, 3, $\supset$E
5	$(\exists x)Gx$	4, $\exists$I

The universal quantifier which is eliminated must be the main operator of the formula. In addition, every occurrence of the variable in question must be replaced in order to avoid being left with a variable which is not within the scope of a quantifier. Another important point is that all the occurrences of the variable being replaced must be replaced by the same term. Some examples of common mistakes in using $\forall$E are shown below:

1	$\sim (\forall x)Fx$	P
2	Fa	P
3	$Fa \supset (\forall x)Rx$	P
4	$(\forall x)(\forall y)Pxy$	P
5	$(\forall x)Fx \supset Rk$	P
6	$(\forall x)Bxx$	P
7	Bjk †††	6, $\forall$E
8	$\sim Fa$ †††	1, $\forall$E
9	$(\forall x)Pxa$ †††	4, $\forall$E
10	$Fa \supset Rk$ †††	5, $\forall$E
11	$Fa \supset Ra$ †††	3, $\forall$E

The same variables in a universally quantified formula are replaced by different constants in the formula on line 7, and this is not a legitimate use of ∀E. This error is intuitively clear in English if one lets '(∀x)Bxx' represent 'Everything is as big as itself.' Plainly this does not allow one to infer that Cambridge is as big as Oxford. Line 8 is incorrect because the main operator of the formula at line 1 is a tilde. Line 9 is incorrect because the main operator of '(∀x)(∀y)Pxy' is '(∀x)' and not '(∀y)'. The main operator of the formula at line 5 is the horseshoe, and thus ∀E is misapplied at line 10. There is exactly the same problem with the appeal to ∀E at line 11.

It is possible to derive 'Fa ⊃ Ra' from 'Fa ⊃ (∀x)Rx' legitimately, and this is done in the following derivation:

1	Fa ⊃ (∀x)Rx	P
2	Fa	A
3	Fa ⊃ (∀x)Rx	1, R
4	(∀x)Rx	2, 3, ⊃E
5	Ra	4, ∀E
6	Fa ⊃ Ra	2–5, ⊃I

The rule of universal quantifier elimination is very easy to remember. In most cases, mistakes are the result of failure to look carefully for the main operator of the formula under consideration.

§5.4: EXISTENTIAL QUANTIFIER ELIMINATION

The rule of **existential quantifier elimination**, '∃E', is more complex than the other rules discussed so far, but the underlying idea behind the rule can be explained easily. If one can establish a conclusion from the fact that something has the property Φ with no appeal to other knowledge about that thing, one is entitled to infer that conclusion from '(∃x)Φx'. There is a very common way to make sure that it is only the fact that the thing under consideration has the property Φ which allows one to infer the conclusion. That is to assign a dummy name like 'John Doe' to that thing. Since 'John Doe' is a dummy name which does not stand for an actual thing or person, anything which can be shown to follow from the fact that John Doe is Φ is established.

The lower-case letters 'u', 'v', 'w', supplemented if need be by subscripted letters like 'w_2', are **parameters** and serve the same sort of purpose as do dummy names. The best way to see how parameters work is to examine a simple derivation which uses ∃E:

1	$(\exists x)Fx$	P
2	$(\forall x)(Fx \supset Gk)$	P
3	u| Fu	A
4	$(\forall x)(Fx \supset Gk)$	2, R
5	$Fu \supset Gk$	4, $\forall$E
6	Gk	3, 5, $\supset$E
7	Gk	1, 3–6, $\exists$E

The assumption at line 3 is the rough equivalent of saying 'Let us give the dummy name "u" to the thing which is F.' The scope line which begins with this assumption is flagged with the parameter 'u'. The flagged scope line serves as a **parameter barrier**, in this case a 'u'-barrier. This indicates that no information about u, no formula containing 'u', is allowed to be moved across the scope line. Although '$(\forall x)(Fx \supset Gk)$' was reiterated across the 'u'-barrier, this move was legitimate because the dummy name 'u' does not occur anywhere in '$(\forall x)(Fx \supset Gk)$'. Because the steps at lines 4, 5 and 6 are made to the right of the 'u'-barrier, one can be sure that 'u' functions as a dummy name, that no additional information about u has been introduced. Accordingly, whatever follows from 'Fu', in this case 'Gk', follows from '$(\exists x)Fx$'. Since the dummy name 'u' does not occur anywhere in 'Gk', 'Gk' can be moved back to the scope line on which '$(\exists x)Fx$' appeared.

In the following derivation, the letter 'v' is used as a parameter and the scope line which begins with the assumption is flagged with a 'v' to create a 'v'-barrier. This means that no formula with a 'v' in it can be reiterated across the scope line. That is irrelevant in this derivation, since no formulas are reiterated.

1	$(\exists x)Mx$	P
2	v| Mv	A
3	$Mv \vee Rv$	2, $\vee$I
4	$(\exists x)(Mx \vee Rx)$	3, $\exists$I
5	$(\exists x)(Mx \vee Rx)$	1, 2–4, $\exists$E

The formula on line 4, '$(\exists x)(Mx \vee Rx)$', was obtained with no information about v other than the initial assumption 'Mv'. Since 'v' does not occur anywhere in '$(\exists x)(Mx \vee Rx)$', the 'v'-barrier can be ended and the formula can be moved to the scope line immediately to the left of the ended scope line. The assumption 'Mv' was made on a scope line immediately to the right of the scope line on which the existentially quantified formula appeared, and thus the formula which was obtained from 'Mv' is moved back to that same scope line, indicating that '$(\exists x)(Mx \vee Rx)$' was derived from '$(\exists x)Mx$'.

Now that some examples of existential quantifier elimination have been given, the rule can be formally stated:

∃E

One can write the formula 'ψ' on any given scope line, provided that **all** of the following conditions are met:

1 An existentially quantified formula '(∃χ)Φχ' is already on the same scope line.

2 Immediately to the right of the given scope line there is a subderivation of 'ψ' from 'Φτ', where 'τ' is any parameter which does not occur in '(∃χ)Φχ' and 'Φτ' is the result of removing the existential quantifier from '(∃χ)Φχ' and replacing every occurrence of 'χ' by 'τ'.

3 The scope line of the subderivation is flagged with the same parameter 'τ', and no formula containing the parameter 'τ' is moved across this scope line.

4 'ψ' does not contain any occurrences of the parameter 'τ'.

The justification for the new line consists of an appeal to the number of the line on which '(∃χ)Φχ' appears, the range of numbers of the subderivation of 'ψ' from 'Φτ' and the rule, '∃E'.

Although the formal statement of ∃E is somewhat complex, the rule is easy to remember once it has been used a few times. In the following derivation, ∃E is used twice to derive '(∃x)(∃y)Kyx' from '(∃x)(∃y)Kxy':

```
1 | (∃x)(∃y)Kxy                    P
2 |   u| (∃y)Kuy                   A
3 |      v| Kuv                    A
4 |         (∃y)Kyv                3, ∃I
5 |       | (∃x)(∃y)Kyx            4, ∃I
6 |     | (∃x)(∃y)Kyx              2, 3–5, ∃E
7 | (∃x)(∃y)Kyx                    1, 2–6, ∃E
```

It is important to remember that the subderivation must be on a scope line immediately to the right of the existentially quantified formula, that the parameter of the assumption must be the same as the parameter of the barrier, and that the conclusion which is reached and moved back to the scope line on which the existentially quantified formula appears must not contain an occurrence of that parameter. A common mistake in using ∃E is now exemplified:

1	(∃x)(∃y)Kxy	P
2	u⌐ (∃x)Kxu	A
3	v⌐ Kvu	A
4	(∃y)Kyu	3, ∃I
5	(∃x)(∃y)Kyx	4, ∃I
6	(∃x)(∃y)Kyx	2, 3–5, ∃E
7	(∃x)(∃y)Kyx †††	1, 2–6, ∃E

The mistake at line 7 is that there is an attempt to use ∃E on the existential quantifier which is not the main operator of the formula. The mistake stems from the assumption of '(∃x)Kxu' at line 2. This assumption, while not strictly speaking a mistake, is certainly useless and likely to lead to mistakes later in the derivation.

The correct way to derive '(∃x)(∃y)Kyx' from '(∃x)(∃y)Kxy' has already been shown. In what follows, there is an attempt to use ∃E on a formula whose main operator is a tilde and not an existential quantifier:

1	~ (∃x)Rx	P
2	u⌐ ~ Ru	A
3	~ Ru ∨ Ku	2, ∨I
4	(∃x)(~ Rx ∨ Kx)	3, ∃I
5	(∃x)(~ Rx ∨ Kx) †††	1, 2–4, ∃E

If one makes sure that one is dealing with an existentially quantified formula, and pays attention to the various points concerning parameters and barriers, learning to use ∃E correctly is much less difficult than it may seem at first.

§5.5: UNIVERSAL QUANTIFIER INTRODUCTION

Like existential quantifier elimination, the rule of **universal quantifier introduction**, '∀I', uses barriers and parameters. To see how these work in ∀I, one can consider the following argument:

$$(\forall x)(Fx \supset Gx)$$
$$\overline{(\forall x)(Fx \supset (Gx \lor Hx))}$$

The validity of the argument is obvious. If John Doe is F, then he is G. This follows by applying ∀E to the premiss. If he is G, then by ∨I he is either G or H. Thus, if John Doe is F, John Doe is either G or H. Since 'John Doe' is used here as a dummy name, the same considerations apply to anything one chooses. Therefore, for anything one chooses, if it is F, then it is G or H.

A parameter serves as a dummy name in deriving the conclusion of the argument from the premiss. The 'u'-barrier in this example serves essentially the same purpose as a barrier used in ∃E, but it is not introduced with an assumption.

1	(∀x)(Fx ⊃ Gx)	P
2	u‖ (∀x)(Fx ⊃ Gx)	1, R
3	Fu ⊃ Gu	2, ∀E
4	Fu	A
5	Fu ⊃ Gu	3, R
6	Gu	4, 5, ⊃E
7	Gu ∨ Hu	6, ∨I
8	Fu ⊃ (Gu ∨ Hu)	4–7, ⊃I
9	(∀x)(Fx ⊃ (Gx ∨ Hx))	8, ∀I

It should be noted that the missing outer brackets in the formula on line 8 were added when ∀I was used. Strictly speaking, ∀I was used on '(Fu ⊃ (Gu ∨ Hu))'.

Sometimes, in the course of a derivation which uses ∀I, a barrier is introduced at the same point in a derivation as an assumption. When this is done, however, separate scope lines are drawn, one as a barrier line and one as the line which starts with the assumption. This pattern is shown in the following derivation, which derives the same conclusion from the same premiss in a slightly more economical way:

1	(∀x)(Fx ⊃ Gx)	P
2	u‖ Fu	A
3	(∀x)(Fx ⊃ Gx)	1, R
4	Fu ⊃ Gu	3, ∀E
5	Gu	2, 4, ⊃E
6	Gu ∨ Hu	5, ∨I
7	Fu ⊃ (Gu ∨ Hu)	2–6, ⊃I
8	(∀x)(Fx ⊃ (Gx ∨ Hx))	7, ∀I

An assumption was introduced at line 2 at the same point at which the 'u'-barrier was introduced, but this is simply a coincidence. 'Fu' was assumed only in order to obtain 'Fu ⊃ (Gu ∨ Hu)' by ⊃I, and the scope line which was started with the assumption of 'Fu' was ended before the barrier line was ended.

Barriers used in connection with universal quantifier introduction are scope lines; formulas can be reiterated to them and from them just as formulas are reiterated to and from other scope lines. The only restriction on reiteration is that no formula containing the parameter of the barrier may be reiterated across the barrier. A barrier can be introduced at any point in a derivation; setting up a 'u'-barrier is like saying 'No formula with a "u" in it will be allowed to cross this line.' This ensures that the parameter really does function as a dummy name; that no information about 'u' is smuggled in during the course of the derivation. The function of a barrier is shown again as $\forall$I is used in deriving the conclusion of the following argument:

$$\frac{(\forall x)(\forall y)(Lx \land (Ly \supset My))}{(\forall x)Mx}$$

The derivation is quite simple:

1	$(\forall x)(\forall y)(Lx \land (Ly \supset My))$	P
2	u $(\forall x)(\forall y)(Lx \land (Ly \supset My))$	1, R
3	$(\forall y)(Lu \land (Ly \supset My))$	2, $\forall$E
4	$Lu \land (Lu \supset Mu)$	3, $\forall$E
5	Lu	4, $\land$E
6	$Lu \supset Mu$	4, $\land$E
7	Mu	5, 6, $\supset$E
8	$(\forall x)Mx$	7, $\forall$I

The formal statement of the rule of universal quantifier introduction follows:

$\forall$I

One can write the formula '$(\forall \chi)\Phi\chi$' on any given scope line, provided that **all** of the following conditions are met:

1 Immediately to the right of the given scope line there is a 'τ'-barrier which was not introduced as the scope line of an assumption.

2 '$\Phi\tau$' is a formula containing 'τ' which appears against the 'τ'-barrier.

3 Every occurrence of 'τ' in '$\Phi\tau$' is replaced by 'χ', where 'χ' is any variable which does not occur in '$\Phi\tau$'.

4 The same variable 'χ' follows the '$\forall$' in '$(\forall \chi)\Phi\chi$'.

The justification for the new line is the number of the line on which '$\Phi\tau$' appears and the rule, '$\forall$I'.

$\forall$I can be used several times in the same derivation, as the following example shows:

1				$(\forall x)(\forall y)(\forall z)Rxyz$	P
2	u		v	w	$(\forall x)(\forall y)(\forall z)Rxyz$	1, R
3				$(\forall y)(\forall z)Rwyz$	2, $\forall$E
4				$(\forall z)Rwvz$	3, $\forall$E
5				Rwvu	4, $\forall$E
6			$(\forall z)Rzvu$		5, $\forall$I
7		$(\forall y)(\forall z)Rzyu$			6, $\forall$I
8	$(\forall x)(\forall y)(\forall z)Rzyx$				7, $\forall$I

Only one parameter at a time can be replaced by a variable. The parameter which is replaced by the variable of the universal quantifier must be the parameter of the barrier which is ended. Some mistakes in using $\forall$I are shown in what follows:

1			$(\forall x)(\forall y)Kxy$	P
2	u	v	$(\forall x)(\forall y)Kxy$	1, R
3			$(\forall y)Kuy$	2, $\forall$E
4			Kuv	3, $\forall$E
5		$(\forall x)Kxx$ †††		4, $\forall$I
6		$(\forall x)Kxv$ †††		4, $\forall$I
7	$(\forall y)(\forall x)Kxy$ †††			6, $\forall$I

Line 5 is mistaken because both of the parameters 'u' and 'v' are replaced by a single variable. Line 6 is wrong because the parameter which is replaced is not the parameter of the barrier. Line 7 is wrong for exactly the same reason.

In introducing the universal quantifier, one must remember that the scope of the quantifier is the entire formula. It is important, therefore, to be sure that the formulas which are going to be universally quantified are properly bracketed. If one keeps in mind the reason for having parameters and barriers – that parameters must function as dummy names and that parameter barriers prevent information about parameters from being reiterated – the use of $\forall$I is completely straightforward.

§5.6: IDENTITY INTRODUCTION

The predicate used to express identity differs importantly from other predicates in that there are introduction and elimination rules connected with it.

The rule of **identity introduction**, '=I', is extremely simple. It is far more useful than it might appear at first:

=I
At any point in a derivation, one can write '$\tau = \tau$', where 'τ' is any constant or parameter.   The justification for the new line is simply the rule, '=I'.

As an example of the correct use of =I, the conclusion of the following argument is derived from the premiss:

$$(\forall x)(Rx \supset \sim a = a)$$
$$\overline{\sim Ra}$$

1	$(\forall x)(Rx \supset \sim a = a)$	P
2	$Ra \supset \sim a = a$	1, ∀E
3	$\quad$ Ra	A
4	$\quad$ $Ra \supset \sim a = a$	2, R
5	$\quad$ $\sim a = a$	3, 4, ⊃E
6	$\quad$ $a = a$	=I
7	$\sim Ra$	3, 5, 6, ~I

The rule of identity introduction is so simple that mistakes in using it are extremely rare.

§ 5.7: IDENTITY ELIMINATION

The rule of **identity elimination**, '=E', is easy to learn:

=E
One can write the formula '$\Phi\tau_2$' on any given scope line, provided that **both** of the following conditions are met:

1 On that scope line there is a formula '$\Phi\tau_1$'
2 On that scope line there is a formula '$\tau_1 = \tau_2$' or '$\tau_2 = \tau_1$'
3 '$\Phi\tau_2$' is the result of replacing all or some of the occurrences of 'τ_1' by 'τ_2' in '$\Phi\tau_1$'.

The justification for the new line consists of an appeal to the number of the line where '$\tau_1 = \tau_2$' or '$\tau_2 = \tau_1$' occurs, the number of the line where '$\Phi\tau_1$' occurs and the rule, '=E'.

All of the following uses of =E are correct:

1	m = j	P
2	Rj	P
3	Kmj	P
4	Rm	1, 2, =E
5	Kmm	1, 3, =E
6	Kjj	1, 3, =E
7	Kjm	1, 6, =E

The rule of identity elimination is intuitively obvious, and mistakes in using it are usually the result of simple inattention.

§ 5.8: EXERCISES

Supply the missing justifications in the following derivations.

Question 1

1	~ (∀x)Fx	P
2	~ (∃x)~ Fx	?
3	u ~ Fu	?
4	(∃x)~ Fx	?
5	~ (∃x)~ Fx	?
6	~ ~ Fu	?
7	Fu	?
8	(∀x)Fx	?
9	~ (∀x)Fx	?
10	~ ~ (∃x)~ Fx	?
11	(∃x)~ Fx	?

Question 2

1	(∃x)Lxc	P
2	(∃x)Lxj	P
3	(∀x)~ (Lxc ∧ Lxj)	P
4	u Luc	?
5	(∃x)Lxj	?
6	v Lvj	?
7	w (∀x)~ (Lxc ∧ Lxj)	?
8	~ (Lwc ∧ Lwj)	?
9	Luc	?
10	Lvj	?
11	Luc ∧ Lvj	?
12	(Luc ∧ Lvj) ∧ ~ (Lwc ∧ Lwj)	?
13	(∀z)((Luc ∧ Lvj) ∧ ~ (Lzc ∧ Lzj))	?
14	(∃y)(∀z)((Luc ∧ Lyj) ∧ ~ (Lzc ∧ Lzj))	?
15	(∃y)(∀z)((Luc ∧ Lyj) ∧ ~ (Lzc ∧ Lzj))	?
16	(∃x)(∃y)(∀z)((Lxc ∧ Lyj) ∧ ~ (Lzc ∧ Lzj))	?
17	(∃x)(∃y)(∀z)((Lxc ∧ Lyj) ∧ ~ (Lzc ∧ Lzj))	?

Question 3

1	(∀x)(Fx ∧ Gx)	P
2	u⌐ (∀x)(Fx ∧ Gx)	?
3	Fu ∧ Gu	?
4	Fu	?
5	Gu	?
6	(∀x)Fx	?
7	(∀x)Gx	?
8	(∀x)Fx ∧ (∀x)Gx	?

Question 4

1	(∃y)(∀x)Rxy	P
2	u⌐ (∀x)Rxu	?
3	v⌐ (∀x)Rxu	?
4	Rvu	?
5	v = v	?
6	Rvu ∧ v = v	?
7	(∃y)(Rvy ∧ v = v)	?
8	(∀x)(∃y)(Rxy ∧ x = x)	?
9	(∀x)(∃y)(Rxy ∧ x = x)	?

Question 5

1	(∃x)(Px ∧ (∀y)(Py ⊃ x = y))	P
2	u⌐ Pu ∧ (∀y)(Py ⊃ u = y)	?
3	Pu	?
4	(∀y)(Py ⊃ u = y)	?
5	v⌐ Pv	?
6	(∀y)(Py ⊃ u = y)	?
7	Pv ⊃ u = v	?
8	u = v	?
9	u = v	?
10	Pu	?
11	Pv	?
12	Pv ≡ u = v	?
13	(∀y)(Py ≡ u = y)	?
14	(∃x)(∀y)(Py ≡ x = y)	?
15	(∃x)(∀y)(Py ≡ x = y)	?

§5.9: DERIVATION STRATEGIES

Derivations in predicate logic tend to be more complex than derivations in sentence logic. There are more rules to be considered and there is the added complication of barriers. However, if one approaches derivations rationally, dealing with one problem at a time and never introducing assumptions without some idea of what one is trying to do, the additional complexities raise no serious difficulties.

The same general approach to constructing derivations which was suggested in Chapter 3 will work in connection with derivations in predicate logic. As a general but flexible rule, when one needs a formula 'Φ', one should go through the following steps in order:

1 See if one can reiterate 'Φ'.

2 See if one can use an elimination rule to obtain 'Φ'. In general, whenever one has an existentially quantified formula available, the best strategy is to use $\exists$E immediately.

3 See if one can use an introduction rule to obtain 'Φ'.

4 See if one can obtain 'Φ' by an indirect proof.

The best way to learn the art of producing derivations in predicate logic is to work through some examples. Deriving the conclusion of the following argument is a good beginning:

$(\forall x)(Fx \supset Gx)$
$(\forall x)(Gx \supset Hx)$
_____
$(\forall x)(Fx \supset Hx)$

Just as with derivations in sentence logic, the first step is to set up a skeleton of the derivation:

1 | $(\forall x)(Fx \supset Gx)$ P
2 | $(\forall x)(Gx \supset Hx)$ P

Z | $(\forall x)(Fx \supset Hx)$?

There are no secondary scope lines, and thus reiteration is not possible. The only elimination rule one can use is $\forall$E. One could obtain something like 'Fa $\supset$ Ga' from line 1 and something like 'Ga $\supset$ Ha' from line 2, but neither of these formulas would be of any help in deriving the conclusion. One must turn to an introduction rule, in this case $\forall$I. If one had 'Fu $\supset$ Hu' against a 'u'-barrier, one could obtain '$(\forall x)(Fx \supset Hx)$' by $\forall$I. The sketch of the derivation is expanded to show this:

```
1 | (∀x)(Fx ⊃ Gx)                            P
2 | (∀x)(Gx ⊃ Hx)                            P
3 |   u|
  ┊     ┊
Y ┊   | Fu ⊃ Hu                              ?
Z | (∀x)(Fx ⊃ Hx)                            Y, ∀I
```

Once again, one cannot use an elimination rule to obtain what is needed, so one must look to an introduction rule. The appropriate introduction rule is ⊃I, and so one should assume 'Fu' and try to obtain 'Hu'. The outline of the derivation shows this:

```
1 | (∀x)(Fx ⊃ Gx)                            P
2 | (∀x)(Gx ⊃ Hx)                            P
3 |   u|    | Fu                             A
  ┊     ┊   ┊
X ┊     ┊   | Hu                             ?
Y ┊     | Fu ⊃ Hu                            3–X, ⊃I
Z | (∀x)(Fx ⊃ Hx)                            Y, ∀I
```

A glance at what is available shows that 'Hu' can be obtained only from the second premiss. If one used ∀E on the formula on line 2, one could have 'Gu ⊃ Hu', but a formula with 'u' in it cannot be reiterated across the 'u'-barrier. Accordingly, '(∀x)(Gx ⊃ Hx)' should be reiterated before ∀E is used. What is needed now is 'Gu', and the sketch of the derivation is amended appropriately:

```
1 | (∀x)(Fx ⊃ Gx)                            P
2 | (∀x)(Gx ⊃ Hx)                            P
3 |   u|    | Fu                             A
4 |        | (∀x)(Gx ⊃ Hx)                   2, R
5 |        | Gu ⊃ Hu                         4, ∀E
  ┊     ┊   ┊
W ┊     ┊   | Gu                             ?
X ┊     ┊   | Hu                             5, W, ⊃E
Y ┊     | Fu ⊃ Hu                            3–X, ⊃I
Z | (∀x)(Fx ⊃ Hx)                            Y, ∀I
```

To obtain 'Gu', one must reiterate the first premiss and use ∀E to obtain 'Fu ⊃ Gu'. To get 'Gu' from this formula, one needs 'Fu', and 'Fu' is already on the scope line. The derivation can therefore be completed:

1	$(\forall x)(Fx \supset Gx)$		P
2	$(\forall x)(Gx \supset Hx)$		P
3	u⌐	Fu	A
4		$(\forall x)(Gx \supset Hx)$	2, R
5		$Gu \supset Hu$	4, $\forall$E
6		$(\forall x)(Fx \supset Gx)$	1, R
7		$Fu \supset Gu$	6, $\forall$E
8		Gu	3, 7, $\supset$E
9		Hu	5, 8, $\supset$E
10		$Fu \supset Hu$	3–9, $\supset$I
11	$(\forall x)(Fx \supset Hx)$		10, $\forall$I

In dealing with derivations in sentence logic, it was suggested that if one has a disjunctive formula available, it is a good strategy to apply ∨E to that formula immediately. Since an existentially quantified formula is like a disjunction – it claims that a predicate is true of one thing or another in the domain – it should be no surprise that in general one should immediately use ∃E when one has an existentially quantified formula. This is done in deriving the conclusion of the following argument:

$$(\forall x)(Kx \supset Ks)$$
$$(\exists x)Kx$$
$$\overline{}$$
$$Ks$$

As before, the premisses and conclusion are set out in the sketch of the derivation:

1	$(\forall x)(Kx \supset Ks)$	P
2	$(\exists x)Kx$	P
Z	Ks	?

Since one has an existentially quantified formula, one should try to obtain 'Ks' by ∃E. The skeleton of the derivation is suitably amended:

1	$(\forall x)(Kx \supset Ks)$	P
2	$(\exists x)Kx$	P
3	u⌐ Ku	A
Y	Ks	?
Z	Ks	2, 3–Y, ∃E

It should be noted that moving 'Ks' from line Y to line Z is legitimate, because the parameter 'u' does not occur in 'Ks'.

What is needed now is a way of getting 'Ks' from 'Ku'. 'Ku ⊃ Ks' can be obtained from '(∀x)(Kx ⊃ Ks)' by ∀E. Bearing in mind the 'u'-barrier, '(∀x)(Kx ⊃ Ks)' must be reiterated from line 1 before ∀E is used. It is then a simple matter to complete the derivation by obtaining 'Ks' at line Y by ⊃E. Once this is done, all that remains is to number the lines and justifications:

1	(∀x)(Kx ⊃ Ks)	P
2	(∃x)Kx	P
3	u⎸ Ku	A
4	(∀x)(Kx ⊃ Ks)	1, R
5	Ku ⊃ Ks	4, ∀E
6	Ks	3, 5, ⊃E
7	Ks	2, 3–6, ∃E

In §5.8, '(∃x)~ Fx' was derived from '~ (∀x)Fx' with the missing justifications left to be supplied as an exercise. It is intuitively obvious that these two formulas are quantificationally equivalent; saying that something is not F comes to the same thing as saying that it is false that everything is F. Accordingly, it should be possible to derive '~ (∀x)Fx' from '(∃x)~ Fx'. Since one has an existentially quantified formula, using ∃E would be a sensible strategy. On the other hand, since what one needs is a negated formula, it would be reasonable to assume '(∀x)Fx' and look for a contradiction. Both strategies work, and both will be developed.

If one starts out by using ∃E to obtain '~ (∀x)Fx', one should assume '~ Fu' against a 'u'-barrier and try to obtain '~ (∀x)Fx' on that scope line. Since there is no 'u' in '~ (∀x)Fx', the scope line can be ended once '~ (∀x)Fx' is obtained and this formula can be moved one scope line to the left. This strategy is sketched in what follows:

1	(∃x)~ Fx	P
2	u⎸ ~ Fu	A
Y	~ (∀x)Fx	?
Z	~ (∀x)Fx	1, 2–Y, ∃E

What is needed at line Y cannot be reiterated or obtained by an elimination rule. The appropriate introduction rule is ~I, since the main operator of what is needed is a tilde. One should, therefore, assume '(∀x)Fx' and look for a contradiction:

```
1  | (∃x)~ Fx                                    P
2  |   u| ~ Fu                                   A
3  |      |  (∀x)Fx                              A
W  |      |  Φ                                   ?
X  |      |  ~ Φ                                 ?
Y  |      | ~ (∀x)Fx                             3, W, X, ~I
Z  | ~ (∀x)Fx                                    1, 2–Y, ∃E
```

An obvious candidate for a contradiction is the pair 'Fu' and '~ Fu'. '~ Fu' can be reiterated from line 2 and 'Fu' can be obtained by ∀E from line 3. The derivation is completed using this contradictory pair:

```
1  | (∃x)~ Fx                                    P
2  |   u| ~ Fu                                   A
3  |      |  (∀x)Fx                              A
4  |      |  Fu                                  3, ∀E
5  |      |  ~ Fu                                2, R
6  |      | ~ (∀x)Fx                             3, 4, 5, ~I
7  | ~ (∀x)Fx                                    1, 2–6, ∃E
```

The other possible strategy in deriving '~ (∀x)Fx' from '(∃x)~ Fx' is to assume '(∀x)Fx' immediately and look for a contradiction. The outline of the derivation follows:

```
1  | (∃x)~ Fx                                    P
2  |   |  (∀x)Fx                                 A
X  |   |  Φ                                      ?
Y  |   |  ~ Φ                                    ?
Z  | ~ (∀x)Fx                                    2, X, Y, ~I
```

'(∀x)Fx' by itself holds no promise of a contradiction. Accordingly, one must reiterate '(∃x)~ Fx' and use ∃E to try to get a contradictory pair. Once '(∃x)~ Fx' has been reiterated, and '~ Fu' assumed against a 'u'-barrier, an easy contradiction is apparent. One has '~ Fu' and one can obtain 'Fu' simply by reiterating '(∀x)Fx' from line 2 and using ∀E. The skeleton of the derivation is amended to show this:

```
1 │ (∃x)~ Fx                              P
2 │    │ (∀x)Fx                           A
3 │    │ (∃x)~ Fx                         1, R
4 │    │  u│ ~ Fu                         A
5 │    │    │ (∀x)Fx                      2, R
6 │    │    │ Fu                          5, ∀E
X ┊    ┊ Φ                                ?

Y ┊    ┊ ~ Φ                              ?
Z │ ~ (∀x)Fx                             2, X, Y, ~I
```

'~ Fu' and 'Fu' are certainly a contradictory pair, but they are on the wrong scope line. The contradiction has to appear on the scope line which begins at line 2, under the assumption of '(∀x)Fx'. Since both formulas contain 'u', neither can be moved onto that scope line by a legitimate appeal to ∃E. The problem of obtaining a contradiction on that scope line remains. It may appear to be insoluble. Under the assumption of '(∀x)Fx' at line 2, a contradictory pair could not be obtained without reiterating '(∃x)~ Fx' and assuming '~ Fu' against a 'u'-barrier. As soon as this is done, one is on the wrong scope line. Although it may seem that either one cannot get a contradiction at all or one can get it only in the wrong place, there is no need to abandon the derivation; the contradictory pair, 'Fu' and '~ Fu', can be used.

Neither '~ Fu' nor 'Fu' can be moved to the scope line which begins at line 2 because they both contain the parameter of the barrier. Any contradictory pair which does not contain 'u', however, could be moved. For example, if one obtained 'Fa' and '~ Fa' on the scope line which begins at line 4, one could move both of those formulas. It would be easy to obtain 'Fa'. One would simply assume '~ Fa', reiterate 'Fu' and '~ Fu', and obtain '~ ~ Fa' by ~I. One could then obtain 'Fa' by ~E. Similarly, it would be easy to obtain '~ Fa'. One would assume 'Fa', reiterate 'Fu' and '~ Fu', and obtain '~ Fa' by ~I. The derivation is completed by following this procedure:

1	$(\exists x)\sim Fx$		P
2	$(\forall x)Fx$		A
3	$(\exists x)\sim Fx$		1, R
4	u ⎡ $\sim Fu$		A
5	$(\forall x)Fx$		2, R
6	Fu		5, $\forall$E
7	$\sim Fa$		A
8	Fu		6, R
9	$\sim Fu$		4, R
10	$\sim \sim Fa$		7, 8, 9, $\sim$I
11	Fa		10, $\sim$E
12	Fa		A
13	Fu		6, R
14	$\sim Fu$		4, R
15	$\sim Fa$		12, 13, 14, $\sim$I
16	Fa		3, 4–11, $\exists$E
17	$\sim Fa$		3, 4–15, $\exists$E
18	$\sim (\forall x)Fx$		2, 16, 17, $\sim$I

Looking back at the completed derivation, it can be seen that the step at line 11 was unnecessary; '$\sim \sim Fa$' and '$\sim Fa$' would have served as a contradictory pair. An even greater economy is possible. Rather than finding a contradictory pair, one could obtain a formula which would form a contradictory pair with something that is already on the scope line which begins at line 2. Since neither '$\sim (\exists x)\sim Fx$' nor '$\sim (\forall x)Fx$' contains 'u', and both of the formulas contradict a formula which is on the scope line which begins at line 2, obtaining either one of them would be a sensible strategy. The shorter version of the derivation follows:

```
1  | (∃x)~ Fx                          P
2  |   | (∀x)Fx                        A
3  |   | (∃x)~ Fx                      1, R
4  |       u| ~ Fu                     A
5  |       | (∀x)Fx                    2, R
6  |       | Fu                        5, ∀E
7  |           | (∀x)Fx                A
8  |           | Fu                    6, R
9  |           | ~ Fu                  4, R
10 |       | ~ (∀x)Fx                  7, 8, 9, ~I
11 |   | ~ (∀x)Fx                      3, 4–10, ∃E
12 | ~ (∀x)Fx                         2, 2, 11, ~I
```

Even this shorter version of the derivation of '~ (∀x)Fx' from '(∃x)~ Fx' took twelve steps. The version which started out by immediately assuming '~ Fu' and obtaining '~ (∀x)Fx' by ∃E took seven steps. This fact supports the suggestion made earlier in this section that immediately using ∃E is usually the best strategy when one has an existentially quantified formula available.

Just as in sentence logic one may have to do disjunction eliminations within disjunction eliminations, so in predicate logic one may have to do existential quantifier eliminations within existential quantifier eliminations. This will be necessary in deriving the conclusion from the premises of the following argument. Clearly, the argument is quantificationally valid; if something is F and something is not F, there are at least two distinct things.

$$(\exists x)Fx$$
$$(\exists x)\sim Fx$$
$$\overline{(\exists x)(\exists y)\sim x = y}$$

The derivation can be started by listing the premises and the conclusion:

```
1 | (∃x)Fx                            P
2 | (∃x)~ Fx                          P
  |
Z | (∃x)(∃y)~ x = y                   ?
```

'(∃x)(∃y)~ x = y' appears nowhere in what is available, and thus it might appear that no elimination rule can be used. In order to use the introduction rule, ∃I, one would need something like '~ a = b', and there seems to be no way of getting such a formula. Since the argument is quantificationally valid, there has to be a way of getting the conclusion from the premises. The thing to do in a situation like this is to start by using the appropriate rule even though it is not clear how one's strategy will develop. In this case, the appropriate rule is ∃E. There are two existentially quantified formulas, and no apparent reason for using one before the other. As an arbitrary choice, one can start with the first premiss, assuming 'Fu' against a 'u'-barrier. The conclusion does not contain 'u', so if one can obtain it against the 'u'-barrier, it can be brought back to the primary scope line. Since it is clear that the second premiss is necessary to obtain the conclusion, one can reiterate it and assume '~ Fv' against a 'v'-barrier. The outline of the derivation follows:

1	(∃x)Fx	P
2	(∃x)~ Fx	P
3	u⌐ Fu	A
4	(∃x)~ Fx	2, R
5	v⌐ ~ Fv	A
X	(∃x)(∃y)~ x = y	?
Y	(∃x)(∃y)~ x = y	4, 5–X, ∃E
Z	(∃x)(∃y)~ x = y	1, 3–Y, ∃E

What is needed at line X could be obtained by two applications of ∃I if one had any negation of an identity formula. The obvious candidate is '~ u = v'. This formula cannot be reiterated, nor does it appear as part of a formula which can be reiterated. Since the main operator of the needed formula is a tilde, one should try to obtain it by ~I. The skeleton of the derivation shows this:

1	(∃x)Fx	P
2	(∃x)~ Fx	P
3	u⌐ Fu	A
4	(∃x)~ Fx	2, R
5	v⌐ ~ Fv	A
6	u = v	A
T	Φ	?
U	~ Φ	?
V	~ u = v	6, T, U, ~I
W	(∃y)~ u = y	V, ∃I
X	(∃x)(∃y)~ x = y	W, ∃I
Y	(∃x)(∃y)~ x = y	4, 5–X, ∃E
Z	(∃x)(∃y)~ x = y	1, 3–Y, ∃E

It is easy to find a contradictory pair to take the place of 'Φ' and '~ Φ'. For example, one can obtain 'Fu' and '~ Fu' simply by reiterating 'Fu' and '~ Fv' and using =E on '~ Fv' to obtain '~ Fu'. The derivation is completed using this contradictory pair:

```
 1 │ (∃x)Fx                              P
 2 │ (∃x)~ Fx                            P
 3 │   u│ Fu                             A
 4 │    │ (∃x)~ Fx                       2, R
 5 │    │   v│ ~ Fv                      A
 6 │    │    │   │ u = v                 A
 7 │    │    │   │ Fu                    3, R
 8 │    │    │   │ ~ Fv                  5, R
 9 │    │    │   │ ~ Fu                  6, 8, =E
10 │    │    │ ~ u = v                   6, 7, 9, ~I
11 │    │    │ (∃y)~ u = y               10, ∃I
12 │    │    │ (∃x)(∃y)~ x = y           11, ∃I
13 │    │ (∃x)(∃y)~ x = y                4, 5–12, ∃E
14 │ (∃x)(∃y)~ x = y                     1, 3–13, ∃E
```

§ 5.10: EXERCISES

For each of the following arguments, derive the conclusion from the premiss(es).

1   $(\forall x)(\forall y)Kxy$
    _____
    $(\forall y)(\forall x)Kxy$

2   $(\forall x)(\forall y)(Fx \supset Gy)$
    _____
    $(\forall x)Fx \supset (\forall y)Gy$

3   $(\forall x)(Kx \supset Lx)$
    $(\forall x)~ Lx$
    _____
    $(\forall x)~ Kx$

4   $(\exists x)(\exists y)(\exists z)Rxyz \supset Raas$
    $Raaa$
    _____
    $(\exists x)Rxxs$

5   $(\exists x)Mx \supset Mk$
    _____
    $(\exists x)Mx \equiv Mk$

6 $(\forall x)(\forall y)(Rxy \supset \sim Ryx)$
   Rab
   _____
   $\sim Rba$

7 $(\forall x)(Px \equiv Qx)$
   $\sim (\exists x)Qx$
   _____
   $\sim Pa$

8 $(\forall x)(Mx \supset Vx)$
   $\sim (\forall x)Vx$
   _____
   $\sim (\forall x)Mx$

9 $(\forall x)(Fx \supset Gx)$
   $(\exists x)(Fx \wedge Hx)$
   _____
   $(\exists x)(Gx \wedge Hx)$

10 $(\exists x)(\exists y)Rxy$
    _____
    $(\exists y)(\exists x)Rxy$

11 $\sim (\exists x)Fx$
    _____
    $(\forall x)\sim Fx$

12 $(\exists x)Fx \supset Ra$
    _____
    $(\forall x)(Fx \supset Ra)$

13 $(\forall x)(Fx \supset Ra)$
    _____
    $(\exists x)Fx \supset Ra$

14 $(\exists x)(Lx \supset Mx)$
    $(\forall x)\sim Mx$
    _____
    $(\exists x)\sim Lx$

15 $(\exists x)(\exists y)(Fxy \vee Fyx)$
    _____
    $(\exists x)(\exists y)Fxy$

§5.11: MORE DERIVATION STRATEGIES

In the discussion of the position of quantifiers in Chapter 4, various claims about equivalent translations were made. One was that the following two formulas are quantificationally equivalent:

$(\exists x)((Wx \wedge Ax) \wedge (\forall y)(My \supset \sim Dyx))$
$(\exists x)(\forall y)((Wx \wedge Ax) \wedge (My \supset \sim Dyx))$

It is instructive to derive each of these formulas from the other.

One can begin by taking the first as a premiss and trying to derive the second. The derivation is outlined in the usual way:

1 | (∃x)((Wx ∧ Ax) ∧ (∀y)(My ⊃ ~ Dyx))   P

Z | (∃x)(∀y)((Wx ∧ Ax) ∧ (My ⊃ ~ Dyx))   ?

Following the strategy of using existential quantifier elimination when one has an existentially quantified formula, the outline of the derivation is developed:

1 | (∃x)((Wx ∧ Ax) ∧ (∀y)(My ⊃ ~ Dyx))   P
2 | u| (Wu ∧ Au) ∧ (∀y)(My ⊃ ~ Dyu)   A

Y | | (∃x)(∀y)((Wx ∧ Ax) ∧ (My ⊃ ~ Dyx))   ?
Z | (∃x)(∀y)((Wx ∧ Ax) ∧ (My ⊃ ~ Dyx))   1, 2–Y, ∃E

What is needed at line Y is an existentially quantified formula. To obtain this by ∃I, one needs a universally quantified formula in which every occurrence of 'x' in the existentially quantified formula is either the same constant or the same parameter. A glance at what one has on line 2 shows that this term should be the parameter 'u'. The outline of the derivation is expanded to show this:

1 | (∃x)((Wx ∧ Ax) ∧ (∀y)(My ⊃ ~ Dyx))   P
2 | u| (Wu ∧ Au) ∧ (∀y)(My ⊃ ~ Dyu)   A

X | | (∀y)((Wu ∧ Au) ∧ (My ⊃ ~ Dyu))   ?
Y | | (∃x)(∀y)((Wx ∧ Ax) ∧ (My ⊃ ~ Dyx))   X, ∃I
Z | (∃x)(∀y)((Wx ∧ Ax) ∧ (My ⊃ ~ Dyx))   1, 2–Y, ∃E

Since the new formula one needs is a universally quantified formula which cannot be obtained by an elimination rule, one should use universal quantifier introduction. A 'u'-barrier is already in place, so one should introduce a 'v'-barrier in order to use ∀I. What is available at line 2 will have to be used to the right of the 'v'-barrier, so it can be reiterated now:

1 | (∃x)((Wx ∧ Ax) ∧ (∀y)(My ⊃ ~ Dyx))   P
2 | u| (Wu ∧ Au) ∧ (∀y)(My ⊃ ~ Dyu)   A
3 | | v| (Wu ∧ Au) ∧ (∀y)(My ⊃ ~ Dyu)   2, R

W | | | (Wu ∧ Au) ∧ (Mv ⊃ ~ Dvu)   ?
X | | (∀y)((Wu ∧ Au) ∧ (My ⊃ ~ Dyu))   W, ∀I
Y | | (∃x)(∀y)((Wx ∧ Ax) ∧ (My ⊃ ~ Dyx))   X, ∃I
Z | (∃x)(∀y)((Wx ∧ Ax) ∧ (My ⊃ ~ Dyx))   1, 2–Y, ∃E

What is needed at line W is a conjunction. The left conjunct is identical to the left conjunct of the conjunction on line 3 and can be obtained by ∧E. The right conjunct of what is needed can be obtained from the right conjunct of the conjunction on line 3 simply by using ∀E. Accordingly, the derivation can be completed by using ∧E twice and ∀E on '(∀y)(My ⊃ ~ Dyu)' One can then obtain the formula one needs by ∧I:

1	(∃x)((Wx ∧ Ax) ∧ (∀y)(My ⊃ ~ Dyx))	P
2	u⌐ ((Wu ∧ Au) ∧ (∀y)(My ⊃ ~ Dyu))	A
3	v⌐ (Wu ∧ Au) ∧ (∀y)(My ⊃ ~ Dyu)	2, R
4	Wu ∧ Au	3, ∧E
5	(∀y)(My ⊃ ~ Dyu)	3, ∧E
6	Mv ⊃ ~ Dvu	5, ∀E
7	(Wu ∧ Au) ∧ (Mv ⊃ ~ Dvu)	4, 6, ∧I
8	(∀y)((Wu ∧ Au) ∧ (My ⊃ ~ Dyu))	7, ∀I
9	(∃x)(∀y)((Wx ∧ Ax) ∧ (My ⊃ ~ Dyx))	8, ∃I
10	(∃x)(∀y)((Wx ∧ Ax) ∧ (My ⊃ ~ Dyx))	1, 2–9, ∃E

The next derivation problem is to derive the formula on line 1 of the above derivation from the formula on line 10. Once again, one has an existentially quantified formula and one needs an existentially quantified formula. Thus, this new derivation will be similar to the previous one. The outline of the derivation reflects this:

1	(∃x)(∀y)((Wx ∧ Ax) ∧ (My ⊃ ~ Dyx))	P
2	u⌐ (∀y)((Wu ∧ Au) ∧ (My ⊃ ~ Dyu))	A
Y	(∃x)((Wx ∧ Ax) ∧ (∀y)(My ⊃ ~ Dyx))	?
Z	(∃x)((Wx ∧ Ax) ∧ (∀y)(My ⊃ ~ Dyx))	1, 2–Y, ∃E

An existentially quantified formula is needed at line Y. In order to obtain this by ∃I, one needs a conjunctive formula, one part of which is a universally quantified formula. This universally quantified formula can be obtained only by ∀I, so it appears that the most sensible thing to do is to start a 'v'-barrier and try to obtain the universally quantified formula. The sketch of the derivation is expanded appropriately:

```
1 | (∃x)(∀y)((Wx ∧ Ax) ∧ (My ⊃ ~ Dyx))              P
2 |   u| (∀y)((Wu ∧ Au) ∧ (My ⊃ ~ Dyu))              A
3 |        v| (∀y)((Wu ∧ Au) ∧ (My ⊃ ~ Dyu))         2, R
4 |         | (Wu ∧ Au) ∧ (Mv ⊃ ~ Dvu)               3, ∀E

Y |        | (∃x)((Wx ∧ Ax) ∧ (∀y)(My ⊃ ~ Dyx))      ?
Z | (∃x)((Wx ∧ Ax) ∧ (∀y)(My ⊃ ~ Dyx))              1, 2–Y, ∃E
```

It seems clear now what formula one should try to obtain in order to use ∃I at line Y: it is the conjunction of 'Wu ∧ Au' and '(∀y)(My ⊃ ~ Dyu)'. The outline of the derivation is expanded by adding this conjunctive formula at line X and the two conjuncts which are needed at line W and line V:

```
1 | (∃x)(∀y)((Wx ∧ Ax) ∧ (My ⊃ ~ Dyx))              P
2 |   u| (∀y)((Wu ∧ Au) ∧ (My ⊃ ~ Dyu))              A
3 |        v| (∀y)((Wu ∧ Au) ∧ (My ⊃ ~ Dyu))         2, R
4 |         | (Wu ∧ Au) ∧ (Mv ⊃ ~ Dvu)               3, ∀E

V |        | (∀y)(My ⊃ ~ Dyu)                         ?

W |        | Wu ∧ Au                                  ?
X |        | (Wu ∧ Au) ∧ (∀y)(My ⊃ ~ Dyu)            V, W, ∧I
Y |        | (∃x)((Wx ∧ Ax) ∧ (∀y)(My ⊃ ~ Dyx))      X, ∃I
Z | (∃x)((Wx ∧ Ax) ∧ (∀y)(My ⊃ ~ Dyx))              1, 2–Y, ∃E
```

If one ended the 'v'-barrier and used ∀I with the variable 'y' on the formula on line 4, the result would be exactly what one has at line 2. It is clear that this strategy would be pointless. Clearly, it is necessary to break up the conjunction on line 4. The outline of the derivation is expanded:

```
1 | (∃x)(∀y)((Wx ∧ Ax) ∧ (My ⊃ ~ Dyx))              P
2 |   u| (∀y)((Wu ∧ Au) ∧ (My ⊃ ~ Dyu))              A
3 |        v| (∀y)((Wu ∧ Au) ∧ (My ⊃ ~ Dyu))         2, R
4 |         | (Wu ∧ Au) ∧ (Mv ⊃ ~ Dvu)               3, ∀E
5 |         | Wu ∧ Au                                 4, ∧E
6 |         | Mv ⊃ ~ Dvu                              4, ∧E

V |        | (∀y)(My ⊃ ~ Dyu)                         ?

W |        | Wu ∧ Au                                  ?
X |        | (Wu ∧ Au) ∧ (∀y)(My ⊃ ~ Dyu)            V, W, ∧I
Y |        | (∃x)((Wx ∧ Ax) ∧ (∀y)(My ⊃ ~ Dyx))      X, ∃I
Z | (∃x)((Wx ∧ Ax) ∧ (∀y)(My ⊃ ~ Dyx))              1, 2–Y, ∃E
```

It is easy to obtain '$(\forall y)(My \supset \sim Dyu)$' by $\forall I$ from the formula on line 6. The problem is with the formula which is needed at line W. There is no rule which allows one to move 'Wu $\wedge$ Au' from line 5 to the scope line which begins at line 2. If one tries to conjoin this formula with the formula on line 6, to bring it over by the $\forall I$ rule, one ends up with the formula one had at line 2. The formula at line 5 is simply of no use, and it can be erased from the outline. One should use $\forall I$ to obtain '$(\forall y)(My \supset \sim Dyu)$' from 'Mv $\supset \sim$ Dvu', and then turn to the problem of obtaining 'Wu $\wedge$ Au' without the complication of the 'v'-barrier. The outline of the derivation reflects this strategy:

1	$(\exists x)(\forall y)((Wx \wedge Ax) \wedge (My \supset \sim Dyx))$		P
2	u⌐ $(\forall y)((Wu \wedge Au) \wedge (My \supset \sim Dyu))$		A
3		v⌐ $(\forall y)((Wu \wedge Au) \wedge (My \supset \sim Dyu))$	2, R
4		$(Wu \wedge Au) \wedge (Mv \supset \sim Dvu)$	3, $\forall E$
5		Mv $\supset \sim$ Dvu	4, $\wedge E$
6		$(\forall y)(My \supset \sim Dyu)$	5, $\forall I$
W		Wu $\wedge$ Au	?
X		$(Wu \wedge Au) \wedge (\forall y)(My \supset \sim Dyu)$	6, W, $\wedge I$
Y		$(\exists x)((Wx \wedge Ax) \wedge (\forall y)(My \supset \sim Dyx))$	X, $\exists I$
Z	$(\exists x)((Wx \wedge Ax) \wedge (\forall y)(My \supset \sim Dyx))$		1, 2–Y, $\exists E$

There remains only the problem of obtaining 'Wu $\wedge$ Au' at line W. This problem is easily solved. It can be obtained from the formula on line 2 by $\forall E$ and $\wedge E$ just as it was before, but this time the formula is not first reiterated across a 'v'-barrier. In using $\forall E$ here, it does not matter what term replaces 'y'. When the $\forall E$ step is completed, the result will be a conjunction. The conjunct one needs, 'Wu $\wedge$ Au', can be extracted by $\wedge E$, and it is unaffected by the choice of the term which replaces 'y'. That part of the conjunctive formula which is affected by this choice will not be used. The derivation is completed by arbitrarily picking 'k' as the replacement for 'y' in the application of $\forall E$, and going on to use $\wedge E$ to extract what one needs:

1	$(\exists x)(\forall y)((Wx \wedge Ax) \wedge (My \supset \sim Dyx))$	P
2	$^u (\forall y)((Wu \wedge Au) \wedge (My \supset \sim Dyu))$	A
3	$^v (\forall y)((Wu \wedge Au) \wedge (My \supset \sim Dyu))$	2, R
4	$(Wu \wedge Au) \wedge (Mv \supset \sim Dvu)$	3, $\forall$E
5	$Mv \supset \sim Dvu$	4, $\wedge$E
6	$(\forall y)(My \supset \sim Dyu)$	5, $\forall$I
7	$(Wu \wedge Au) \wedge (Mk \supset \sim Dku)$	2, $\forall$E
8	$Wu \wedge Au$	7, $\wedge$E
9	$(Wu \wedge Au) \wedge (\forall y)(My \supset \sim Dyu)$	6, 8, $\wedge$I
10	$(\exists x)((Wx \wedge Ax) \wedge (\forall y)(My \supset \sim Dyx))$	9, $\exists$I
11	$(\exists x)((Wx \wedge Ax) \wedge (\forall y)(My \supset \sim Dyx))$	1, 2–10, $\exists$E

In Chapter 4 other points about equivalent translations were made. One was the claim that the following two formulas are quantificationally equivalent:

$(\exists x)(Px \wedge (\forall y)(Py \supset x = y))$

$(\exists x)(\forall y)(Py \equiv x = y)$

'$(\exists x)(\forall y)(Py \equiv x = y)$' was derived from '$(\exists x)(Px \wedge (\forall y)(Py \supset x = y))$' in §5.8, with most of the justifications left to be supplied as an exercise. Since these formulas are quantificationally equivalent, one can derive '$(\exists x)(Px \wedge (\forall y)(Py \supset x = y))$' from '$(\exists x)(\forall y)(Py \equiv x = y)$'.

The standard procedure for dealing with an existentially quantified formula is followed in starting the derivation:

1	$(\exists x)(\forall y)(Py \equiv x = y)$	P
2	$^u (\forall y)(Py \equiv u = y)$	A
Y	$(\exists x)(Px \wedge (\forall y)(Py \supset x = y))$	?
Z	$(\exists x)(Px \wedge (\forall y)(Py \supset x = y))$	1, 2–Y, $\exists$E

To obtain the formula on line Y, one should use $\exists$I on a conjunction. Since a 'u'-barrier is in place, 'u' seems like a reasonable choice for the term which is to be replaced by the variable when $\exists$I is used. The outline of the derivation is expanded accordingly:

```
1  │ (∃x)(∀y)(Py ≡ x = y)                           P
2  │    u│ (∀y)(Py ≡ u = y)                         A
   │     ┊
V  │     ┊ Pu                                       ?
   │     ┊
W  │     │ (∀y)(Py ⊃ u = y)                         ?
X  │     │ Pu ∧ (∀y)(Py ⊃ u = y)                    V, W, ∧I
Y  │     │ (∃x)(Px ∧ (∀y)(Py ⊃ x = y))              X, ∃I
Z  │ (∃x)(Px ∧ (∀y)(Py ⊃ x = y))                    1, 2–Y, ∃E
```

There are now two problems to be addressed. Approaching one problem at
a time, one can deal first with the matter of obtaining 'Pu'. One could get
'Pu' by using ∀E and then ≡E on the formula on line 2, provided one had
'u = u'. This is an occasion on which the rule of =I is useful; one can simply
write 'u = u' and justify this step by =I. The outline of the derivation is
developed to show how the first problem is solved:

```
1  │ (∃x)(∀y)(Py ≡ x = y)                           P
2  │    u│ (∀y)(Py ≡ u = y)                         A
3  │     │ u = u                                    =I
4  │     │ Pu ≡ u = u                               2, ∀E
5  │     │ Pu                                       3, 4, ≡E
   │     ┊
W  │     │ (∀y)(Py ⊃ u = y)                         ?
X  │     │ Pu ∧ (∀y)(Py ⊃ u = y)                    5, W, ∧I
Y  │     │ (∃x)(Px ∧ (∀y)(Py ⊃ x = y))              X, ∃I
Z  │ (∃x)(Px ∧ (∀y)(Py ⊃ x = y))                    1, 2–Y, ∃E
```

The other formula which is needed is '(∀y)(Py ⊃ u = y)'. It is a universally
quantified formula which cannot be obtained by an elimination rule. One
should, therefore, introduce a barrier with a parameter which has not been
used, and try to obtain '(∀y)(Py ⊃ u = y)' by ∀I. 'Pv ⊃ u = v' against a
'v'-barrier would serve. To obtain this formula, one should assume 'Pv' and
try to obtain 'u = v'. The outline of the derivation is amended to show this:

1	$(\exists x)(\forall y)(Py \equiv x = y)$	P
2	u| $(\forall y)(Py \equiv u = y)$	A
3	$u = u$	=I
4	$Pu \equiv u = u$	2, $\forall$E
5	Pu	3, 4, $\equiv$E
6	v| | Pv	A
U	$u = v$	?
V	$Pv \supset u = v$	6–U, $\supset$I
W	$(\forall y)(Py \supset u = y)$	V, $\forall$I
X	$Pu \wedge (\forall y)(Py \supset u = y)$	5, W, $\wedge$I
Y	$(\exists x)(Px \wedge (\forall y)(Py \supset x = y))$	X, $\exists$I
Z	$(\exists x)(Px \wedge (\forall y)(Py \supset x = y))$	1, 2–Y, $\exists$E

The obvious way of obtaining 'u = v' is from the formula on line 2. Once this is reiterated, an application of $\forall$E yields 'Pv $\equiv$ u = v' which, together with 'Pv', allows one to obtain 'u = v' by $\equiv$E. Thus, the derivation can be completed:

1	$(\exists x)(\forall y)(Py \equiv x = y)$	P
2	u| $(\forall y)(Py \equiv u = y)$	A
3	$u = u$	=I
4	$Pu \equiv u = u$	2, $\forall$E
5	Pu	3, 4, $\equiv$E
6	v| | Pv	A
7	$(\forall y)(Py \equiv u = y)$	2, R
8	$Pv \equiv u = v$	7, $\forall$E
9	$u = v$	6, 8, $\equiv$E
10	$Pv \supset u = v$	6–9, $\supset$I
11	$(\forall y)(Py \supset u = y)$	10, $\forall$I
12	$Pu \wedge (\forall y)(Py \supset u = y)$	5, 11, $\wedge$I
13	$(\exists x)(Px \wedge (\forall y)(Py \supset x = y))$	12, $\exists$I
14	$(\exists x)(Px \wedge (\forall y)(Py \supset x = y))$	1, 2–13, $\exists$E

Another problem which requires some thought is the derivation of the conclusion from the premiss of the following argument:

$$(\forall x)(Fx \vee Gx)$$
$$\overline{(\forall x)Fx \vee (\exists x)Gx}$$

Just looking at the problem should make it clear that neither of the disjuncts which make up the conclusion can be derived from the premiss; from the claim that everything is either F or G, one can infer neither that everything is F nor that something is G. Trying to obtain one of the disjuncts and using ∨I to get the conclusion, therefore, would be a hopeless strategy. What one must do here is go immediately to an indirect proof. The derivation is started accordingly:

$$
\begin{array}{lll}
1 & (\forall x)(Fx \lor Gx) & P \\
2 & \quad \sim ((\forall x)Fx \lor (\exists x)Gx) & A \\
W & \quad \Phi & ? \\
X & \quad \sim \Phi & ? \\
Y & \sim \sim ((\forall x)Fx \lor (\exists x)Gx) & 2, W, X, \sim I \\
Z & (\forall x)Fx \lor (\exists x)Gx & Y, \sim E
\end{array}
$$

The problem now is to decide which contradictory pair of formulas one should try to obtain to replace 'Φ' and '∼ Φ'. Because the formula on line 2 is a negated formula, nothing within it is accessible. One could reiterate the formula on line 1 and obtain something like 'Fa ∨ Ga' by ∨I, but that formula offers little promise of a contradiction. The most promising candidates to form the contradictory pair are the formula at line 2 itself and '(∀x)Fx ∨ (∃x)Gx'. The outline of the derivation is changed to include this specific contradictory pair:

$$
\begin{array}{lll}
1 & (\forall x)(Fx \lor Gx) & P \\
2 & \quad \sim ((\forall x)Fx \lor (\exists x)Gx) & A \\
X & \quad (\forall x)Fx \lor (\exists x)Gx & ? \\
Y & \sim \sim ((\forall x)Fx \lor (\exists x)Gx) & 2, 2, X, \sim I \\
Z & (\forall x)Fx \lor (\exists x)Gx & Y, \sim E
\end{array}
$$

What is needed now is a disjunctive formula, the very formula one wanted at the beginning of the derivation. Then, it was plain that one could not obtain one of the disjuncts and go on to use ∨I. Now, however, the information at line 2 is available, and it makes sense to try to obtain one of the disjuncts and obtain '(∀x)Fx ∨ (∃x)Gx' by ∨I. The question now is whether one should try to obtain '(∀x)Fx' or '(∃x)Gx'. If one reiterated the formula on line 1 and applied ∀E to it, one would have a disjunction, say 'Fa ∨ Ga'. Assuming one of the disjuncts, 'Ga', one could obtain '(∃x)Gx' by ∃I. However, there seems to be no easy way of obtaining '(∃x)Gx' from the assumption of 'Fa'. A more promising strategy is to try to obtain

'($\forall$x)Fx'. In the expanded outline of the derivation, a 'u'-barrier is set up, '($\forall$x)(Fx $\vee$ Gx)' is reiterated, and 'Fu $\vee$ Gu' is obtained by $\forall$E:

1	($\forall$x)(Fx $\vee$ Gx)	P
2	$\sim$ (($\forall$x)Fx $\vee$ ($\exists$x)Gx)	A
3	u| ($\forall$x)(Fx $\vee$ Gx)	1, R
4	Fu $\vee$ Gu	3, $\forall$E
V	Fu	?
W	($\forall$x)Fx	V, $\forall$I
X	($\forall$x)Fx $\vee$ ($\exists$x)Gx	W, $\vee$I
Y	$\sim$ $\sim$ (($\forall$x)Fx $\vee$ ($\exists$x)Gx)	2, 2, X, $\sim$I
Z	($\forall$x)Fx $\vee$ ($\exists$x)Gx	Y, $\sim$E

The problem now is to obtain 'Fu' from 'Fu $\vee$ Gu' by $\vee$E. Since the first disjunct is exactly the formula which is needed, the sole problem is to obtain 'Fu' from 'Gu'. The only option that seems possible at this point is an indirect proof. The outline of the derivation is expanded to include the assumption of '$\sim$ Fu':

1	($\forall$x)(Fx $\vee$ Gx)	P
2	$\sim$ (($\forall$x)Fx $\vee$ ($\exists$x)Gx)	A
3	u| ($\forall$x)(Fx $\vee$ Gx)	1, R
4	Fu $\vee$ Gu	3, $\forall$E
5	Fu	A
6	Gu	A
7	$\sim$ Fu	A
R	Φ	?
S	$\sim$ Φ	?
T	$\sim$ $\sim$ Fu	7, R, S, $\sim$I
U	Fu	T, $\sim$E
V	Fu	4, 5–5, 6–U, $\vee$E
W	($\forall$x)Fx	V, $\forall$I
X	($\forall$x)Fx $\vee$ ($\exists$x)Gx	W, $\vee$I
Y	$\sim$ $\sim$ (($\forall$x)Fx $\vee$ ($\exists$x)Gx)	2, 2, X, $\sim$I
Z	($\forall$x)Fx $\vee$ ($\exists$x)Gx	Y, $\sim$E

The contradictory pair to replace 'Φ' and '$\sim \Phi$' can easily be found. The formula on line 2 and its negation can be obtained without difficulty. One can reiterate '$\sim ((\forall x)Fx \lor (\exists x)Gx)$' from line 2 and reiterate 'Gu' from line 6. From 'Gu', one can obtain '$(\exists x)Gx$' by $\exists$I, and from this one can obtain '$(\forall x)Fx \lor (\exists x)Gx$' by $\lor$I. The derivation is completed in this way:

1	$(\forall x)(Fx \lor Gx)$	P
2	$\sim ((\forall x)Fx \lor (\exists x)Gx)$	A
3	u $(\forall x)(Fx \lor Gx)$	1, R
4	Fu $\lor$ Gu	3, $\forall$E
5	Fu	A
6	Gu	A
7	$\sim$ Fu	A
8	Gu	6, R
9	$(\exists x)Gx$	8, $\exists$I
10	$(\forall x)Fx \lor (\exists x)Gx$	9, $\lor$I
11	$\sim ((\forall x)Fx \lor (\exists x)Gx)$	2, R
12	$\sim \sim$ Fu	7, 10, 11, $\sim$I
13	Fu	12, $\sim$E
14	Fu	4, 5–5, 6–13, $\lor$E
15	$(\forall x)Fx$	14, $\forall$I
16	$(\forall x)Fx \lor (\exists x)Gx$	15, $\lor$I
17	$\sim \sim ((\forall x)Fx \lor (\exists x)Gx)$	2, 2, 16, $\sim$I
18	$(\forall x)Fx \lor (\exists x)Gx$	17, $\sim$E

One should always be ready to abandon a given strategy in a derivation when it looks as though that strategy will either fail or be extremely difficult to bring to completion. When a more promising strategy suggests itself, one has a clear reason for abandoning a strategy. The derivation which was just completed is a case in point. In the course of producing that derivation, the strategy of reiterating '$(\forall x)(Fx \lor Gx)$', getting 'Fa $\lor$ Ga' by $\forall$E, and then obtaining '$(\exists x)Gx$' from each disjunct was abandoned. Rather than simply abandoning this strategy, one could have amended it to try to obtain '$(\forall x)Fx \lor (\exists x)Gx$' from each disjunct. If that strategy had been pursued, the conclusion could have been reached in twenty-five steps, rather than the eighteen steps which were taken. The long derivation follows:

1	$(\forall x)(Fx \lor Gx)$	P
2	$\sim ((\forall x)Fx \lor (\exists x)Gx)$	A
3	$(\forall x)(Fx \lor Gx)$	1, R
4	$Fa \lor Ga$	3, $\forall$E
5	Ga	A
6	$(\exists x)Gx$	5, $\exists$I
7	$(\forall x)Fx \lor (\exists x)Gx$	6, $\lor$I
8	Fa	A
9	$u\ (\forall x)(Fx \lor Gx)$	1, R
10	$Fu \lor Gu$	9, $\forall$E
11	Fu	A
12	Gu	A
13	$\sim Fu$	A
14	Gu	12, R
15	$(\exists x)Gx$	14, $\exists$I
16	$(\forall x)Fx \lor (\exists x)Gx$	15, $\lor$I
17	$\sim ((\forall x)Fx \lor (\exists x)Gx)$	2, R
18	$\sim \sim Fu$	13, 16, 17, $\sim$I
19	Fu	18, $\sim$E
20	Fu	10, 11–11, 12–19, $\lor$E
21	$(\forall x)Fx$	20, $\forall$I
22	$(\forall x)Fx \lor (\exists x)Gx$	21, $\lor$I
23	$(\forall x)Fx \lor (\exists x)Gx$	4, 5–7, 8–22, $\lor$E
24	$\sim \sim ((\forall x)Fx \lor (\exists x)Gx)$	2, 2, 23, $\sim$I
25	$(\forall x)Fx \lor (\exists x)Gx$	24, $\sim$E

§5.12: EXERCISES

For each of the following arguments, derive the conclusion from the premiss(es).

1 $(\forall x)(Rkx \supset Rkc)$
$\underline{Rkc \supset (\forall x)Rxk}$

$(\forall x)(Rkx \supset Rck)$

2 $\underline{(\forall x)\sim Kx}$

$\sim (\exists x)Kx$

3 $\underline{(\exists x)Fx \lor (\exists x)Gx}$

$(\exists x)(Fx \lor Gx)$

4   $(\forall x)(Lx \lor Ma)$
   _____
   $\sim (\exists x)Mx \supset (\exists x)Lx$

5   $(\exists x)(Fx \lor Gx)$
   _____
   $(\exists x)Fx \lor (\exists x)Gx$

6   $(\forall x)Fx \land (\forall x)Gx$
   _____
   $(\forall x)(Fx \land Gx)$

7   $(\forall x) \sim Rxx$
   $(\forall x)(\forall y)((\exists z)(Rxz \land Rzy) \supset Rxy)$
   _____
   $(\forall x)(\forall y)(Rxy \supset \sim Ryx)$

8   $(\forall x)(Ax \supset Bx)$
   $(\forall x) \sim (Bx \lor Cx)$
   _____
   $\sim (\exists x)Ax$

9   $(\forall x)(Gx \supset (\exists y)Rxy)$
   $(\forall x)(\forall y)(Ryx \supset Ryy)$
   _____
   $(\forall x)(Gx \supset Rxx)$

10 $(\forall x)(Mxa \supset Mxb)$
   $(\exists x)(Mxa \lor Mxc)$
   _____
   $(\exists x)(Mxb \lor Mxc)$

11 $(\forall x)Fx \lor (\forall x) \sim Fx$
   _____
   $(\exists x)Fx \supset (\forall x)Fx$

12 $d = e \supset (\exists x)(Fx \land \sim Fx)$
   _____
   $\sim d = e$

13 $(\forall x)(\forall y)(((Fx \land Fy) \land (\sim Gx \land \sim Gy)) \supset x = y)$
   $\sim a = b$
   $Fa \land Fb$
   _____
   $Ga \lor Gb$

14 $j = k \lor j = m$
   $\sim k = m$
   _____
   $(\exists x) \sim j = x$

15 $(\exists x)(Mx \land (\exists y) \sim Qxy)$
   $(\forall x)(Mx \supset (\forall y)(Py \supset Qxy))$
   _____
   $\sim (\forall x)Px$

16 ($\forall$x)(Ax $\supset$ ($\exists$y)(Dy $\wedge$ Cxy))
    ($\forall$x)(Ax $\supset$ ($\forall$y)(Dy $\supset$ ~ Cxy))
   —————————————————————
    ($\exists$x)Ax $\supset$ ~ ($\forall$x)Fx

17 ($\forall$x)((Fx $\wedge$ Gx) $\supset$ Rx)
    ~ ($\forall$x)Rx
   —————————————————————
    ($\exists$x)~ Fx $\vee$ ($\exists$x)~ Gx

18 ($\exists$x)(Fx $\vee$ Gx) $\supset$ ($\exists$x)Hx
    ($\forall$x)(Hx $\supset$ Ix)
    ($\exists$x)Fx
   —————————————————————
    ($\exists$x)Ix

19 ($\exists$x)Fx $\supset$ ($\exists$x)Gx
   —————————————————————
    ($\forall$x)($\exists$y)(Fx $\supset$ Gy)

20 ($\forall$x)~ Fx
    ($\forall$x)~ Gx
   —————————————————————
    ~ (Fa $\vee$ Ga)

§ 5.13: CATEGORICAL DERIVATIONS IN PREDICATE LOGIC

Categorical derivations in predicate logic are very similar to categorical derivations in sentence logic. They are used to derive quantificational truths and they almost always begin with an assumption. That everything is either F or not F is intuitively obvious, and it should be possible to produce a categorical derivation of '($\forall$x)(Fx $\vee$ ~ Fx)'. To obtain this formula, one needs 'Fu $\vee$ ~ Fu' against a 'u'-barrier, which means that the problem is no more difficult than a categorical derivation in sentence logic. The derivation follows:

1	u	~ (Fu $\vee$ ~ Fu)	A
2		Fu	A
3		Fu $\vee$ ~ Fu	2, $\vee$I
4		~ (Fu $\vee$ ~ Fu)	1, R
5		~ Fu	2, 3, 4, ~I
6		Fu $\vee$ ~ Fu	5, $\vee$I
7		~ ~ (Fu $\vee$ ~ Fu)	1, 1, 6, ~I
8		Fu $\vee$ ~ Fu	7, ~E
9	($\forall$x)(Fx $\vee$ ~ Fx)		8, $\forall$I

In predicate logic, just as in sentence logic, indirect proof is often very useful in producing categorical derivations. Indirect proof is used again to derive '$(\forall x)(\exists y)Rxy \lor (\exists x)(\forall y)\sim Rxy$':

1	$\sim ((\forall x)(\exists y)Rxy \lor (\exists x)(\forall y)\sim Rxy)$	A
2	u $\sim (\exists y)Ruy$	A
3	v Ruv	A
4	$(\exists y)Ruy$	3, $\exists$I
5	$\sim (\exists y)Ruy$	2, R
6	$\sim$ Ruv	3, 4, 5, $\sim$I
7	$(\forall y)\sim Ruy$	6, $\forall$I
8	$(\exists x)(\forall y)\sim Rxy$	7, $\exists$I
9	$(\forall x)(\exists y)Rxy \lor (\exists x)(\forall y)\sim Rxy$	8, $\lor$I
10	$\sim ((\forall x)(\exists y)Rxy \lor (\exists x)(\forall y)\sim Rxy)$	1, R
11	$\sim \sim (\exists y)Ruy$	2, 9, 10, $\sim$I
12	$(\exists y)Ruy$	11, $\sim$E
13	$(\forall x)(\exists y)Rxy$	12, $\forall$I
14	$(\forall x)(\exists y)Rxy \lor (\exists x)(\forall y)\sim Rxy$	13, $\lor$I
15	$\sim \sim ((\forall x)(\exists y)Rxy \lor (\exists x)(\forall y)\sim Rxy)$	1, 1, 14, $\sim$I
16	$(\forall x)(\exists y)Rxy \lor (\exists x)(\forall y)\sim Rxy$	15, $\sim$E

The only categorical derivations which do not begin with an assumption are those which begin with a line which is justified by identity introduction. The derivation of the obvious truth that something is identical to something follows:

1	$a = a$	=I
2	$(\exists y)a = y$	1, $\exists$I
3	$(\exists x)(\exists y)x = y$	2, $\exists$I

The derivation of the claim that everything is identical to something is equally short:

1	u $u = u$	=I
2	$(\exists y)u = y$	1, $\exists$I
3	$(\forall x)(\exists y)x = y$	2, $\forall$I

That identity is **reflexive** – that everything is identical to itself – can be easily shown:

1	u $u = u$	=I
2	$(\forall x)x = x$	1, $\forall$I

Another feature of identity is that it is **symmetric**. The symmetry of identity, expressed in the formula '$(\forall x)(\forall y)(x = y \supset y = x)$', can also be easily shown:

1	u	v		u = v	A
2				v = v	=I
3				v = u	1, 2, =E
4				u = v ⊃ v = u	1–3, ⊃I
5			$(\forall y)(u = y \supset y = u)$		4, ∀I
6	$(\forall x)(\forall y)(x = y \supset y = x)$				5, ∀I

The formula '$(\forall x)(\forall y)(\forall z)((x = y \land y = z) \supset x = z)$' expresses yet another feature of identity, that it is **transitive**. The following derivation demonstrates the transitivity of identity:

1	u	v	w		u = v ∧ v = w	A
2				u = v	1, ∧E
3				v = w	1, ∧E
4				u = w	2, 3, =E
5				(u = v ∧ v = w) ⊃ u = w	1–4, ⊃I
6			$(\forall z)((u = v \land v = z) \supset u = z)$		5, ∀I
7		$(\forall y)(\forall z)((u = y \land y = z) \supset u = z)$			6, ∀I
8	$(\forall x)(\forall y)(\forall z)((x = y \land y = z) \supset x = z)$				7, ∀I

The quantificational falsity of '$(\exists x)(Fx \land \sim Fx)$' is shown in the following derivation:

1			(∃x)(Fx ∧ ~ Fx)	A
2		u	Fu ∧ ~ Fu	A
3			(∃x)(Fx ∧ ~ Fx)	A
4			Fu ∧ ~ Fu	2, R
5			Fu	4, ∧E
6			~ Fu	4, ∧E
7			~ (∃x)(Fx ∧ ~ Fx)	3, 5, 6, ~I
8		~ (∃x)(Fx ∧ ~ Fx)		1, 2–7, ∃E
9	~ (∃x)(Fx ∧ ~ Fx)			1, 1, 8, ~I

§5.14: EXERCISES

Provide categorical derivations of the following formulas.

1 $(\forall x)\sim (Fx \wedge \sim Fx)$

2 $(\forall x)((\forall y)Sxy \supset Sxx)$

3 $(\forall x)\sim (\forall y)\sim x = y$

4 $\sim (\exists x)(\forall y)\sim x = y$

5 $(\forall x)Kx \vee (\exists x)\sim Kx$

6 $(\forall x)(\sim Fx \vee Gx) \supset (\forall x)(Fx \supset Gx)$

7 $(\forall x)(\exists y)(Fx \supset Gy) \supset ((\forall x)Fx \supset (\exists y)Gy)$

8 $(\forall x)(Fx \supset Gx) \vee (\exists y)Fy$

9 $(\forall x)(Fx \supset (\exists y)(x = y \wedge Fy))$

10 $(\forall x)((\exists y)(x = y \wedge Fy) \supset Fx)$

11 $Sm \supset (\forall x)(x = m \supset Sx)$

12 $(\forall x)(Lx \supset (\sim Lx \supset Mx))$

13 $(\forall x)\sim Px \supset (\exists x)(Px \supset Qx)$

14 $(\forall x)\sim Px \supset (\forall x)(Px \supset Qx)$

15 $(\exists x)(Fx \supset (\forall y)Fy)$

§5.15: SUMMARY OF TOPICS

With a few possible exceptions to make the summary clearer, the topics appear in the order in which they appear in the text.

Existential quantifier introduction (See p. 178): A rule, $\exists$I, which serves to create a formula which has an existential quantifier as its main operator. Every use of existential quantifier introduction requires an appeal to exactly one line. The general pattern of $\exists$I follows:

m | $\Phi\tau$

n | $(\exists\chi)\Phi\chi$ m, $\exists$I

Universal quantifier elimination (See p. 181): A rule, ∀E, which serves to create a new formula from a formula which has a universal quantifier as its main operator. Every use of universal quantifier elimination requires an appeal to exactly one line. The general pattern of ∀E follows:

m | (∀χ)Φχ

n | Φτ   m, ∀E

Parameter (See p. 183): A dummy name used to name a variable in a derivation. The lower-case letters 'u', 'v' and 'w' are reserved for use as parameters.

Parameter barrier (See p. 184): A scope line flagged with a parameter to prevent any occurrences of the parameter crossing the scope line.

Existential quantifier elimination (See p. 183): A rule, ∃E, which serves to create a new formula from a formula which has an existential quantifier as its main operator. Use of existential quantifier elimination involves obtaining a formula from an assumption which is the existentially quantified formula with the quantifier removed and each occurrence of the variable of the quantifier replaced by a parameter. The scope line of the assumption is flagged with the parameter. Every use of ∃E requires an appeal to exactly one line and the range of the subderivation which starts with the assumption. An example of ∃E follows:

m | (∃χ)(Φχ ∧ Ψχ)

n | ᵘ| Φu ∧ Ψu   A

o | | Φu   n, ∧E

p | | (∃χ)Φχ   o, ∃I

q | (∃χ)Φχ   m, n −p, ∃E

Universal quantifier introduction (See p. 186): A rule, ∀I, which serves to create a universally quantified formula from a formula on a parameter barrier which does not begin with an assumption. Use of universal quantifier introduction involves replacing every occurrence of the parameter of the formula on the barrier with a variable which does not already occur in that formula. The barrier is then ended and a universal quantifier with the new variable is placed before the result of the replacement. Every use of universal quantifier introduction requires an appeal to exactly one line. An example of ∀I follows:

```
m  | (∀χ)(Φχ ∧ Ψχ)

n  |  u| (∀x)(Φχ ∧ Ψχ)              m, R

o  |   | Φu ∧ Ψu                    n, ∀E

p  |   | Φu                         o, ∧E

q  | (∀χ)Φχ                         p, ∀I
```

Identity introduction (See p. 190): A rule, =I, which allows one to write 'Φ = Φ' anywhere in a derivation with no appeal to a line number. An example of =I follows:

```
m  | p = p ⊃ Φτ

n  | p = p                          =I

o  | Φτ                             m, n, ⊃E
```

Identity elimination (See p. 191): A rule, =E, which allows one to replace any term, 'τ₁', in a formula such as 'Φτ₁', with another term, 'τ₂', provided that an identity formula, 'τ₁ = τ₂', is already on the current scope line. Every use of identity elimination requires an appeal to exactly two lines. An example of =E follows:

```
m  | (∃χ)Φac

n  | c = d

o  | (∃χ)Φad                        m, n, =E
```

CHAPTER SIX

MISCELLANEOUS MATTERS

§6.1: THE SCOPE OF THE TEXT

Essentials of Symbolic Logic was written to provide students with a short introduction to the vast and sometimes bewildering field of symbolic logic. Those students who pursue the subject further will find some unfamiliar vocabulary, conventions and symbols. This chapter is provided to make things a little easier for such students.

Those students who approach metatheory will find several unfamiliar symbols. Any decent discussion of metatheory will explain the meaning of such symbols as they are introduced, so they will not be discussed here.

Some systems of derivations use very few rules and make appeals to axioms. *The Elements,* Euclid's study of geometry, provides the most famous examples of proofs which appeal to axioms. The system of derivations used in this book is called a system of 'natural deduction' because it uses rules without any appeals to axioms. In this respect, it resembles everyday reasoning. Some natural deduction systems use scope lines and make frequent use of reiteration, while others do not. Some of these variations are discussed in this chapter. However, the student should be aware that *Essentials of Symbolic Logic* is a short introductory text, and there is much which is not even mentioned.

§6.2: EXISTENCE AND TRANSLATION PROBLEMS

In §4.13, it was pointed out that 'Mary is in terror of werewolves' could not be adequately translated using either the universal or existential quantifier, since such translations would either be trivially true or assert the existence of werewolves. There, the problem was avoided by the simple expedient of using the one-place predicate, 'Tm', to translate the entire sentence. There are other problems about existence in the discussion of definite descriptions in §4.12 and the rule of existential quantifier introduction in §5.2.

In general, there is no problem in using the existential quantifier to translate expressions such as 'the first man to climb Mount Everest'. However, it is possible to use a definite description in a sentence such as 'The dog which is smarter than Einstein is old.' There is no such dog and it would be misleading to assert the existence of such a dog. Problems of this sort have concerned logicians for years; there are serious questions which can be addressed in the logic of fiction and other areas. These topics cannot be addressed in a book of this sort. 'The dog which is smarter than Einstein is old' can be translated as: '$(\exists x)(Sxe \wedge (Dx \wedge Ox))$'. To deny that there is such a dog one can write: '$\sim (\exists x)(Sxe \wedge (Dx \wedge Ox))$'.

The rule of existential quantifier introduction can lead to similar puzzles. From 'John is a thief', one can derive '$(\exists x)Tx$'. However, from 'Atlantis is a lost continent', it would be wrong the assert the existence of a lost continent: '$(\exists x)(Cx \wedge Lx)$'. The easiest way to avoid such problems is to avoid using the names of non-existent people and things. Not using such names, of course, makes dealing with fictional people and things impossible.

One final problem: from 'John read a big book carefully', one cannot derive 'John read a big book', 'John read a book carefully' or even 'John read a book', although these are intuitively correct inferences. The predicate logic discussed in this text cannot deal well with modifiers, and is unable to reflect the connections between reading carefully and reading, or between big books and books. To deal with inferences of this sort, one needs a more advanced system of logic. A short introductory text can only point out a few such limitations and the need for a more sophisticated predicate logic.

§6.3: THE NAMES OF THE RULES

There is a minor problem with the names of some of the rules in *Essentials of Symbolic Logic* and in other texts. For example, strictly speaking, conjunction introduction does not introduce a conjunction; it introduces the caret, and should be called 'caret introduction'. Since using this terminology would be eccentric, it is not used in this book. The following list provides rule names in English which could be used to avoid a rather pedantic objection.

1 '~E' could be called 'tilde elimination'.

2 '~I' could be called 'tilde introduction'.

3 '∧E' could be called 'caret elimination'.

4 '∧I' could be called 'caret introduction'.

5 '∨E' could be called 'vel elimination'.

6 '∨I' could be called 'vel introduction'.

7 '=E' could be called 'identity symbol elimination'.

8 '=I' could be called 'identity symbol introduction'.

§6.4: UNFAMILIAR TERMINOLOGY AND SYMBOLS

For the most part, this book has avoided eccentric terminology and symbols. However, many authors use different names for rules which operate in much the same way as the rules of this book, and use symbols which are slightly different from the symbols used in this book.

A few of the more common variations in the names of rules are listed below:

1 'Conjunction elimination' is called 'simplification', or 'Simp'.

2 'Conjunction introduction' is called 'conjunction', or 'Conj'.

3 'Negation elimination' is called 'double negation', or 'DN'.

4 'Negation introduction' is abbreviated as 'NI'.

5 'Disjunction elimination' is called 'constructive dilemma', or 'CD'.

6 'Disjunction introduction' is called 'addition', or 'Add'.

7 'Horseshoe elimination' is called *'modus ponens'*, or 'MP'.

8 'Horseshoe introduction' is called 'conditional proof', or 'CP'.

9 'Triplebar elimination' is called 'biconditional elimination', or 'BE'.

10 'Triplebar introduction' is called 'biconditional introduction', or 'BI'.

11 'Indirect proof' is often called *'reductio ad absurdum'*, or 'RAA'.

12 'Universal quantifier introduction' is called 'universal generalization', or 'UG'.

13 'Universal quantifier elimination' is called 'universal instantiation', or 'UI'.

14 'Existential quantifier introduction' is called 'existential generalization', or 'EG'.

15 'Existential quantifier elimination' is called 'existential instantiation', or 'EI'.

Some more examples of variations in symbols and terminology follow.

Some authors use a system of ranking which reduces the need for brackets. For example, one can stipulate that '⊃' outranks '∧'. Given this stipulation, 'A ⊃ B ∧ C' is not ambiguous; it is to be read as 'A ⊃ (B ∧ C)'. Fortunately, this practice seem to be falling into disuse. Another practice which students may come across is the use of different kinds of brackets. '(~ (A ∨ ~ (B ⊃ C)) ≡ D) ∨ A' is sometimes written as '{~ [A ∨ ~ (B ⊃ C)] ≡ D} ∨ A'. Students can decide for themselves whether this increases clarity.

Many authors use a few lower-case letters and subscripts for sentence letters rather than the upper-case letters used in this book. Some authors refer to sentence letters as 'propositional variables'. Rather than use 'T's and 'F's in truth tables, some authors use '1's and '0's or 'T's and '⊥'s. Neither of these practices should confuse students. Rather than use '~', some authors use '¬'. Both '&' and '•' are often used instead of '∧', '⇒' and '→' are often used instead of '⊃', and '⇔' and '↔' are often used instead of '≡'.

In predicate logic, many authors use '(∃x)' and '(x)', rather than '(∃x)' and '(∀x)'. An open sentence is sometimes said to express a 'propositional function', and many authors use 'propositional function' in the way that 'open sentence' is used in this book. When a variable in an open sentence is not linked to a quantifier, it is often called a 'free variable'. When a variable is linked to a quantifier, it is often called a 'bound variable'. Some derivation systems use free variables in much the way that parameters are used in derivations in this book.

A notation which is very different from that of *Essentials of Symbolic Logic* is Polish notation. It will strike most students as very odd, but it does have the advantage that all formulas of sentence logic can be produced on a standard typewriter. Polish notation uses lower-case letters for sentence letters and requires no brackets. A few examples follow:

'~ P' is written as 'Np'.
'P ⊃ Q' is written as 'Cpq'.
'P ∧ Q' is written as 'Kpq'.
'P ∨ Q' is written as 'Apq'.
'P ≡ Q' is written as 'Epq'.
'P ⊃ (Q ⊃ R)' is written as 'CpCqr'.
'(P ⊃ Q) ⊃ R' is written as 'CCpqr'.

As might be guessed from the last two examples, the first upper-case letter of a formula is the main operator. Any good discussion of Polish notation explains how the position of the upper-case letters makes brackets unnecessary. The formulas of predicate logic can also be written in Polish notation, but a standard typewriter is inadequate for this. A variation of Polish notation is sometimes used in electronic calculators.

In Chapter 2, truth-functionally true, truth-functionally false and truth-functionally indeterminate formulas were discussed, as were truth-functionally equivalent formulas. In Chapter 4, analogous concepts in predicate logic were introduced: quantificational truth, quantificational falsehood, quantificational indeterminacy and quantificational equivalence. Both truth-functional truths and quantificational truths are often called 'theorems', 'tautologies' or 'valid formulas'. Sometimes they are called 'logical', 'analytic' or 'necessary' truths. Both truth-functional falsehoods and quantificational falsehoods are sometimes said to be 'logically', 'analytically' or 'necessarily' false. Both truth-functionally indeterminate and quantificationally indeterminate formulas are often called 'contingent' or 'logically contingent'. Similarly, the term 'valid argument' is often used to describe both truth-functionally valid arguments and quantificationally valid arguments. The student should be aware that there is considerable variation in the way that the terms mentioned in this paragraph are used. For example, some authors use 'analytic' and 'necessary' as synonyms, while others use the different terms to make what they consider to be an important distinction.

Necessity and contingency are notions dealt with by modal logic, a topic which has not been addressed in this book. Students who continue in logic will come across the three symbols: '$\Box$', '$\Diamond$' and '$\dashv$'. 'A $\supset$ A' is necessarily true, and this necessary truth can be expressed in terms of modal logic as '$\Box$ (A $\supset$ A)'. '$\Box$ (A $\supset$ A)' can also be expressed as 'A $\dashv$ A' which is read as 'A strictly implies A.' Similarly, the necessary falsehood of 'A $\wedge$ ~ A' can be expressed as '$\Box$ ~ (A $\wedge$ ~ A)'. What is necessarily false is not possibly true. Accordingly, this same necessary falsehood can be expressed in terms of '$\Diamond$', the possibility symbol: '~ $\Diamond$ (A $\wedge$ ~ A)'.

Besides being necessarily true or necessarily false, a statement can also be contingent, meaning that it is possibly true and possibly false. The mark of a contingent statement is that its truth value cannot be determined by logical considerations alone. For example, a formula such as 'A $\vee$ B' is contingent; it is possibly true and possibly false. In the symbols of modal logic, these two possibilities can be expressed as '$\Diamond$ (A $\vee$ B) $\wedge$ $\Diamond$ ~ (A $\vee$ B)'. Since '$\Diamond$ ~ (A $\vee$ B)' is true, '$\Box$ (A $\vee$ B)' is false.

Turning to predicate logic, '($\forall$x)(Fx $\vee$ ~ Fx)' is necessarily true, and this can be expressed as '$\Box$ ($\forall$x)(Fx $\vee$ ~ Fx)' or as '~ $\Diamond$ ~ ($\forall$x)(Fx $\vee$ ~ Fx)'. Similarly, the necessary truth of '($\forall$x)(Fx $\supset$ Fx)' can be expressed as '$\Box$ ($\forall$x)(Fx $\supset$ Fx)'. The necessary falsity of '($\exists$x)(Fx $\wedge$ ~ Fx)' can be expressed as '$\Box$ ~ ($\exists$x)(Fx $\wedge$ ~ Fx)' or as '~ $\Diamond$ ($\exists$x)(Fx $\wedge$ ~ Fx)'. The contingency of '($\exists$x)Fx' can be expressed in terms of modal logic as '$\Diamond$ ($\exists$x)Fx $\wedge$ $\Diamond$ ~ ($\exists$x)Fx'.

§6.5: ADDITIONAL DERIVATION RULES

Systems of logic frequently use more rules than the elimination and introduction rules of this book. Using more rules allows for shorter derivations, but requires that one remember more rules. The extra rules were avoided in this book for three reasons. First, the system of having a single introduction rule and a single elimination rule for each sentence operator is straightforward and easily understood. Second, the set of rules presented in this book is a minimal set; each rule is necessary and everything that can be done with additional derivation rules can be done without them. Third, all the rules of this book are presented with what is intended to be a justification for their use. To learn a large number of rules which are to be accepted on faith does nothing to increase one's understanding. It is possible in principle to make all derivations extremely short. For every derivation, one would need a rule allowing one to derive the conclusion from the premiss or premisses. Obviously, it would be impossible in practice to formulate a complete set of such rules. Between this ridiculous extreme and the minimal set of rules in this book, it is possible to make derivations shorter by adding a few rules which are commonly used. In this section, three additional rules are discussed. It should be clear that anything which can be derived with these rules can be derived using the rules of Chapter 3.

1 Hypothetical Syllogism is usually abbreviated as 'HS'. In this derivation, '$\Phi \supset \Omega$' is derived from '$\Phi \supset \Psi$' and '$\Psi \supset \Omega$' using this rule:

1	$\Phi \supset \Psi$	P
2	$\Psi \supset \Omega$	P
3	$\Phi \supset \Omega$	1, 2, HS

2 Disjunctive Syllogism is usually abbreviated as 'DS'. This rule is used in the next derivation to obtain 'Φ' from '$\Phi \vee \Psi$' and '$\sim \Psi$'.

1	$\Phi \vee \Psi$	P
2	$\sim \Phi$	P
3	Ψ	1, 2, DS

3 *Modus Tollens* is usually abbreviated as 'MT'. In the next derivation, '$\sim \Phi$' is derived from '$\Phi \supset \Psi$' and '$\sim \Psi$' using this rule.

1	$\Phi \supset \Psi$	P
2	$\sim \Psi$	P
3	$\sim \Phi$	1, 2, MT

§6.6: REPLACEMENT RULES

As well as the additional derivation rules, some systems of logic have replacement rules, rules which allow one to replace *part* of a formula with something which is logically equivalent. A typical example is double negation, abbreviated as 'DN'. This rule is used in the following derivation:

1	A ⊃ ~ ~ B	P
2	A	P
3	A ⊃ B	1, DN
4	B	2, 3, ⊃E

As with the additional derivation rules, anything derived with replacement rules can be derived using the rules of Chapter 3 and Chapter 5. Four dots are usually used to signify that replacement is permissible. Thus, the rule of double negation is usually stated as '~ ~ Φ :: Φ'. What is on the left of the four dots can always be replaced by what is on the right, and *vice versa*. It should be clear that, for every replacement rule, there is a corresponding biconditional formula which is truth-functionally or quantificationally true. For example, the truth-functionally true formula, '~ ~ Φ ≡ Φ', corresponds to the rule of double negation. A few of the more common replacement rules are listed below:

1 Double Negation (DN)
   ~ ~ Φ :: Φ

2 Commutation (Comm)
   Φ ∨ ψ :: ψ ∨ Φ
   Φ ∧ ψ :: ψ ∧ Φ

3 De Morgan (De M)
   ~ (Φ ∨ ψ) :: ~ Φ ∧ ~ ψ
   ~ (Φ ∧ ψ) :: ~ Φ ∨ ~ ψ

4 Distribution (Dist)
   Φ ∧ (ψ ∨ Ω) :: (Φ ∧ ψ) ∨ (Φ ∧ Ω)
   Φ ∨ (ψ ∧ Ω) :: (Φ ∨ ψ) ∧ (Φ ∨ Ω)

5 Contraposition (Cont)
   Φ ⊃ ψ :: ~ ψ ⊃ ~ Φ

6 Association (Ass)
   (Φ ∨ ψ) ∨ Ω :: Φ ∨ (ψ ∨ Ω)
   (Φ ∧ ψ) ∧ Ω :: Φ ∧ (ψ ∧ Ω)

7 Exportation (Exp)
   (Φ ∧ ψ) ⊃ Ω :: Φ ⊃ (ψ ⊃ Ω)

8 Implication (Imp)

   $\Phi \supset \Psi :: \sim \Phi \lor \Psi$

9 Equivalence (Equiv)

   $\Phi \equiv \Psi :: (\Phi \supset \Psi) \land (\Psi \supset \Phi)$

10 Quantificational Equivalence (QE)

   $(\forall\chi)\Phi\chi :: \sim (\exists\chi)\sim \Phi\chi$

   $(\exists\chi)\Phi\chi :: \sim (\forall\chi)\sim \Phi\chi$

   $\sim (\forall\chi)\Phi\chi :: (\exists\chi)\sim \Phi\chi$

   $\sim (\exists\chi)\Phi\chi :: (\forall\chi)\sim \Phi\chi$

§6.7: AVOIDING REITERATION

Some systems of logic do not require reiteration. In these systems, one can appeal to any formula which can be reiterated according to the rules of Chapter 3 and Chapter 5. Using reiteration makes stating the rules simpler, and many students find it less confusing when appeals to rules such as ∧I and ⊃E always involve formulas on the current scope line. An example of how reiteration is avoided in some systems follows. It should be noted that ∧I′, ⊃E′, ∧E′ and ∨I′ are not the regular rules of *Essentials of Symbolic Logic* in that each of them allows appeals to other scope lines.

1	D ∧ B	P
2	N ⊃ C	P
3	B ⊃ M	P
4	K	P
5	N	A
6	K ∧ N	4, 5, ∧I′
7	C	2, 5, ⊃E′
8	B	1, ∧E′
9	K ∧ (B ⊃ M)	3, 4, ∧I′
10	K ∨ R	4, ∨I′
11	(K ∧ (B ⊃ M)) ∧ (K ∨ R)	9, 10, ∧I
12	N ⊃ ((K ∧ (B ⊃ M)) ∧ (K ∨ R))	5–11, ⊃I

Rather than having formulas on different scope lines, some systems of logic have all formulas in a numbered list and use lines at the side to keep track of assumptions. Very often these systems mark assumptions with a note explaining why the assumption is made. In the following derivation, some of the rules discussed in §6.4 and §6.5 are used in a derivation which does not use secondary scope lines.

1	~ Q ∨ ~ R	P
2	Q ⊃ R	P
3	(~ S ∧ ~ L) ⊃ Q	P
4	M	A (CP)
5	Q	A (NI)
6	R	2, 5, MP
7	~ R	1, 5, DS
8	R ∧ ~ R	6, 7, Conj
9	~ Q	5–8, NI
10	~ (~ S ∧ ~ L)	3, 9, MT
11	M ⊃ ~ (~ S ∧ ~ L)	4–10, CP

§6.8: JOINT DENIAL AND THE SHEFFER STROKE

In §2.18, it was demonstrated that two sentence operators could do the work of the five discussed in Chapter 2. In particular, it was shown that the tilde and the horseshoe would serve to do anything done by the entire set of five operators. A major theoretical interest of logicians and computer scientists is the possibility of reducing the number of operators. There are two well-known ways of reducing the five sentence operators to a single operator: joint denial and alternative denial.

The joint denial of 'Φ' and 'Ψ' is the claim that 'Φ' and 'Ψ' are both false; that neither 'Φ' nor 'Ψ' is true. Sometimes joint denial is simply known as 'nor'. The symbol for joint denial is a downward-pointing arrow, '↓'. The truth-table definition of the joint denial symbol follows:

Φ	Ψ	$\Phi \downarrow \Psi$
T	T	F
T	F	F
F	T	F
F	F	T

Since 'Φ ↓ Ψ' is true only when flanked by two false formulas, one can use '↓' to express negation. The truth table for '~ Φ' using the joint denial symbol follows:

Φ	~ Φ	Φ ↓ Φ
T	F	F
F	T	T

The truth table for 'Φ ⊃ Ψ' using the joint denial symbol follows. The correctness of each column on this table can be checked against the truth-table definition of joint denial.

Φ	Ψ	Φ ⊃ Ψ	((Φ ↓ Ψ) ↓ Ψ) ↓ ((Φ ↓ Ψ) ↓ Ψ)				
T	T	T	F	F	T	F	F
T	F	F	F	T	F	F	T
F	T	T	F	F	T	F	F
F	F	T	T	F	T	T	F
			5	3	1	4	2

Since anything done with '∨', '∧' and '≡' can be done using just the tilde and the horseshoe. It follows that anything done with '∨', '∧' and '≡' can be done using just joint denial. Enthusiastic readers with lots of scrap paper may care to develop joint denial equivalents of '∨', '∧' and '≡'.

Alternative denial is best known by its symbol, the Sheffer stroke, '|'. Computer people sometimes use the expression 'nand' to mean 'not both' and the Sheffer stroke represents this. The truth-table definition of the Sheffer stroke follows:

Φ	Ψ	Φ | Ψ
T	T	F
T	F	T
F	T	T
F	F	T

From this definition of the Sheffer stroke it can be seen that the negation of 'Φ' can be expressed as 'Φ | Φ' and this is shown on the truth table below.

Φ	~ Φ	Φ | Φ
T	F	F
F	T	T

The truth table for '$\Phi \supset \Psi$' using the Sheffer stroke follows. As with the table for joint denial, the correctness of each column on this table can be checked against the truth-table definition of the Sheffer stroke.

Φ	Ψ	$\Phi \supset \Psi$	$\Phi \mid (\Phi \mid \Psi)$	
T	T	T	T	F
T	F	F	F	T
F	T	T	T	T
F	F	T	T	T
			1	2

Just as anything done with '$\vee$', '$\wedge$' and '$\equiv$' can be done using just joint denial, anything done with these symbols can be done using the Sheffer stroke. Some readers, particularly those with an interest in computer science, can work out truth tables for '$\vee$', '$\wedge$' and '$\equiv$' using the Sheffer stroke.

Enthusiasts, of course, can work on expressing very complicated formulas using only joint denial and the Sheffer stroke. As an added challenge, one can translate back and forth between formulas using joint denial and formulas using the Sheffer stroke. Doing this will convince anyone that it is a good thing that computers have no logical intuitions and never get bored.

§6.9: CONSISTENCY AND TRUTH TREES

Logicians use the notion of consistency much in the way it is used when people say things such as that the suspect's story was inconsistent. A set of formulas is truth-functionally inconsistent if there is no line of a complete truth table on which all the formulas are true. The set of formulas may have just one element. To give some simple examples, the set of formulas having just '$P \vee \sim P$' as a member is a consistent set, while the set of formulas having only '$P \wedge \sim P$' as a member is an inconsistent set. Similarly, '$\{C, \sim R, C \supset R\}$' is an inconsistent set. The consistency or inconsistency of a set can easily be determined on a truth table.

A truth tree works in much the same way as a truth table. Just as a truth table requires that the truth value of a complex formula be determined from the truth value of its sentence letters and the definition of the sentence operators, a truth tree breaks up complicated formulas and deals with the parts. A tree consists of the 'trunk' on which a set of formulas is placed sequentially. The tree has downward-pointing branches (which might better be called 'roots') on which all the parts of every member of the set appear.

Conjunctions are broken up on a single branch, while disjunctions are broken up on a divided branch. When conjunctions are broken up, this is justified by a rule often known as 'conjunction decomposition' or simply as

'∧D'. This rule works in much the same way as ∧E works in derivations. When a divided branch is formed from a disjunction, the division is justified by a rule often known as 'disjunction decomposition' or simply as '∨D'. Since 'C ⊃ R' is truth-functionally equivalent to '~ C ∨ R', conditional formulas can be dealt with much as disjunctive formulas are, using the rule of 'conditional decomposition', '⊃D'. Whenever a complex formula is broken up into its components, it is marked with a check mark, '✓', to show that it needs no further attention.

As mentioned, '{C, ~ R, C ⊃ R}' is truth-functionally inconsistent. On the following tree, all the members of this set are placed on the 'trunk'. Conditional decomposition is used to form two branches from 'C ⊃ R'. When this is done, '✓' is placed at line 3 to show that it needs no further attention.

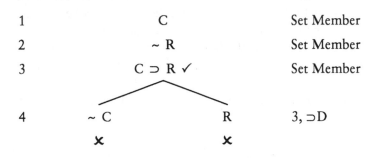

1	C	Set Member
2	~ R	Set Member
3	C ⊃ R ✓	Set Member
4	~ C R	3, ⊃D

One can now trace a path from each of the formulas on line 4 to the top of the tree. The checked line 3 can be ignored, since other lines have replaced it. Both of the formulas on line 4 are marked with a cross, '✗'. These marks indicate that both branches are closed. In a closed branch, there is no path which does not include a contradictory pair. On the left branch, this pair is 'C' on line 1 and '~ C' on line 4. On the right branch, the pair is '~ R' on line 2 and 'R' on line 4. What this shows is that there is no assignment of truth values which can make all the members of '{C, ~ R, C ⊃ R}' true.

In tracing a path from the lower end of a branch to the top of a tree, the only formulas which need to be considered are atomic formulas and the negations of atomic formulas. If the tree has been completed properly, all other formulas will be marked with a '✓', indicating that they have been replaced by simpler formulas.

All of the decomposition rules needed for trees in sentence logic are illustrated below. It can be seen that many of these rules resemble the replacement rules discussed in §6.6.

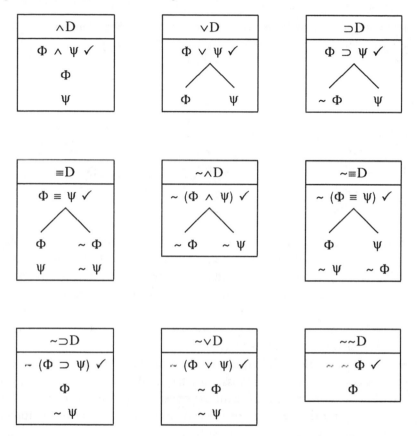

If '(A ⊃ B) ∧ (B ⊃ C)' were put on a truth table, there would be at least one 'T' under the main operator. The fact that '(A ⊃ B) ∧ (B ⊃ C)' is not truth-functionally false can be shown on a tree.

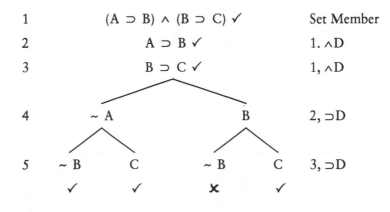

1	(A ⊃ B) ∧ (B ⊃ C) ✓	Set Member
2	A ⊃ B ✓	1. ∧D
3	B ⊃ C ✓	1, ∧D
4	~ A B	2, ⊃D
5	~ B C ~ B C	3, ⊃D

It should be noted that the conditional decomposition of line 3 appears twice at line 5, on both of the branches formed at line 4. This is to ensure that all necessary branches are included in the tree. All of the open branches are marked with '✓' just as the closed branch is marked with '✗'. '(A ⊃ B) ∧ (B ⊃ C)' is not truth-functionally false because there is at least one open branch. This means that there is at least one assignment of truth values on which the formula is true.

A truth-functionally valid argument is one in which there is no row of a truth table on which all the premises are true and on which the conclusion is false. Put in terms of truth-functional consistency, a set consisting of all the premises and the negation of the conclusion of any truth-functionally valid argument is bound to be inconsistent.

The following argument is truth-functionally valid:

P ⊃ (Q ∧ R)
P
―――――――
Q

The truth-functional validity of the argument is shown on the following truth tree.

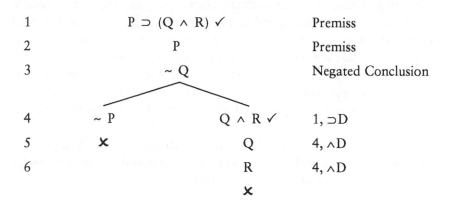

1	P ⊃ (Q ∧ R) ✓	Premiss
2	P	Premiss
3	~ Q	Negated Conclusion
4	~ P Q ∧ R ✓	1, ⊃D
5	✗ Q	4, ∧D
6	R	4, ∧D
	✗	

Since all branches close, the argument is valid.

By contrast, the following argument is truth-functionally invalid:

$$P \supset (Q \wedge R)$$
$$\sim P$$
_____
$$\sim Q$$

As before, the premisses are followed by the negation of the conclusion.

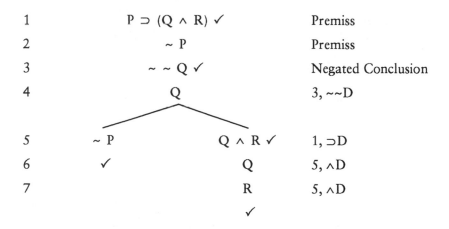

1	P ⊃ (Q ∧ R) ✓	Premiss
2	~ P	Premiss
3	~ ~ Q ✓	Negated Conclusion
4	Q	3, ~~D
5	~ P Q ∧ R ✓	1, ⊃D
6	✓ Q	5, ∧D
7	R	5, ∧D
	✓	

Since there is at least one open branch, the argument is invalid.

In the discussion of predicate logic and interpretations in §4.17, it was shown how universally quantified formulas are replaced by conjunctions and existentially quantified formulas are replaced by disjunctions. This suggests that trees can be used to assess quantified formulas within interpretations. In some cases – but only in some cases – trees can be used to show quantificational validity and consistency, and even to determine the necessary domains. However, such trees can rapidly expand to an unwieldy size. In many cases, trees expand to an infinite size. Using trees to deal with interpretations is a complex procedure, involving many issues. A serious discussion of these matters is beyond the scope of this book.

Even when one is dealing with sentence logic, trees can grow to unmanageable proportions. It is easy to run out of room on the page or else be reduced to writing in such small characters and symbols that the tree becomes unreadable. Trees have been mentioned in this chapter so that students will not be completely bewildered when they see one. As a practical technique for dealing with such things as arguments and interpretations, the method of using trees has serious deficiencies.

INDEX

TECHNICAL TERMS

When a technical term is first introduced, it is printed in bold face. The following pages contain such occurrences of technical terms. Terms which are mentioned only in Chapter 6 are not included.